TREES

and

THE

Environment

Another Perspective

MICHAEL GRAHAM MSC.

authorHOUSE®

AuthorHouse™
1663 Liberty Drive
Bloomington, IN 47403
www.authorhouse.com
Phone: 833-262-8899

Published by AuthorHouse 03/10/2022

ISBN: 978-1-6655-5429-9 (sc)
ISBN: 978-1-6655-5428-2 (e)

Library of Congress Control Number: 2022904584

Print information available on the last page.

Contents

Abbreviations

1.	ABRAF	Associacao Brasileira de Produtores de Floresta Plantadas/Brazilian Association of Planted Forest Producers
2.	AD	ANNO DOMINI (In the year of the Lord)
3.	AC	Alternation Current
4.	ACLUMP	Australian Collaborative Land Use Management Program
5.	ALB	Asian Longhorn Beetle
6.	AP	Associated Press
7.	ATP	Adenosine triphosphate
8.	BC	Before Christ
9.	BCE	Before the Common Era
10.	C	Carbon
11.	CCS	Carbon Capture and Storage
12.	CE	Common Era
13.	CH_2O	Formaldehyde
14.	$C_6H_{12}O_6$	Glucose
15.	CIA	Central Intelligence Agency (US)
16.	CIAM	
17.	CO	Carbon Monoxide
18.	CO_2	Carbon Dioxide
19.	CSP	Concentrated Solar Power
20.	CU	Unconfined Cohesive Strength (CU-Structural Soil
21.	$^{\circ}C$	Degree Centigrade or Celsius
22.	DAC	Direct Air Capture

23.	DFTM	Douglas fir Tussock Moth
24.	DRC	Democratic Republic of the Congo
25.	EESC	European Economic and Social Committee
26.	EOR	Enhanced Oil Recovery
27.	EUROSTAT	European Statistical
28.	FAO	Food and Agricultural Organization
29.	FAOSTAT	Food and Agricultural Organization Statistic- Food and Agriculture Data
30.	FDR	Franklin Delano Roosevelt
31.	FSC	Forest Stewardship Council
32.	°F	Degree Fahrenheit
33.	GDP	Gross Domestic Product
34.	GFMA	Global Financial Markets Association
35.	GHG	Green House Gases
36.	GGWI	Great Green Wall Initiative
37.	$GtCO_2$	Gigatons Carbon Dioxide
38.	GW	Gigawatt
39.	H	Hydrogen
40.	HWA	Hemlock Wooly Adelgid
41.	IBGE	Instituto Brasileiro de Geographia e Estatistica/ Brazilian Institute of Geography and Statistics
42.	ICONE	Instituto de Estudio do Comercio e Negociacoes Internacionais/ Institute of Trade Studies and International Negotiations (Brazil)
43.	IFAD	International Fund for Agricultural Development
44.	IPCC	Intergovernmental Panel on Climate Change
45.	KW	Kilowatt
46.	MMA	Mobile Marketing Association of Brazil
47.	MW	Megawatt
48.	N_2	Nitrogen
49.	NASA	National Aeronautics and Space Administration
50.	NADPH	Nicotinamide adenine dinucleotide phosphate
51.	NRCS	National Resources Conservation Service
52.	NOAA	National Oceanic and Atmospheric Administration

53.	NO_x	Nitrogen Oxides
54.	O_2	Oxygen
55.	O_3	Ozone
56.	ODS	Ozone Depleting Substances
57.	PCE	Perchloroethylene
58.	PG&E	Pacific Gas & Electric Company
59.	PM	Particulate Matter
60.	PSI	Photo Systems I
61.	PV	Photovoltaic
62.	SLM	Sustainable Land Management
63.	SO_2	Sulfur Dioxide
64.	TCE	Trichloroethylene/Tetrachloroethylene/Trichloroethane
65.	UC	University of California
66.	UN	United Nations
67.	UNCCD	United Nations Convention to Combat Desertification
68.	UNDP	United Nations Development Program
69.	UNESCO	United Nation Educational Scientific and Cultural Organization
70.	USA/US	United States of America/United States
71.	USDA	United States Department of Agriculture
72.	USEIA	United States Energy Information Administration
73.	USEPA	United States Environmental Protection Agency
74.	USGS	United States Geological Survey
75.	UV	Ultraviolet

Abstract

Plants inclusive of trees have been and continues to be very rich natural resources for humans and the other animals that call Earth home, as they have provided habitat, food and raw material from the beginning of time that both humans and animals have used as such, resources to be used only, however, time and experience is indicating that plants inclusive of trees are more than just very valuable natural resources to be used up and cast aside, as experience and scientific evidence is indicating that plants inclusive of trees are an integral part of the natural environment similar to rocks, soils, mountains, rivers, lakes, oceans and the atmosphere. While plants play a very vital role in shaping life on Earth, unfortunately, it appears that until relatively recent times, 300–400 years, even the most advanced human societies appear to lack an appreciation of the importance of trees to the environment, human and animal life and how human and animal activities can negatively impact the ability of trees and plants to continue providing their lifegiving support. Recently uncovered archaeological evidence indicates that places such as the Sahara Desert were once very green and full of life and according to Lloyd (2018) "Before the Sahara changed into a desert there were also trees such as ash, cedar, oak, walnut, myrtle and lime in the region." This green and verdant place was destroyed by very early humans to fill their needs for the creation of open fields for agriculture, habitat for humans, monuments of stones glorifying dead men and mining for minerals. With the growth of human population in the region more trees and other natural resources were destroyed to facilitate the necessary expansion in agriculture and habitat building required to meet human needs and the life of flora and fauna in these places diminished and eventually faded away. According to Gavin

Schmidt, a NASA Climate Scientist, the cause of Sahara's desertification was a shift in the earth's orbit which may have occurred 8–10,000 years ago, however, based on the rate of desertification that is occurring today, without any shift in the earth's orbit, it is very likely that the change in the Sahara could have occurred due to the same problems that are causing desertification today. The destruction of 3.5 million square miles of well-watered arable land, hundreds of species of animals, trees and plants, the Sahara covers an area of approximately 3.5 million square miles, for the purpose of agriculture, construction and mining over an extended period of time, tens of thousands of years, could easily have led to fragmentation of natural forests resources, desertification, a major change in climatic conditions in the region and eventually the creation of the largest dry desert on the planet.

Current data from the Food and Agricultural Organization (FAO, UN), clearly indicates that this scenario described was quite probable, as according to the FAO "An estimated 92,000 hectares of forests and woodlands as well as 2 billion metric tons of fertile soils are lost every year in Ethiopia due to improper land use, poor land management practices, population pressure, overgrazing, deforestation and climate change."

Introduction

The current list of known and accepted plant species consists of 374,000 plants inclusive of 308,312 vascular plants of which 295,383 are flowering plants (angiosperms) and 1079 species of gymnosperms (Christenhusz and Byng 2016). Of these, approximately 60,065 species are trees (Kinver, April 2017, Botanical Gardens Conservation International List of Trees) spread across all land masses, with exception of Antarctica and the Arctic region, inclusive of continents and islands, occupied and unoccupied landmasses, and this presence of trees everywhere indicates a certain special relationship with the planet and the tree inhabitants of the planet. Historical and scientific data indicates that plants predates both animal and human life everywhere on the planet and also that the majority of tree species have a much longer life span than any animal or human, with the Bristle Cone Pine living for as long as 5000 years.

Plants have been and continues to be very rich natural resources for humans and the other animals that call planet Earth home, as they have provided habitat, food and raw material from the beginning of time that both humans and animals have used as such, resources to be used only, however, time and experience is indicating that plants are more than just very valuable natural resources to be used up and cast aside, as experience and scientific evidence is indicating that plants are an integral part of the natural environment similar to rocks, soils, mountains, rivers, lakes, oceans and the atmosphere and also performs some very important roles. While plants play a very vital role in shaping life on Earth, unfortunately, it appears that until in relatively recent times, 300–400 years, even the most advanced human societies appear to lack an appreciation of the importance of trees to the environment, human and animal life and how human and animal activities can negatively impact the ability of plants to continue providing their lifegiving support. Recently uncovered archaeological evidence indicates that places such as the Sahara Desert were once very green and full of life and according to Lloyd (2018) "Before the Sahara changed into a desert there were also trees such as ash, cedar, oak, walnut, myrtle and lime in the region." This green and verdant place was destroyed by very early humans to fill their needs for the creation of open fields for agriculture, habitat for humans, grazing for their domesticated animals, monuments of stones glorifying dead men and mining for minerals. With the growth of human population in the region more trees and other natural resources were destroyed to facilitate the necessary expansion in agriculture and the growth in habitat construction to meet human needs, thereby causing the life of flora and fauna in these places to diminish and eventually faded away. According to Gavin Schmidt, a NASA Climate Scientist, the cause of Sahara's desertification was a shift in the earth's orbit which may have occurred 8-10,000 years ago, however, based on the rate of desertification that is occurring today, without any shift in the earth's orbit, it is very likely that the change in the Sahara could have occurred due to the same problems that are causing desertification today. The destruction of 3.5 million square miles of well-watered arable lands, hundreds of species of animals, trees and plants, the Sahara covers an area of approximately 3.5 million square miles, for the purpose of agriculture, construction and mining over an extended period of time, probably tens of thousands of years, could easily have led to fragmentation of natural forests resources, desertification, a major change in climatic conditions in the region and eventually the creation of the largest hot desert on the planet.

Current data from the Food and Agricultural Organization (FAO, UN), clearly indicates that this scenario described was quite probable, as according to the FAO "An estimated 92,000 hectares of forest and woodlands as well as 2 billion metric tons of fertile soils are lost every year in Ethiopia due to improper land use, poor land management practices, population pressure, overgrazing, deforestation and climate change." Using Ethiopia's data, it can be shown that desertification of the Sahara could easily have occurred over a period of 10,000 years without the theoretical shift in the earth's orbit and according to Kemp

(1994) desertification is usually caused by a combination of natural and anthropogenic activities. At a rate of 92,000 hectares per year the loss of forest lands over a 10,000year period would have resulted in the loss of 920,000,000 hectares which is equivalent to 2,272,400,000 acres. The Sahara Desert is 3.5 million square miles which is equivalent to (3,500,000 x 640) 2,240,000,000 acres and any higher rate of loss would have seen the destruction happening in even shorter spans of time.

The harm caused to forests due to the use of the land for agriculture, while absolutely necessary to feed humans, became significantly worse with the rapid growth in human populations as this growth would have required the stripping and clearing of even more lands to meet the nutritional needs of the increasing number of humans. In addition to the trees destroyed to facilitate agriculture, trees were also destroyed to support mining and smelting of metals, the construction of human shelters and the construction of large monuments and temples made from stone, masonry, fired bricks and sundried bricks, with the monuments and temples dedicated to dead men and religions. Trees or tree products were used in all phased of the construction of the big monuments and by all logical assumptions, timber, a product of trees, must have been used to transport the millions of tons of stones that were required to construct and also to build the support systems that were required to raise very heavy stones hundreds of feet into the air, as in the case of the tallest pyramid Khufu at Giza, Egypt (the Great Pyramid) which stood at a height of 481 feet 3 inches when it was completed. These great stone monuments of Egypt, pyramids, monuments and temples, are today worshipped as great works worthy of commendations by the whole world without anyone giving any thought to the millions of trees that were destroyed to create lifeless, useless stone monuments to glorify narcissistic dead men and the same applies to all great monuments around the world that have been built from the most ancient times until today whose functional use is at best questionable.

Desertification, one of the major environmental problems, in almost all hot regions usually begins with the depletion of trees, followed by the curtailment of the hydrologic cycle, followed by the drying out of soils and consequently the relocation of soils by wind and water forces. This loss of trees, plants and water resources would naturally force the relocation of most species of animals and the humans that were dependent on these species of plants and animals, thereby completing the process of the creation of places like the great Sahara Desert. Unfortunately, this sequence of failures appears to have completely escaped the notice of the human occupants of the Sahara region, as it appears that they may have just moved on to other locations which they consequently destroyed as well, continuing a destructive cycle. This pattern of activities was followed by humans all over the world in many different places, inclusive of the Americas, China, Australia, Mesopotamia, India and Pakistan, wherever most hot desert exists, and continued on for many centuries on into modern societies,16th -21st century, with nations depleting most of their trees for agriculture, implements of war, transportation inclusive of shipping, trucking and rail, manufacturing, paper production and the construction of buildings for residential, commercial and institutional purposes.

Historically, many nations depleted their own stock of trees, after which they were forced to acquire wood products to meet all their needs from their neighbors or faraway places, from friend or foe, through means fair or foul. The path taken would depend on the size of the nation in need and its capacity to make war on its neighbors or having the necessary financial resources to purchase required material, however, quite often the resources of their smaller and weaker neighbors was usually taken by force leading to wars, more weapon building, more ship building and consequently the destruction of even more forests and trees. The trees from lands from much further away and from bigger nations would usually be obtained through trade which also required the destruction of more trees to build ships to transport the acquired material. This destruction of trees by humans without any recourse to replanting for extended periods of human history was in direct contradiction to the human approach to animals and other necessary food resources that humans depended on in their transition away from the hunter-gatherer life style, as humans had begun to domesticate certain animals and crops and had successfully developed practices to replenish these animals and crops on an annual cycle or as frequently as possible, yet these same humans made very little or no effort to regrow the trees that were destroyed to create agricultural fields, build houses and build monuments. This lack of thought and effort could be attributed to many things inclusive of the time required to grow a tree to maturity and to the absence of knowledge about the real importance of trees, especially on the global scale. But in general, the main cause of the failure were the policies of early humans that made them focus only on their immediate needs and far less on the future, which given the levels of development in most places could be considered excusable. The policy makers in early human history were head of families, village priests and various types of monarchy, people who lacked an appreciation of things outside of their immediate locations, the lasting impact of human activities on the environment and over all the larger picture of life on Earth. The policies made by these people would include such things as what crop to plant, the location of the plot of land to be used, the source of water for irrigation, who would plant, reap and store the crops. Unfortunately, even with greater increases in knowledge and levels of development this pattern continued even after many great renaissance periods, industrial revolutions, social revolutions and many other human social changes and transformations throughout history.

CHAPTER

1

Anatomy of Trees

According to the Merriam-Webster dictionary a tree is "a woody perennial plant having a single usually elongated main stem generally with few or no branches on its lower part or is a shrub or herb of arborescent form such as rose trees or banana trees." This makes trees a member of the plant kingdom and they are in fact the giants of the plant world standing anywhere from a few inches tall, Dwarf Willow (Salix Herbacea), which is adapted to survive in arctic and sub-arctic regions of the world inclusive of the North Atlantic, North-East Asia, Northern Europe, Greenland and Eastern Canada, to the nearly 400 feet tall, Hyperion, Sequoia Sempervirens or Coast Redwood, which are concentrated in the California region of the American Pacific North West coast. At the highest heights 350 plus feet "Trees are the tallest self-supporting organisms in the world" Gul et al (2017).

Anatomy of Trees: The basic anatomy of a tree consists of roots, trunks, limbs, branches, twigs and leaves (foliage), buds, blossoms and fruits or seeds and according to Bales (2012) trees are made up leaves – 5%, limbs - 15%, trunk – 60%, woody roots – 15% and absorbing roots – 5%.

Roots

The roots are structurally the foundation of the tree as they connects the tree to the ground and supports the vertical loads transferred from all parts of the crown and the trunk and they also provide structural lateral support and resistance for the tree against strong winds and all forms of horizontal loads that may impact a tree. The roots also have the responsibility for absorbing and transferring nutrients and water from the soil to the crown to ensure the continued growth and maturity of the tree during all stages of the plant's life, the growing, fruit bearing and the declining years of the plant. While all plants have roots, the roots of all plants are not identical and will differ according to the specie of the plants and trees and are divided into two main groups monocotyledon roots and dicotyledon roots and are further subdivided into another two categories, namely primary and adventitious roots. Mono and di refers to the number of cotyledons, seed leaves, in the seed of a plant with monocotyledons have one cotyledon and dicotyledons having two cotyledons. Dicotyledon roots usually refers to the root systems that are associated with trees and are usually called primary and adventitious roots. Monocotyledon roots refer to the fibrous roots systems associated with the grass family inclusive of grain crops, vegetables, bamboo, sugar cane, banana and the palm family, all of which have adventitious roots which usually grow from the stem of the plant.

Primary Roots

The primary root, the first root developed by a plant grows in the opposite direction to the stem, which grows upward towards the sky, going down into the soil to different levels based on the type of soil, clay, sandy or a mixture and the hardness or softness of the soil. The primary root in gymnosperms and dicotyledons usually forms and develops as a tap root from which several lateral branching roots with root hairs will grow creating the tap root system that all such plants are totally dependent upon. The functions of the primary roots include anchoring of the plant to the earth, absorbing water and nutrients from the soil and acting as a storehouse of food material for the plant.

The type of roots and how they grow in relation to the tree will be a function of the type of soil, sandy or clay, the depth of the soil and the availability of water and nutrients. The following are all possible:

- The tree may have a one large tap root.
- The tap root will grow lateral or branch roots covered with root hairs
- The sinker roots hold the tree in place
- 20% of the mass of a tree is located underground in the root system.
- Fibrous roots have the greatest responsibility for providing water and nutrients to the tree and consist of 5% of the tree's mass.
- Fibrous roots extend out 2-3 times the height of the tree, with the total distance being determined by the type of soil, with sandy soil allowing greater width.
- Water and nutrient are taken up by plant roots by the process of osmosis.
- The depths of a tap root system can extend to over 8 feet.

Adventitious Roots

Adventitious roots are usually produced by plants, both monocotyledons and dicotyledons, with a natural disposition to grow adventitious roots such as the grass family of plants inclusive bamboo, banana, sugarcane and the cereal crops and not all plants can produce adventitious roots. The production of adventitious roots occurs naturally in some plants, such as crown roots on cereal plants, while on other plants they are usually triggered by adverse situations and conditions such as flooding, nutrient deprivation and deliberate or accidental wounding of the plant. These adventitious roots usually spring from organs on the stem of the plant above the ground as they do not necessarily require soil to spring and grow. Some features of adventitious roots are as follows:

- There are a set of adventitious plants inclusive of cereal and mangroves which do not need adverse conditions to grow adventitious roots as they produce constitutive adventitious roots naturally and they tend to develop these roots in ordered segments. These plants frequently have segmented stems for the growth of organized adventitious roots.

- Some adventitious plants will only produce adventitious roots in adverse environmental conditions such as flooding, deliberate or unintentional wounding or the absence of adequate water and nutrients.
- Cuttings for propagation from different plants sometimes require different conditions to be successful and example of these are succulent cutting which require just open air to produce roots and devil vine which must be submerged in water.

Trunks

The trunk of the tree act as a natural link between the roots and the crown of the tree and supports the crown literally as a structural member, by storing and transporting food, water and nutrients up and down the tree. The trunk consists of several very important elements that act together to provide the services required by the tree and includes:

- Bark – This is usually the tough outer skin on the tree and usually have different colors and textures depending on the species of the tree. The main function of the bark is to protect the inner cells that are responsible for production of cells, transportation and storage of food.
- Cork Cells- The cork cells are directly below the bark on the inside of the bark and provides secondary protection in the event of damage to the bark.
- Phloem - These are cells that are directly below, on the inside, of the cork cell and they act as the conduit for transporting food produced in the leaves around and down the tree, running from the leaves down to the roots.
- Xylem – These are cells that are located on the inside of the phloem cells that run from the roots of the plant right up to its

leaves and which are responsible for the transportation of water and nutrients from the soil up through the tree.

- Cambium – These are the cells that are directly below the phloem cells and are usually only one cell thick. Cambium cells have the responsibility to produce phloem cells for the outside and xylem cells for the inside as both of these cells die and must be regularly replenished to prevent the death of the tree.
- Heartwood – Provides the structural strength of the tree and consist basically of old and non-functional xylem cells.

Crown

The crown is supported by the trunk or stem of the tree and consists of limbs, branches, twigs, leaves, buds and fruits and it is responsible for the overall growth and development of each tree. The limbs, branches and twigs provide the structural framework that supports, the buds, leaves and fruits, while the leaves are responsible, through the process of photosynthesis, for the production of food and energy that fosters the growth and development of the trees and the production of fruits and seeds. the limbs are the portions of the tree that grows out directly from the trunk while the branches are the divisions of limbs and the twigs are the attachments at the tip of the branches. The limbs and branches are anatomically the same as the trunks as they consist of bark, several layers of different cell material and a hardwood core with the major difference being the size and maturity of limbs and branches relative to the trunk with the trunk being the most developed and matured followed by the limbs, branches and twigs.

Limbs, Branches and Twigs

The limbs, branches and twigs are all woody offshoots from the trunk and basically consists of the same materials as the trunk, bark, cork, phloem, xylem, cambium and heartwood as they must all perform the same functions of taking water and nutrients to the leaves and taking glucose and related food products from the leaves to the rest of the tree. The limbs are directly connected to the trunk, while the branches are the divisions that form on the limbs and the twigs are the small tender end points on the branches on which leaves, buds, blossoms and fruits are formed. Structurally the strength in these members is greatest in the limb and reduces going from limb to branches and lowest in the twigs, which must still be fairly strong as the twigs must support the fruits, fruits that can be quite heavy, that the tree produces.

Leaves (Foliage)

Leaves are numerically in great abundance on most trees and they represent a tree's center of manufacturing, as leaves are where water, nutrient, chlorophyl and sunlight meets to create the starches and sugars that are required for tree growth and the production of fruits, nuts and other edible products. They also provide shade for the tree undergrowth, the creator of undergrowth nurseries for new life forms, both as green leaves on the branch and as dry fallen leaves on the ground, habitat for many species and a tool in the creation of the hydrological system. The basic components of this most important member of most trees and most plants are as follows:

- Leaf Blade. The blades are the center of operation of all leaves as they contain the chemicals and physical infrastructure in which all the processes of photosynthesis occur. The blade typically consists of several components inclusive of cuticle, upper epidermis, lower epidermis, mesophyll -palisade and spongy, veins (xylem and phloem) and stoma.
- Petiole. The petiole is the main structural support of the leaf that connects it to the stem and directly connect to the leaf through the midrib, the main vein of the leaf. The petiole also carries xylem and phloem that connect the leaf to the main vascular system of the tree.
- Veins. The veins form the main structural support within a leaf structure and carries both xylem and phloem which connects every section of the leaf to the vascular system. The pattern of the veins on the leaves also varies based on whether they are monocotyledons (monocots) or dicotyledons (dicots) with

monocots having leaves with parallel veins, parallel venation, that may meet at the apex of the leaf. Dicots have veins that are connected and branched veins from one or more midrib, netted veins. Dicots have three vein patters, pinnately netted venation, palmately netted venation and dichotomous venation.

- Stomata. Stomata are holes on the bottom of the leaf that opens and close to control gas exchange in the leaves and to prevent the loss of water from the leaf.
- Margin. The margin forms the outer boundaries or edge of the leaf and can be either rough or smooth, lobed, serrated, undulate, entire, revolute or crenate.
- Apex and base. These are the end points of the leaf with the base directly connected to the petiole and the apex completely free.
- Texture. The texture of each leaf will be hairy, waxy, rough, smooth, thick or thin.
- Shape. Leaves can be found in many shapes inclusive of linear, oval, oblong, ovate, obovate, deltoid, cordate, elliptical, lanceolate, dentate or lobed.

While leaves are common to all trees and plants, all leaves are not the same and varies based on the species of the plant, gymnosperm versus angiosperm, monocotyledons versus dicotyledons and evergreen versus deciduous species of plants. Typical leaf classifications include simple and compound leaves and are as follows:

- Simple Leaves. These leaves have one blade per petiole and can either be a pinnate or palmate netted venation type which can be in one of several shapes.
- Compound Leaves. Compound leaves have multiple blades or leaflets per petiole and can be one of three types, one pinnately compound type or two palmately compound types and they can have one of many shapes.
- Needle-like or scale-like leaves. These leaves are from evergreen trees

The arrangement of leaves on a stem also varies in one of four grouping:

- Opposite. The leaves are directly across from each other, two leaves per node.
- Alternate. The leaves are spaced out in an alternate pattern on the stem, one leaf per node.
- Subopposite. The spacing of the leaves on the stem are in pattern that is in between opposite and the alternate arrangement, closely spaced nodes with one leaf per node.
- Whorled. The leaves are arranged in a grouping of three or more per node.

Vascular System

The vascular system of plants, consists of the xylem and phloem cells and goes from the roots of the plants to the leaves to ensure the transportation of required water and nutrients from the soil through the roots right up to the leaves and the transportation of the products of photosynthesis, glucose, from the leaves down to the twigs, branches, limbs, the stem and the roots and according to Rost (UC DAVIS) the vascular system of plants "consists of an interconnected network of cells that traverse the entire body of the plant". This interconnected network supplies the water and nutrients, through the xylem, to meet the needs of plant cells and supplies the carbohydrates produced by the leaves to supply energy for the growth of the plant through the phloem, from the leaves. The xylem and phloem cells, while separate entities, forms the circulatory, or vascular system of most plants, however, not all plants have vascular systems. Plants with vascular systems have roots, stems, leaves, vascular bundles that can transport water and nutrients, are better able to store water in cells and are larger, thus making trees vascular plants. Plants without vascular systems have no roots, stems, leaves or vascular bundles, must live in damp conditions and are smaller in size.

Chemical Content of Trees (Wood)

In general, the chemical composition of a tree will vary with the parts of the tree (roots, trunk, branch and leaves), the specie of the tree, the geographic location, the climate, and the soil conditions in which the tree is grown. However, as a general guide, "wood has an elemental composition of approximately 50% Carbon, 6 % Hydrogen, 44% Oxygen and trace amounts of several metal ions" Pettersen (1984).

Lifespan of Trees

The life of a tree begins when the seed of that tree species germinates and sends out it first root followed by its first leaves and ends when the tree dies and decomposes back to carbon and between the beginning of life and death, the tree goes through several physiological changes which includes rapid growth in its early years, followed by constant slow growth, followed by maturity and final decline. During the rapid growth period the tree will have high photosynthetic rates, high growth rates, high foliar efficiency utilizing optimum leaf sizes, high gas exchange rates and a high utilization of carbon resources- (Johnson and Abrahams (2009), Kaufman (1996), Ryan and Yoder (1997), Carrer and Urbinati (2004), & Martinez-Vilalta et al (2007). This early period is followed by reduction in all rates inclusive of photosynthetic, growth, foliar efficiency, leaf sizes, gas exchange and utilization of carbon resources. During the life of trees, they operate between 8-12 hours per day, depending on their location and hours of daylight that is available to them, taking carbon dioxide from the air through their leaves, water and nutrients through their root from the soil, combining them with chlorophyll, which is built into the leaves, and sunlight to create carbohydrates, through the process of photosynthesis for the continuous growth and development of the tree. The conversion of carbon dioxide into carbohydrates that supply the tree with energy for growth, also solidifies to become a part of the structure of the tree which ensure that the carbon is stored in the structure of the tree for the life of the tree. During the life span of each tree, it will shed leaves every year or every three years depending on their status as a deciduous or an evergreen species.

Deciduous Trees. Deciduous trees are generally said to have broad flat leaves and these leaves fall from the trees with the onset of cold weather in autumn. With the coming of the shorter darker days the deciduous trees transition into a rest period or tree-hibernation and during this transition the leaves change color after the disappearance of the chlorophyll, followed by the shedding of all of their leaves after which they remain dormant until the return of brighter longer days in Spring. Another characteristic of deciduous trees is that they usually take much longer to grow and mature and usually produced wood that are hard to work, thus the moniker of hardwood trees. The products made from these hardwood trees tend to be more difficult to make, has a longer life and are relatively more expensive. A deciduous forest is usually made up of broadleaf, hardwood trees that shed their leaves each Autumn and the decomposition of these leaves create a very fertile soil that supports a rich variety of flora and fauna that thrives in the undergrowth of these forests.

Evergreen Trees. Evergreen trees are usually conifers that are generally said to have needle-like leaves with some species having broad flat leaves and these conifers are said to grow relatively faster and are usually much more upright than deciduous trees, which makes the wood from them more suitable for the construction of many elements of a building inclusive of floors, walls, sidings, structural frames and commercial and residential furniture. The wood from an evergreen tree is usually relatively easy to work and is generally referred to as softwood although a few species produce wood that is as hard as or harder than timber produced from many hardwood trees. The shorter, darker, colder days of fall and winter does not have the same impact on evergreen trees as they do on deciduous trees as the leaves of the evergreen tree have much smaller surface areas, are much tougher and more resistant cold and moisture loss. In comparison, while the deciduous trees are tree-hibernating, evergreen trees will continue to grow, with adequate water resources.

2

History of Trees

Human history evolved in the presence of plants, inclusive of trees, as plants were the major producers of the oxygen that humans and animals developed to use in their respiratory systems and this dependency of humans upon the oxygen produced by plants formed an eternal symbiotic relationship. According to Thomas (2000), the first vascular plants appeared on earth during the Silurian about 400 million years ago and "From these the first trees evolved in the early Devonian around 390 million years ago" and by general consensus the first humans or humanlike creatures appeared somewhere between 2.5 to 7 million years ago. According to Harari (2014) "Animals much like modern humans first appeared about 2.5 million years ago". These time periods 390 million years and 2.5-7 million years, indicate that trees predated human existence by hundreds of millions of years, that their established presence over that period of time provided a great base upon which human and animal lives evolved and these trees also provided a foundation upon which to build human lives and many civilizations. Trees and plants have been directly or indirectly providing shelter, clothing, heat and food for humans for many tens of thousands of years and has also been responsible for the preservation of lands, flora, fauna and the environments that have served as the cradle for human existence and civilizations for even much longer periods of time.

According to Thomas (2000) life in the post Devonian period saw 100 million years of trees expanding across coal-producing swamps of the Carboniferous in many different species including tree ferns, giant horsetails and clubmosses and other species, some of which have disappeared today, and this period also saw the development of the first primitive conifers and later, about 250 million years ago, the development of trees such as the cycads, ginkgo and monkey puzzles. This development of different species of tree continued with the following species:

- Pines – 180-135 million years ago
- Early hardwood species – 65-25 million years ago. The development of hardwood species was aided by the warm humid global climate of that period that saw a great expansion in the growth of hardwood trees, this period of expansion helped hardwood species to outpace conifers.

These early trees survived chemical, biological, environmental, climate, temperature, geological and geographical changes to evolve into the plants that they have become in modern times and the best example of these various changes was the breaking up the supercontinent Pangaea over 200 million years ago (King 2005), to form Laurasia and Gondwanaland, followed by the breaking up of the super-continent off-springs 135 million years later, Laurasia to form the northern hemisphere continents and Gondwanaland to form the Southern hemisphere continents all of which led to the creation of the current land masses, geographies, hemispheres and hydrological systems. According to Thomas (2000) all of these changes significantly influenced how trees evolved and developed with each species adjusting and growing in their new environment with the biological, chemical and climatic conditions associated with this new environment to produce the many different species of trees. This period of gigantic changes saw conifers being trapped mostly in the northern hemispheres and the dispersion of the other tree species into varying climate zones. These varying climate zones produced significant differences in the species, for example hardwoods from the northern and southern hemisphere are quite different from each other based on the climatic conditions in which they developed.

Tree Types

The early environmental, geographical, geological, chemical and temporal conditions all converged to create two basic types of trees, Angiosperms – Hardwood Trees and Gymnosperms – Softwood Trees. Around 250 million years ago three species of conifers appeared in those very early forests followed closely by the primitive ancestors of the ginkgo tree, which fossil records have shown to be almost the same as todays ginkgo trees. Botanist Peter Crane (2013) described the ginkgo tree as "a living fossil that has been essentially unchanged for more than 200 million years." These early conifers were the fore runners of the group called gymnosperms or softwood trees which have evolved into the species of softwood trees now grown widely today for their many and varied uses. Angiosperms or hardwood trees first appeared around 150-200 million years ago, which was about the time that the super-continent Pangaea was breaking up and causing the dispersion of angiosperms over a much wider geographical area than gymnosperms. This dispersion continued even further with the breaking up of Laurasia, which formed the northern continents and Gondwanaland which formed the southern continents and gave hardwoods a great dispersion all around the globe. These geographical and geological changes created a proliferation of hardwood trees 95 million years ago beginning with species such as Magnolias, Laurels, Maples Sycamore and Oaks (Nix 2018) and continued until hardwood became the dominant tree type on the planet.

Gymnosperms.

Gymnosperms are seed producing plants that are autotrophic, photosynthetic organisms with a vascular system consisting of roots, xylem and phloem, that use fairly small amounts of water during their lifetime. There are 900 species of gymnosperms (naked seed) or softwoods trees belonging to four linages or types inclusive of Cycads, Ginkgo, Conifers and Gnetophytes, with conifers being the most popular, numbering approximately 650 species, and the most widely used gymnosperm today. The conifers include pines, firs, spruces, hemlocks, redwood, cedars, cypress, yews, and several Southern Hemisphere genera and are both economically and ecologically very important and all have the following general characteristics:

- Scaly or needle like leaves
- Non-flowering seed plants
- Non-fruit producing (one or two exceptions)
- Woody cones in which seeds are produced (few exceptions junipers, podocarps, yews and plum yews).
- Produces both male and female cones, with female cones on the higher branches and male cones on the lower branches
- They are pollinated by the wind.
- Are evergreen and retain leaves during cold months (a few exceptions Larches, Bald Cypress and Dawn Redwood)
- They produce softer timber.

The typical gymnosperms also include Pine (Pinus), Spruce (Picea), Larch (Larix), Fir (Abies), Redwood (Sequoia, Metasequoia, Sequoiadendron), and Douglas-Fir (Psuedotsuga) Cycads (Cycas, Dion, Zamia), Maidenhair Tree (Ginkgo), Cedar (Cedrus), Juniper (Juniperus) and Mormon Tea or Joint Fir (Ephedra). Gymnosperms are present in most ecosystems but are prominent in cool temperate forests.

Angiosperms

Angiosperms are woody and herbaceous flowering seed plants with the seeds embedded in a fruit and they make up more than 80% of the earth's vegetation and consist of basal angiosperms inclusive of Amborella, water lilies, star anise and related species and core angiosperms consisting of three clades magnoliids, monocots, eudicots and have a total of 257,000 species in 14,000 genera. Angiosperms have been and still are of exceptional importance to the growth and development of human societies as they have provided all of the plant food and most of the medicines that have fostered human progress to date and are also vitally important to the natural environment and ecology. Angiosperm trees are hardwood trees that have very high economic values and in general angiosperms plants have the following characteristics:

- Broad leaves which can be simple or compound
- Flowering plants with seeds embedded in a fruit
- Leaves change color and fall of each year (Deciduous) in temperate climates
- Two types of angiosperms monocotyledonous and dicotyledonous plants
- Trees are dicotyledonous.
- Angiosperms are the most developed plants in the world
- The most diverse group of land plants.
- Produces hardwood timber.

The following are a few of the angiosperm species Oaks (Quercus), Ash (Fraxinus), Maple (Acer), Birch (Betula), Beech (Fagus), Cottonwood and Aspen (Populus) and fruit trees which form a very large group of angiosperms that is too long to enumerate here.

Historical Use of Trees.

Since the emergence of the human species, they have made use of trees and the products of trees in many ways inclusive of heating and cooking, construction of shelters, the creation of garments, consumption of the edible fruits and nuts and using wood for religious and social purposes, however, the process of using plants inclusive of trees as a natural resource was not automatic or immediate but developed over significant periods of time. "Crop plants are our greatest heritage from prehistory" (Jannick 2005; Harlan 1992; Diamond 2002), but, unfortunately, the exact location and time when all crop plants were domesticated or first used is fairly hard to determine and science is only now slowly being used to revealed some of the answers through new and more invasive technologies. These new technologies will, however, not provide all of the answer as the connections to some ancient and currently domesticated species have become fairly obscured over many millennia. Molecular biology is currently being used to trace the origins of some ancient grains that were first domesticated in Neolithic time (Janick 2005 and Gepts 2003) and to date, archeological digs have unearthed data indicating probable locations for the early development of agriculture which includes place like Mesopotamia, Indus Valley, Nile, China, Central America, East and West Africa and New Guinea (Janick 2005 and Diamond 1997, 2002). Diamond's evidence suggests that there may have been a specific order in which these developments occurred, however, since all of the locations focused on different crops and there is no evidence of any interrelationships or sequential order in these developments, it is quite probable that all of these developments in agriculture occurred independently of each. The domestication of tree crops follows a similar path to that taken by other crops however, this would have taken place at a later period in time based on available evidence and would have sparked the fruit culture at about the time of the second Neolithic revolution 6000–3000 BCE in the fertile crescent (Janick 2005 and Childe 1958). Evidence indicates that:

- Date Palm may have been the first cultivated fruit crop in Mesopotamia dating to about 4000 BCE. The Date Palm is a Mediterranean fruit.
- Cultivated olives originated around 6000 years ago in Asia Minor
- The peach was domesticated in China before 3300-2500 BCE
- The citrus family of fruits were domesticated in southeast Asia (East India, Burma and Southern China) before 1000 BCE. Biblical references dated it to about 1200 BCE.
- The mango originated in southeast Asia (Indo Burma region) and has been known for 4-6000 years.
- The Avocado originated from the region of southern Mexico-to Panama with archeological evidence showing that it has been eaten since 7000 BCE with evidence of cultivation from around 2000 BCE

These tree fruit crops show different regions domesticating and using different fruits at different periods in time without any evidence that the domestication of one particular tree crop had any bearing on the domestication of other unrelated tree crops in unconnected areas of the globe.

The Historical Social Value of Trees

Trees have provided much more than material benefits to the development of human societies inclusive of places to meet, rest, contemplate, worship and or meditate and historically the wood from trees were used for religious sacrificial purposes, the creation of a representation of a chosen deity and the creation of places of worship. The use of wood in religious sacrifices is clearly written about in the Jewish bible as follows "Then the fire of the LORD fell and burned up the sacrifice, the wood, the stones and the soil and also licked up the water in the trench" (Bible,1 Kings 18 verse 38). People across the globe, thousands of miles away from Jewish settlements, also offered burnt sacrifices to their deities using wood inclusive of the people of Mesoamerica "Human sacrifice was important in Mayan Culture" (Brown 2014) and "When celebrating mythic events dedicated to their gods, Incas used to make human sacrifices" (Anitei 2008) According to Brown and Anitei, Mesoamerica's history showed that all the major cultures inclusive of the Olmecs, Maya, Aztecs and Incas practiced human sacrifice in which humans were ritually killed and some were burned. According to Nadia Selez Valdana, archeologist, "The sacrifice involved burning or partially burning victims" (Stevenson 2005). These references clearly indicate that human religious rites involving sacrificial offerings utilizing wood to burn the sacrifice. This was, however, not the only way that trees were used in religious encounters as many people all around the globe saw trees as being sacred and holy in themselves. The following are example of this.

- Neem Tree. Neem trees are considered holy and one located in Varanasi, India is considered too holy to cut down and is usually dressed and treated with much veneration.

- Pipal Tree. The Pipal Tree located at Dukh Haran Hanuman Temple in Varanasi, India is believed to embody the monkey god Hanuman and many people pray to the monkey god Hanuman. This tree is also dressed up, protected and venerated by all believers.
- Bunut Bolong. The Bunut Bolong is a sacred tree in West Bali that is actively worshipped by Hindu believers.
- Tane Mahuta. The Tane Mahatu (Lord of the Forest) is a Kauri tree that is found in the remote Waipoua Forest of New Zealand and it is sacred to the Maori people.
- The Incas highly valued the Palo Santo (Bursera Graveolens) and the Willows, native to Peru and ranked trees plants such as cocoa plants, rose and seeds as sacred.
- The natives of tribes of the north American continent valued highly the Arbutus or Madrone trees, Cottonwood trees and Cedar trees among their most important trees.
- The Japanese people value ancient Japanese Cypress trees as sacred
- The aboriginal people of Australia highly value the Djap Wurrung Trees
- The Celtics had a very strong tree culture and most trees were revered and thought to have special powers. The Celtic calendar year consists of thirteen lunar months representing the cycles of the moon and each lunar month was linked to one of the sacred Celtic trees and this was used as the basis of the Celtic Tree Astrology. The astrology included Birch the Achiever(Dec24 -January 20), Rowan the Thinker(January 21-Feb 17), Ash the Enchanter(Feb 18- Mar 17), Alder the Trailblazer(Mar 18- April 14), Willow the Observer (April 15- May 12), Hawthorne the Illusionist(May 13- June 9), Oak the Stabilizer(June 10 – July 7), Holly the Ruler(July 8- August 4), Hazel the Knower(August 5- Sept 1), Vine the Equalizer(Sept 2-Sept 29), Ivy the Survivor(Sept 30-Oct 27), Reed the Inquisitor(Oct 28- Nov 24) and Elder the Seeker(Nov 25- Dec 23). In addition to their tree astrology, they also had a trilogy of most sacred trees which includes the Ash, Oak and Hawthorne.

- The Druids love all species of trees, their name "Druids" can be translated as "One with the knowledge of oak" or "Wise person of the oak" and those who had knowledge of oak were thought to have knowledge of all trees and they developed their own lore and knowledge systems about trees.

The above represent only a few of the many trees that were and are still considered either sacred or holy by the many aboriginal peoples of the world inclusive of Celtics, Druids, Germanic tribes and other aboriginal people of Europe, Australia, New Zealand, the Americas, continental Africa and Asia. These different peoples worshiped or valued very highly some particular trees due to one of many attributes of the tree inclusive of longevity, the height, the overall size, the material value that they produced, the medicinal value or properties and the food value of a particular trees, while many other civilizations and societies, such as the Incas of South America, consider all trees and plants to be very sacred beings. Some of the natives of North America also considered all trees to be important based upon their understanding of the roles of trees, and according to poet Richard Olafson, one native American legend says "The trees webbed roots hold the splintered earth together" which shows a very high level of understanding of trees and their roles by these original peoples of the Americas.

In addition to the sacred and religious values of trees, trees were also valued for many other social and sentimental reason some of which are shown below.

- Meeting Trees. Huge trees with wide canopies that can shelter a large number of people were used as village meeting places as they provided shelter and were held as common property to all. One such example are large mango trees in some African villages, inclusive of one in Naunde, Mozambique.
- Loved by Community. A 1200- 1300 years old Montezuma Cypress, that has a circumference of 138 feet, located in Mexico, is so well beloved by the community that a main highway was re-routed to avoid it.

- Memorial Trees. A Monkey Pod tree in Cambodia is used as a memorial for children killed by the Khmer Rouge. Items representing each child is hung on this tree by the bereaved family members.

While some people place great value on specific trees or species of trees, others place greater value on groves of trees or whole forest, based on their religious beliefs, which may include the worship of trees, worship of a god that dwells among the trees, worship of a god the dwells in a specific tree or worshipping their god among the trees as a place of reverence. Based on these different preferences many groups of people around the globe have made groves of trees their place of worship and veneration, thus making these places sacred and holy to them. The consecration of these forests, called sacred groves, usually take these locations away from the normal everyday usage with each group developing their own list of prohibitions based on their set of religious or social tenets. These prohibitions varied from not using any product from within the sacred spaces inclusive of wood, fruits, leaves or animals that live in the forest, to being allowed to use dead wood, fruits, leaves and animals but never destroying any life within the space, with other variations depending on the people who develop these prohibitions. These "Sacred Groves" thus became conservation spaces for many species of plants and animals through many thousands of years and in general, "Sacred Groves are tracts of virgin forest with rich diversity which have been protected by local peoples for centuries for their cultural, religious beliefs and taboos that the deities reside in them and protect the villages from different calamities" Khan et al (2008). In general "sacred groves" have been created, preserved and utilized by people with polytheistic and animistic religious beliefs from the earliest development of human life with significant references made to these groves by different cultures inclusive of Judaism, a monotheistic religion that saw sacred groves as evil as they were used to worship gods that were different from the one that they believe in "Whilst their children remember their altars and their groves by the green trees upon the high hills" (Jeremiah chapter 17 verse 2, Jewish Bible). Tacitus, the Roman historian, referred to the Germans and their groves in his writings "In the country of the latter is a grove, consecrated to religious rites of great antiquity". These two references, however, are only two of the many peoples and tribes that have built and maintained "sacred groves" or have a religious position on the subject for many centuries. Other references include:

- Acknowledgement of scared groves as "...important features of the mythological landscape and cult practices of Celtic, Baltic, Germanic, ancient Greeks, Near Eastern, Roman, and Slavic polytheisms and were also used in India, Japan and West Africa" (Corvillo Arroyo 2015),
- Ancient Greece groves "The sacred groves of the ancient Greece were designed for the specific purpose of linking the sacred realm of the gods and the profane world of humans"- Barrett (2007),
- Indian groves "The existence of sacred groves in India is thought likely dates back to an ancient pre-agrarian hunter-gathering era, and their presence has been documented since the early 1800s" Polidor (2004),
- Ghanaian groves "Sacred forests groves dot the otherwise increasingly degraded landscape of Ghana, in West Africa, providing oases of diversity and tradition" (Corbin 2008)
- Ethiopian groves "These 'church forest' (as they are known) are biodiversity preserves of critical importance for the future of Ethiopia" (Goodin et al 2019).

All of the above references indicate quite clearly the wide use of sacred groves or forest by peoples of many nations around the globe, with a very strong polytheistic religious background, with one exception in Ethiopia which currently has a monotheistic religious outlook and deep seated animistic background, who through their religious practices established sacred groves which are now proving to be quite beneficial to forests, the environment and consequently to humans and animals. The main benefits from maintaining sacred forest include:

- The creation of biodiverse hot spot

- They allow for the accumulation of optimum levels of biomass, carbon dioxide (CO_2) and Oxygen (O_2) balances locally.
- They allow for the growth of thick vegetation that provides varying layers of canopy to facilitate the harvesting, absorption and distribution of rainwater.
- The provision of habitat for varying species of birds, pollinating insects and bees.
- The provision of checks on the growth of desertification, the degradation and erosion of soil
- The provision of nurseries for many medicinal plants.
- The provision of sanctuaries for many rare, endangered and endemic species of plants and animals.

MICHAEL GRAHAM MSc.

3

The Impact of Trees

Trees have through many millennia provided so many benefits to humanity that even without citing scientific data, most people can off the top of their heads, name many benefits they have obtained from trees inclusive of fruits and nuts, shelter made from timber and leaves, clothing made from cotton and linen, shading during the hot seasons, natural beauty during spring and fall seasons in temperate climates, all year round beauty in tropical climates, heating obtained from logs during the winter and trees providing winds breaks against strong winds year round. In this same light they can also point to some of the problems associated with trees, such as falling leaves during Autumn, falling trees during heavy storms and the hinderance that trees represent when they desire to use lands covered with trees for agricultural, residential or commercial developments, the construction of an essential infrastructure and services such as roads, rails, schools, hospitals and military facilities. Most people, however, are ignorant about the more essential services provided by trees or their overall impact on the environment, animal and human life, the atmosphere, rainfall, climate, air pollution, clean water supplies, pollination of food crops, soil erosion, desertification and the many other very valuable environmental services provided by trees to support life on this planet.

The benefits provided by trees fall into some basic categories inclusive of social, communal, environmental, ecological and economic.

Social Benefits

All humans have a natural affinity for the presence of trees, of all kinds, due to the many natural offerings the trees have on display, visual beauty, singing birds, insects, flitting butterflies, tree loving animals, the soothing sound of the wind blowing in the leaves, the odor from the trees, all of which can and have combined to sooth the minds and hearts of all human and many animal species for thousands of years. This natural calming effect of trees has been well recognized and recorded for many centuries and has been highlighted by the many recluses, writers, monks, ascetic, hermits and even revolutionaries who wandered off into the wilderness to contemplate and calm their hearts and minds before making life changing decisions that could affect their families and community, cause the loss of lives or make drastic improvements for many. A few of these outstanding people includes Buddha, Jesus and Thoreau.

The Buddha who live from 500-400 BCE, started life as a prince by the name of Siddhartha Gautama who lived the good life but by the age of 29 realized that he was dissatisfied with his existence and walk away from everything and went off into the forest where he wandered for six years before finding enlightenment while sitting under a tree, later called the Bodhi Tree, "It was thus that one evening seated under a tree on the bank of the river Neranjara at Buddha-Gaya at the age of 35 Gautama attained enlightenment after which he was known as the Buddha" (Rahula 1974). The Buddha went on from this enlightenment to start what became one of the world's major religions, Buddhism. The Buddha lived and taught in India all of his life.

Jesus of Nazareth, who lived in the land of Israel in the Middle East, from somewhere between AD 5- 40, was the son of a humble carpenter or woodworker, who by the age of 30 years old completely changed his life after he was baptized, a religious rite for the followers of Judaism, at the beginning of what was to become the most important phase of his life. After this baptism he went on a sojourn into the wilderness, forests, for 40 days and 40 nights from which he emerged energized to take on established Judaism which led to his death and rebirth, "Then was Jesus led up of the Spirit into the wilderness to be tempted of the devil" (Christian Bible, St. Matthew Chapter 4 verse 1). The teachings, philosophies, death and rebirth of Jesus lead to the formation of one of the great and most influential religions of the world, Christianity, that has influenced positively the lives of billions of people all across the globe starting after the resurrection of Jesus. It should be noted that Christianity has also negatively impacted the lives of many indigenous people as it was used by its adherents to subjugate and control in the many new lands that they conquered.

Henry David Thoreau (1817-1862) was an American poet, essayist and practical philosopher who spent two years (1845-1847) of his life living in the woods while writing two of his best and most influential works, an essay called "On the Duty of Civil Disobedience" and a book named "Walden". The essay "On the Duty to Civil Disobedience" significantly influenced the lives of two important world figures Mahatma Gandhi of India and Martin Luther King Junior of the US, while the book "Walden" greatly influenced the early environmental movement in the USA and many refer to him as the father of American environmentalism. According to one biographer, Richard J. Schneider, Thoreau also made several trips into the woods apart from his two years on the Walden Pond "…and his main concern was his daily afternoon walks in the Concord woods." (Schneider).

The works of these three men who sojourned in forests for particular periods of time have provided and continues to provide great social and spiritual benefits which have had long lasting effects upon much of modern eastern and western civilizations.

Communal Benefits of Trees

Modern sociologists have indicated that trees and greenspaces can also have similar calming effects upon not just individuals, such as Thoreau, but also upon groups of people within a locale inclusive of people sharing common spaces like office buildings, apartment buildings, schools, colleges, universities, hospitals and other spaces that are shared by groups of people "Overall, academic institutions and hospitals have found that natural settings and trees result in measurably positive impacts on students and patients" (Bassett 2015; Wolf et al 2014). This effect has been observed in the difference in crime levels in apartment buildings that have trees and greenspaces and those that do not have these amenities. The calming, stress and fatigue reducing effects of trees are also said to do such things as reduce the time to recovery after surgery, reduce stress in traffic and may even reduce the levels of crime in a city "Urban trees improve air quality, cool local air temperatures, filter and retain stormwater, sequester carbon and contribute to healthier and more beautiful cities (Bassett 2015; Nowak et al 2008; McPherson et al 2003). Urban trees are currently being used in many other ways inclusive of providing privacy and blocking out objectionable views, emphasizing particular views and reducing reflections and glares. These urban trees can also be used to highlight architectural designs by providing a background to, softening or enhancing particular features. "To the 75% of the United States population that now live in urban and suburban areas, trees provide many goods and services (Coder 1996). In general, an urban community benefit from urban trees in many ways inclusive of:

- Reduced Heat Island Effect that normally elevates the temperature of cities upto10 degree Fahrenheit above the surrounding countryside, thereby increasing energy demands and creating negative health and environmental impacts.
- Improved air quality caused by the reduction of carbon dioxide in the air, the production of oxygen by the tree and the reduction of other pollutants by the trees.
- Improved hydrological effects as the tree canopies will improve the amount of rainwater that will be absorbed and thereby reduce the amount of water run-off and soil erosion and improve the quality of the water in aquifers, streams, rivers and lakes.
- Wind Control. Trees will reduce the wind impact upon residences and reduce required heating energy each cold season.

- Shade. Shade from trees willing significantly reduce the cooling required during summers as they directly block the heating rays from the sun.
- Improved evaporation will also be provided by trees that will help to improve cooling in the community and ensure more rainfall.
- Improved real estate values, as a trees in the front yard improve the economic value of a property.
- Nosie abatement. The white noise produced by the leaves of trees will abate noise produced from other sources inclusive of noise produced by traffic on a highway, close to residential communities.

Environmental and Ecological Benefits of Trees.

Trees and plants are great benefactors of the natural environment of which they form one of the major components, inclusive of the land, the atmosphere and water and since the first appearance of the forerunners of trees 400 million years ago, they have evolved to contend with all the elements of the Earth, soil, rocks, atmosphere, wind and water to shape the space that all humans and animals would later evolved to occupy. Some of the basic function of trees in the evolutionary process includes:

- Utilizing and or disposing of the chemicals that were naturally produced by the activities that formed and continues to ensure the existence of the earth.
- Holding the soils of the earth together.
- Providing and acting as habitats and nurseries for newly formed animal and plant life.
- Providing two levels of shading for humans, more sensitive animals and plants from the direct rays of the sun, particularly those UV rays with the capacity to destroy life through excessive heating. The first barrier or shade is in the ozone layer of the atmosphere, where oxygen produced by plants and other autotrophs have been converted by solar energy to form ozone which has been deposited high in the atmosphere over millions

of years. This barrier, the ozone layer, reflects much of the sun's solar radiation back into space, thereby limiting the amount of heat that will directly reach the earth. The second layer of shading is provided directly by the canopies of trees on the surface of the earth.

- Continuously removing various chemicals from the soils and from the water to provide suitable resources for humans and animals.
- Continuously removing carbon dioxide and other gases from the atmosphere.
- Continuously producing oxygen that is essential to human and animal life.

Prior to the evolution of human and animal life, a large portion of the oxygen produced by plants inclusive of trees was converted and placed into storage high above the surface of the earth in the stratosphere as ozone, and this ozone created a protective shield around the earth. This process left the atmosphere rich in oxygen, 20 %, to support the evolution and development of animal and humans and provided a very healthy atmosphere that far exceeded the needs of early humans and animal life and established a tree to human and animal ratio that was essential for the early survival of the species. However, with the explosion in the human population this relationship has been significantly altered as theoretically more humans should require more trees and plants to meet their oxygen needs, however, this conflicted with the needs for more trees to be destroyed to facilitate more agriculture to feed the growing human population. This conflict eliminated the possibility of restoring and maintaining the pristine condition of the atmosphere that existed at the start of human and animal life. Current conditions indicate that the reestablishment this theoretical pristine condition is very unlikely under most circumstances and may not be necessary however, this theoretical condition could be used as a benchmark, an unattainable goal, that is used to guide the future actions of humans on the planet.

IN the post evolutionary or creation world the main environmental and ecological benefits of trees and plants, are as follows:

- Maintaining atmospheric conditions to ensure optimum livability for humans, animals and plant life. This would include the process of removing carbon dioxide from the atmosphere and storing it in the biosphere.
- Continuing to create oxygen to maintain human and animal life.
- Maintaining local temperatures through the provision of natural shading under their canopies to ensure livable and safe conditions for humans, animals and plants.
- Acting to prevent soil erosion by their web of roots holding soil together and acting as barriers to wind.
- Acting to ensure a clean water supply by ensuring that storm water runoff volume, speed and silt content is reduced and that more water from precipitation events penetrates the soil to enter underground aquifers than would travel over ground into surface water bodies
- Continuing to providing habitat for mammals, reptiles, amphibians, birds, insect, bees and all tree dwelling animals.
- Preventing desertification and providing an essential element for the reclamation of deserts.

Trees and the Atmosphere

Trees have an enormous capacity to interrelate to all elements of the environment that they are in contact with, inclusive of the soil, rocks, atmosphere, other plants, animals and humans. The relationship between trees and the atmosphere is of special significance as trees access carbon dioxide a greenhouse gas, one of the main components that is used in the manufacture of carbohydrate, plant food, directly from the atmosphere. While removing carbon dioxide from the atmosphere trees have the capacity to simultaneously to remove other chemicals, some described as criteria pollutants inclusive of Particulate Matter (PM), Sulfur Dioxide (SO_2), Nitrogen Oxides (NO_x), Carbon Monoxide (CO) and ground level ozone from it. Trees also use their leaves to block 95% of the UV rays that reach the Earth's surface, thereby creating more hospitable conditions for human and animal health and the development of nurseries for other lifeforms. "A modelling study using hourly meteorological and pollution concentration data from across the coterminous United States demonstrates that urban trees remove large amounts of air pollution that consequently improve urban air quality" (Nowak et al 2006). The study also indicated that the pollutants removed included the six criteria pollutants, with the amount of each pollutant removed being dependent upon the region and the type of trees. According to Nowak et al (2006) the mechanisms used by trees to remove pollutants and carbon dioxide (climate change gas) include the following:

- Uptake of carbon dioxide by leaf stomata
- Uptake of gaseous air pollutants by leaf stomata
- Deposition of gases on trees surfaces
- Deposition of particulate matter on leaves and other tree surfaces
- Absorption of some particulate matter into the tree.
- Adjusting the temperature of the air in the surrounding space to reduce the possibility of the formation of ground level ozone.

The gases taken in by the leaf stomata usually diffuses into the intercellular spaces of the leaves after which it may follow one of two paths, absorption by water film to form acids or reacting with inner leaf surfaces (Smith et al 1990; Nowak et al 2006). The particulate matter intercepted is usually managed in one of three ways, resuspending it into the atmosphere, removal by precipitation to the ground or falling to the ground with dead leaves.

In general, trees can improve the health of humans, animals and the environment by reducing pollutants emissions and formation and by using their leaves to block 95% of incident UV radiation. Trees, however, can and have contributed to air pollution by emitting their natural

VOCs that can facilitate the formation of ground level ozone and therefore when selecting trees for urban environments effort must be made to select the trees that will emit the least VOCs.

Trees and Oxygen

Oxygen, (O_2) is a colorless, odorless, tasteless gas that is essential to all living organisms that utilize cellular respiration, the main method that almost all living organisms utilize to gain energy. The process of cellular respiration is used by all living animals inclusive of insects, birds, fish, mammals, reptiles and amphibians and prior to the presence of oxygen in the atmosphere only plants and other elements that could use carbon dioxide to generate the energy that they needed could exist. According to Yu (2001) oxygen is a relative newcomer as four billion years ago the earth's primeval atmosphere was composed mostly of Carbon Dioxide (CO_2) 98%, a little Nitrogen (N_2) 1.9%, water vapor, trace amounts of other gases and little or no oxygen. The atmosphere currently consists of Nitrogen (N_2) 79%, Oxygen (O_2) 20%, Carbon dioxide (CO_2) 0.035%, trace amounts of other gases and water vapor and this transition from an atmosphere rich in carbon dioxide to an atmosphere rich in nitrogen and relatively rich in oxygen lead to the development of a substantial increase in the amount of complexed living organisms. The transition was fostered by autotrophs, all plants and trees, which utilize inorganic carbon (carbon dioxide) to produce cell material and the energy that they need, with oxygen as a waste product. The process by which plants utilize carbon dioxide to produce energy is called photosynthesis. "Photosynthesis sustains virtually all life on planet Earth providing the oxygen that we breathe and the food we eat" (Johnson 2016). The oxygen produced by the plants in the first 400 million years led to a great buildup of oxygen in the stratosphere where oxygen (O_2) was converted by a process of photodissociation to become ozone (O_3) which formed a protective layer around the earth. This protective layer is responsible for reflecting a large portion of the sun's infrared and UV rays back into space, that would otherwise have made the earth too hot for the development of animal life and probably plant life as well.

Photosynthesis

Photosynthesis is considered to be the most beautiful and enduring process on earth, as it gives the inhabitants of planet Earth life by utilizing the light from the sun, components of the air and the soil and will continue to do so as long as humans ensure the continued existence and growth of all plants, especially our trees.

The leaves of plants are the center of photosynthetic operations as they are responsible for the collection of carbon dioxide (CO_2), mixing the CO_2 with water, nutrients and chlorophyl, natural plant chemical, and exposing the mixture to sunlight and thereby generating all the activities that are involved in the photosynthetic process that creates plant food and oxygen. The steps involved in the photosynthetic process are as follows according to Johnson (2016):

- Leaves, as evolved, expose the largest possible surface area of green tissue to sunlight and carbon dioxide.
- Each leaf has holes in its lower epidermis called stomata which is used to control the flow of carbon dioxide into each leaf.
- The size of the opening of each stoma is variable and is regulated by a pair of guard cells which respond to the water content (turgor pressure) of each leaf.
- When the leaf is hydrated the stomata opens to allow entry of carbon dioxide and closes when the water content falls. The closure of the stomata when water content falls prevents the escape of water from the leaf by the process of evapotranspiration.
- The green tissue of each leaf has cells which contain chloroplast where the process of photosynthesis takes place.
- The chloroplasts have a complex structure with two outer membranes which enclose an aqueous space called the stroma and the stroma contains a third membrane called the thylakoid.
- The thylakoid encloses the lumen which is a single continuous aqueous space.
- The process of photosynthesis involves two subprocesses Light Reaction and Dark Reaction.

- The Light Reaction takes place in the thylakoid membrane and involves light driven electrons and protons.
- The Dark Reaction take place in the stroma and the fixation of carbon dioxide into carbohydrates (Calvin-Benson Cycle).
- The Light and Dark Reactions are mutually dependent on each other.
- The process of photosynthesis begins with the splitting of water by photosystem II (PSII) where PSII is a chlorophyll-protein complex embedded in the thylakoid membrane that uses light to oxidize water to oxygen and reduce the electron acceptor Plastoquinone to Plastoquinol.
- Plastoquinol carries the electrons derived from the reaction with water to another complex protein called cytochrome b_6f ($cytb_6f$).
- The $cytb_6f$ oxidizes plastoquinol to plastoquinone and reduces a small water-soluble electron carrier protein called plastocyanin, which resides in the lumen.
- The second light-driven reaction is then carried out by another chlorophyll protein complex called photosystem I (PSI), where this PSI oxidizes plastocyanin and reduces another soluble electron carrier protein ferredoxin that resides in the stroma

All of these reactions produce carbohydrates, tree food, in the form of glucose, starches and other sugars, and oxygen as a by-product or waste. The outlined processes clearly highlight how plants, inclusive of trees, working together with light, nutrients and water created the environment for animal life, that utilizes oxygen respiration to exist.

Trees and Temperature

Trees are unique in their structure and the mechanisms that make them work as trees and they have unique and significant effects upon the environment inclusive of their ability to affect the temperature and climate around them as an individual tree and more so as a group of trees or a forest. Two of the major activities of a tree that affect the temperature and consequently the environment includes:

- Shading
- Evapotranspiration

Shading

The crown of the tree, all trees inclusive of evergreens and deciduous trees, usually consist of limbs, branches, twigs and leaves or foliage which together act to block the rays of the sun and especially UV ray that can have deleterious effect on human, animals and some plants. This blocking out of direct sunlight and UV rays creates a lower temperature under the trees. "Forest vegetation reduces mean annual temperature five feet above the ground from 0.8- 1.8 FO depending upon character of forest and locality, particularly elevation" (Ansari 2003). According to the USEPA, shaded surfaces could be 20-45degree Fahrenheit cooler than the temporary highest temperatures of unshaded areas or material. Trees therefore, not only produced oxygen for respiration but also provided cooler locations that could facilitate the development of secondary plant and animal life. The typical spaces that are affected by the shade of trees include the forest floor, understory layer of trees, the canopy layer and emergent layers, each of which are the habitats for several species of plants and animals.

- The forest floor shaded by the trees, dead leaves and grass provides a cool moist environment that is a habitat for things like fungi, insects, worms, snails, slugs and other small organisms that live there and function to breakdown forest waste to form new soil that is essential to continuity. Left unshaded most forest floors would dry out eventually and end the cycle for continuous renewal as the fungi, insects, snails and other small organisms would not have required temperature and moisture for growth and existence. The forest floor also acts as an incubator for the seeds of other plants that thrive only in the shade of taller trees, thus ensuring that the forest floor is covered with ecologically vibrant secondary plants and shrubs.
- The understory layer is a layer that is above ground but under leaves that provides a dark, cooler and damp environment for

plants such as shrubs, small or young trees that have adapted to live in the shade of larger trees and is also home to reptiles, insect and other small organisms. These shade loving trees and plants, sciophytes, include such plants as cardamom which is a spice that is widely used in the food world.

- The canopy layer, limbs, branches, twigs and leaves, provides shade and protection for the rest of the forest and it is usually full of life inclusive of birds, insects, reptiles and mammals.
- The emergent layer pokes out much higher than the trees from the canopy layer and is usually the home to many birds and insects.

Evapotranspiration

Water is essential to the life of all plants inclusive of trees and it is usually taken into the plant by the roots from where it travels through the xylem to the leaves where a portion of it is utilized in the process of photosynthesis. The tree's intake of water is usually much greater than its own particular needs as the tree only uses approximately five percent (5%) of its water intake and allows the remaining ninety five percent (95%) to escape as vapor through its leaves. "In the leaves, small pores allow water to escape as a vapor. Of all the water absorbed by plants less than five percent (5%) remains in the plant for growth" (Sterling 2004).

The Cohesion Theory of Sap Ascent that has been used to describe the movement of water through plants, states that "The cohesive properties of water (hydrogen bonding between adjacent water molecules) allow the column of water to be "pulled" up through the plant as water molecules are evaporating at the leaf surface" (Sterling 2004). The process of transpiration is vital to each plant because it allows some very important activities to take place inclusive of:

- Water and nutrient intake
- Strengthening the structural integrity of the tree or plant
- Continuous functioning of the tree or plant
- The intake of Carbon Dioxide
- The provision of the energy required in the process of photosynthesis.

Without transpiration the roots of the tree will not "pull " up the necessary water and nutrients and the tree will lose it structural integrity and collapse, the stomata will not open to take in carbon dioxide as the leaves are not hydrated and the necessary functions such as photosynthesis cannot not be completed as the source of energy to break the strong hydrogen bond, which can only be taken from the exothermic energy release during the process of vaporization of water at the leaf, will not be available.

The process of transpiration ensures the release of energy by vaporization that will cool the leaves, the air surrounding the leaves and consequently the air immediately adjacent to the tree's space. The volume of water released through the leaves will also disperse into the atmosphere immediately adjacent to the tree and will affect the relative humidity and temperature of the atmosphere in and around the trees or plants. The amount of cooling will be dependent upon the amount of water released by each type of plant and the size of the forest or field.

Trees and Soil Erosion.

Soil erosion is the detachment, removal and eventual loss of top soil from one section of land to another section of land or surface waters and the loss of soil from any section of land will lead to the degradation, loss of productivity and loss of value of the portion of land thus affected. This degradation is usually long term and according to one US president, in the middle of a soil erosion crisis, "A nation that destroys its soil destroys itself" (FDR 1937). The president made this comment during a speech he gave while the worst soil erosion events to have ever affected the United States from 1930-1939 in the Southern Plains Region called The Dust Bowl, was affecting the country. The accepted rationale for this soil erosion failure was said to be the result of several bad government policies and poor agricultural practices over a period of approximately 80 years and many very harsh lessons were learnt during this10 years period. According the NRCS of the USDA soil erosion is a two-phase process and are as follows:

- Detachment of individual particle from soil aggregate
- Transportation of released particles by the erosive forces of wind and water.

From all the evidence gathered by local and international soil authorities there are several factors which are responsible for soil degradation and consequently the detachment of soil particles from soil aggregates and these include, deforestation 30%, agriculture 28%, overgrazing 35%, overexploitation 7% and industrialization 1%. The main erosion agents as given by the USDA, were water 55%, wind 29% chemical, acidifications and salts 12% and physical degradation, compaction and crusting 4%.

From the referenced report it can be seen that trees and other plants can play a major role in the reduction of soils erosion as from the data provided it can be seen that the elimination of trees and other plants for legitimate and illegitimate reasons are responsible for ninety three percent (93 %) of soil erosion problems worldwide. Trees and all other plants by design have a natural capacity to prevent soil erosion by water and wind, the two erosion agents responsible for eighty four percent (84%) of all soil erosion worldwide.

Water Erosion

The USDA 1982- 2000 Erosion Report indicates that water is responsible for fifty five percent (55%) of all soil erosion. Trees and other plants combined can significantly reduce the problems of soil erosion by water and we can understand how trees with the vastness of their root systems, roots that go deep and are widely spread with a width of two to three times the height of the tree and depth of up to 8 feet can act to keep soil together. This root system combined with the crown, shrubs undergrowth and debris usually act to significantly reduce the chances of rainwater or stormwater removing top soil as follows:

- The main roots, primary and lateral, combined with the hair roots hold soil in direct contact with them compactly, thus increasing the force required to detach soil particles and thereby reducing the likelihood of soil erosion. The intermeshing of the roots on many trees, shrubs and grass as usually occurs in a forest makes the bonds even stronger.

- The crown of the tree which comes in contact with precipitation first will upon impact reduce the velocity of rain, sleet and snow, but especially rain, and slow the flow velocity significantly before it impacts the soil. Some of the precipitation will be absorbed by the crown, while a portion will flow, relatively slowly down the limbs, branches and the trunks, while some will fall through the leaves making many impacts, hitting many leaves, before it reaches the soil.

- The dead leaves and underbrush that is normally found under most trees on the forest floors will further slow the movement of the liquid precipitation and the resistance created by the dead leaves, other debris, grass and shrubs will allow a proportion of the water to be infiltrated in the soil and into underground receptacle called aquifers while a portion of it will run over the surface to rivers, stream, ponds, lakes and the oceans.

- The reduction of precipitation velocity and volume, due to impact with the crown of tree, before it reaches the forest floor also reduces capacity of the water to break soil bonds and to transport large volumes of soil and silt to other locations, inclusive of surface water bodies such as ponds, streams, rivers, lakes and the oceans.

Wind Erosion

Trees also provide very good resistance to wind erosion, which normally occurs when there is an absence of any type of cover over the soils and the soils have been fractured into a loose state due to poor soil preparation practices and the drying out effect of the sun's heat. Trees by their presence and the resistance that their leaves give to wind, usually act to reduce the velocity of the wind in the vicinity and therefore will reduce the capacity of the wind to lift and remove soil. According the NRCS, USDA 1982-2000 report, wind erosion is responsible for 29% of all erosion, due to the methods of soil preparation used, the large expanse of open uncovered fields and the strong winds that are prevalent across much of the US and many other areas of the world. The effect of wind erosion can be reduced by changing field preparation methods and by creating barriers to wind action and trees can be used as one such barrier. "Barriers help by reducing wind speed on the downwind side of the barrier and by trapping moving soil." (Tatarko). According to Tatarko, barriers can act to reduce wind speed over distances of approximately ten times the height of the barriers thereby reducing the effective field length and creating a protective zone in the direction of the erosive wind. Such barriers can be created by land berms, shrubs, grass and other smaller plant life or other material, but trees with their immensely greater heights would create much larger protective zones and would be much better at reducing soil erosion.

A recent USDA report indicates that approximately 12,000 pounds of top soil per acre was lost in North America (USA and Canada) from 575 million acres of farmlands (1998-1999) and this computes to millions of tons of soil being relocate by wind each year in North America and worldwide this number would be approximately 7 times as much, based on the total acreage of land farmed worldwide. With wind being responsible for 29% of all soil erosion the use of trees, along and between large fields perpendicular to wind direction, could lead to a reduction in this great loss of topsoil.

Trees and Hydrology

Hydrology is the science concerned with the occurrence, distribution, circulation, locations and properties of water in the environment and the main water resources of the earth are in the oceans, lakes, rivers, streams, ponds, groundwater aquifers, glaciers and permanent snow, ground ice and permafrost, swamps, plants, animals and the atmosphere. These resources are fixed and has not increased since the beginning of time and according to the USEPA's the Water Cycle and Water Conservation document page A-1 "The water available to planet Earth is the same water that has always been available and the only water that ever will be available". These water resources are divided as follow:

- Oceans – 97 % (saline water).
- Glaciers, ice caps and snowy mountains – 2% (fresh water)
- Lakes, rivers, streams, groundwater, ponds and swamps - 1% (fresh water)

Trees and plants in general, play an integral part in the occurrence, distribution and circulation of water and the availability of adequate supplies of water to facilitate and maintain life on planet Earth. "Forests occupy approximately one-third of the earth's land area, accounting for over two-thirds of the leaf area of land plants and thus play a very important role on terrestrial hydrology" (Bond et al. 2007). Each tree has its own cycle that sees it absorbing water from the soil and through the process of transpiration sending ninety-five percent (95%) of the collected water into the atmosphere as water vapor and in association with the other trees and plants in a forest, or a particular location, increase the humidity and modify the temperature of that local atmosphere (micro climate) and thereby increasing the likelihood of precipitation. The precipitation then falls first onto trees, leaving a certain portion on the trees, interception water, with the balance falling along the stems and through the canopy to the ground, where it is also divided into two more streams depending on the conditions on the ground beneath the tree canopy.

These two streams are infiltration and runoff water, with infiltration water penetrating the soil to meet the water demands of the trees and plants and to fill underground caverns called aquifers, while the runoff water moves over the ground at a speed dependent on the presence of shrubs, grass and plant debris, to surface water sources such as rivers, streams, lakes and ponds. The portion intercepted by the tree also divides into two streams, a portion that is absorbed by the tree and a portion that is reevaporated back into the atmosphere. The absence or presence of trees directly affect the portions of water that infiltrates the soil and the portion that goes directly over land to rivers, streams, lake and ponds and the presence or absence of trees will also affect the quality of water that reaches the rivers, streams, lakes and ponds, as trees helps to prevents soil erosion and thereby prevents excessive amounts of soil entering the surface water bodies. The trees also play another function in this process as the trees also acts as filters to block debris and remove dissolved chemicals and other pollutants from storm water that is directed to surface water bodies.

Trees, Water and Soil Pollution

The ground and surface water supplies of the world are impacted by many sources of pollution inclusive of soil erosion, air pollutants, fertilizers, pesticides, wastewater, animal waste, manufacturing waste, industrial waste, power generation waste and solid waste disposal and all of these waste streams must be managed or eliminated to ensure a clean public water supply. Trees with their many established capabilities offer a perfect tool that could be utilized in the management of these many waste streams to prevent many of these pollutants from entering the potable water supply system. To provide the required protection of the most vulnerable sites trees are located in watershed areas, along rivers and streams, along the shores of lakes and could be located in airshed areas, on farms, around industrial facilities inclusive of power plants, manufacturing and industrial plants, on solid waste disposal sites and on any other site that emits or receives air and water pollutants.

Since the beginning of the industrial age humans have been producing vast amounts of non-biodegradable wastes that have created significant health and environmental related problems that are seriously compromising the quality of life for a very large sections of the human and animal populations and the natural ecological systems. The major sources of these wastes are transportation, heavy industry, construction, mining, manufacturing, electrical power generation, agriculture and electronic wastes. These many wastes streams have been responsible for the contamination and pollution of soils, water and air in almost every occupied corner of the Earth and have been responsible for the failing health of humans and animals at each location. The levels of pollutants deposited in the environment creates problems with safe supplies of potable water, edible agricultural and natural products and clean breathable air, all of which can consequently cause great harm to the health of humans, animals and the environment. "Unfortunately, polluted water and air are common throughout the world" (European

Public Health Alliance 2008 and Khan et al). This pollution is not limited to water and air but it is also in soils all over the world and soil pollution is defined as "the presence in the soil of a chemical or substance out of place and/or present at a higher-than-normal concentration that has adverse effect on any non-targeted organism" (Rodrigues-Eugenio et al 2018). In general soils are usually polluted by excessive use of agricultural chemicals, biological agents, pesticides, industrial waste, urban waste and e-waste all of which have an enduring negative impact upon the condition of soils inclusive of the ability of soils to produce crops at the expected capacities and the pollutants also affect the life of the microbes that make soils productive, the health of humans, animals and plants in close contact with the polluted soil and any water that may flow through the polluted soil.

Trees and plants naturally "pull" water and nutrients from the soil in which they are located and if they are in polluted areas, they will absorb much of the pollutants dumped into soils, and these pollutants will be gradually absorbed into the tissues of the plants and over time this process could make the soil safer for humans, animals and even some more sensitive plants. The use of trees and plants in this way is referred to as phytoremediation, which "involves the use of plants to remove, transfer, stabilize and/or degrade contaminants in soil, sediment and water" (Hughes et al., 1997; Ali et al., 2018). There are several phytoremediation techniques that are quite useful for the treatment, storage and removal of many environmental pollutants inclusive of heavy metals, organic and inorganic pollutants. These techniques include phytosequestration or phytostabilization, Rhizodegradation, phytohydraulics, phytoextraction, phytovolatilization and phytodegradation. Each of these techniques differ in the way that the plants handle the pollutants (removal, immobilization, storage or degradation) and the type of pollutant that the plant species can treat, organic or inorganic. The operation of each technique is as follows:

- Phytostabilization (phytosequestration) –Involves one of several possible activities inclusive of absorption by roots, adsorption to root surfaces, the production and release of biochemicals which can be used to sequester, precipitate or immobilize pollutants that are in close proximity to the roots, either in soil or in groundwater.

- Phytohydraulics - This involves the use of deep-rooted trees or other plants to contain, sequester or degrade groundwater pollutants which the roots of that tree come into contact with.
- Phytoextraction – In this process plants, using their roots, take up or hyperaccumulate pollutants and use the tissues of their stems and leaves to store them.
- Phytovolatilization – In this process volatile compounds are taken up by the roots of plants and are then transpired, in their original form or as a metabolite, into the atmosphere.
- Phytodegradation – In this process pollutants are taken up by the roots of the plant from where they may be transported to the stems or leaves or remain in the roots where the pollutant is transformed through a process of metabolization.
- Rhizodegardation – In this process excretions from plants prompts rhizosphere bacteria to increase biodegradation of contaminants in soil or groundwater.

No single species of trees has the capacity or the physical and chemical make-up to absorb all of the known chemicals that are quite often spilled in soils and water and therefore the capacity of available trees must be ascertained, and the correct species of plants, tree or trees must be selected for particular remediation duties. Phytoremediation methods have been used on many Superfund clean-up projects in the US with great success for many decades and the data gathered from these projects highlight the type of trees used, the success obtained at each site and the data collected and compiled forms a resource that can be utilized for helping with the reduction or elimination of pollutants at other locations around the world. The US EPA's Introduction to Phytoremediation EPA/600/R-99/107 February 2000, provides several case studies that highlights the types of pollution, type of trees used for each situation and the result achieved.

Trees and Desertification

Trees make the difference between the formation of deserts and the maintenance of good fertile land and as has been demonstrated throughout history- when trees are destroyed leaving land and soil bare and unshaded, the soil will dry out over time killing the nutrients and microscopic life that are essential to plant life, and these losses eventually prevent the regrowth of trees and other plants and thereby creating arid soils which can then be more easily transformed into deserts. This drying out process is brought about by the heat of the sun which drives the continuous evaporation process that is the engine of the hydrologic cycle that takes water from all elements inclusive of trees, plants, seas, lakes, river, streams, ponds, swamps and the soil and recycles it through the atmosphere before it is returned to the firmament as precipitation (Hydrologic Cycle). The evaporation of water from the soil becomes greater when there is nothing shading that soil from the direct rays and heat of the sun and when this occurs over continuous cycles of time the soil is dried out and the bonds holding the grains of soil together is weakened and these bonds are then easily broken by wind and water. Recent evidence of this activity can be found all over the world as indicated in many reports from the USDA, FAO(UN) and other bodies. These reports indicate that along with the many existing deserts there are now many areas across the globe that are currently vulnerable to desertification. The vulnerable areas include:

- Large sections of Western United States,
- Large sections of Mexico and Central America,
- Large sections of Colombia, Brazil, Chile and Argentina
- Large section of the North Africa that is not already a desert, the Sahel Region and most of Sub-Saharan Africa.
- Large areas of Madagascar
- Very large areas of Australia that is not already engulfed in deserts.
- Large swaths of China, India, Pakistan, Afghanistan, Iran, Iraq, Syria, Lebanon, Jordan and Turkey
- Large sections of Europe inclusive all of Spain and Portugal, sections of France, Germany and the Balkans and Russia.

According to an IFAD(UN) report "Desertification occurs when the tree and plant cover that binds soil is removed". This loss of trees and plants usually occurs as a result of the clearing of lands for agricultural purposes, for mining purposes, the utilization of trees as wood or timber for the construction of shelters, residential, commercial, industrial and institutional facilities and for fuel. The process of desertification can happen over long periods of time or over relatively short periods depending on the level of intensity applied to the agricultural and other economic activities, as may have occurred with the migration of Europeans to the Americas, Oceana and Africa over the last five hundred years.

The desertification process usually follows several steps inclusive of vegetation degradation, water erosion, wind erosion, salinization and soil compaction and the creation of a desert in a particular location has a significant impact upon the rest of the environment around them as deserts negatively impact the lives of all plant and animal species, inclusive of humans, as they become quite inhospitable with high temperatures, great swings in diurnal temperatures and the absence of adequate sources of potable water for most species of plant and animals. The conditions in most deserts are such that they usually have high daytime temperatures and very cold nights, a few plants and a few animals, which when combined cannot sustain a significant human and animal populations and with expanding deserts and the creation of new ones there will be even less suitable lands available for human habitation and the survival of many important species. To stop the process of desertification or to reclaim existing deserts only one solution is available, trees, large volumes of trees, as according to the FAO only trees can stop desertification.

Many nations have, in the past and more recently, launched projects to retard, prevent or eliminate desertification, by replanting forests on lands that had been converted to agriculture, (Reforestation), or planting forest on lands that previously had no forest (Afforestation) or to reclaim existing desert lands using current and evolving technologies, however, the success of such projects is heavily dependent upon the science of trees, the availability of finances and the will to persevere against conditions that have broken the will of many ancient peoples who had in the past abandoned most such areas after the onset of desertification. According to the FAO (2007) forest projects, afforestation and reforestation, "Require high rates of financing at the beginning, forest takes some time to deliver revenues and benefits". This is confirmed by Camhi (2009) "Reforestation is expensive, difficult to plan and even harder to execute". Achieving any level of success will always be dependent upon the weather conditions, natural pests, weeds, water supply and all of the other problems that a regular farmer has to deal with and this can be even more difficult as the activity, especially the need for continuous maintenance, is time consuming, expensive to finance and returns can be very slow in coming.

CHAPTER

4

Trees, Climate Change and Carbon Sequestration

According to Seinfeld and Pandis (2006) "The early atmosphere of the earth is believed to have been a mixture of carbon dioxide (CO_2) nitrogen (N_2) and water vapor (H_2O) with trace amounts of hydrogen (H_2) a mixture similar to that emitted by present day volcanoes". Approximately four billion years ago, the estimated percentage of each of these gases in the atmosphere were mostly carbon dioxide, approximately 98%, nitrogen, approximately 1.9 %, water vapor and trace amounts of other gases. Over time the amount of carbon dioxide in the atmosphere was reduced by the processes of weathering, the conversion of carbon dioxide to oxygen by the process of photosynthesis in cyanobacteria (Seinfeld & Pandis 2006) and starting over 400 million years ago, with the evolution of plants and trees, the process of photosynthesis in plants on a very large scale. Weathering is the process where the precipitation of water vapor dissolves atmospheric carbon dioxide creating a relatively weak carbonic acid that on contact with bedrock reacts to produce carbonate compounds and this process locks the carbon into rocks and minerals (Yu). Cyanobacteria are an ancient blue green group of microbes that utilizes carbon dioxide and the process of photosynthesis to create its own food (Vincent 2009), in the same way that plants do, and these microbes occur mostly in inland waters. The combined processes of weathering and photosynthesis in cyanobacteria and plants, however, did not remove all carbon dioxide from the atmosphere and a large portion is still maintained there, along with larger portions in the oceans, rocks, fossil fuels and shale, with a small balance contained in plants and animal life. The carbon balance is as shown in the table below.

Item	Sphere	Relative Units
1	Biosphere	1
2	Atmosphere	70
3	Non-Marine	1
4	Ocean (dissolved carbon dioxide)	4000
5	Fossil Fuels	800
6	Shale	800,000
7	Carbonate Rocks	2,000,000

Table 1. Inventory of Carbon Near the Earth's Surface.

Carbon dioxide, a greenhouse gas (GHG), in association with other greenhouse gases such as methane, nitrous oxide, water vapor, ozone and halocarbons are responsible for the problems associated with the phenomena of Climate Change. Most of these GHGs, with the exception of the halocarbons, are naturally occurring and are very important to life on earth, as combined they are responsible for maintaining the earth at an average temperature of 59° F (15°C) instead of the mathematically more realistic temperature of 0°F (-18°C) as projected by Fourier in1827 (NASA), a temperature at which life on earth may not have been viable. The GHGs have the ability to absorb infrared radiation reflected from the earth's surface and to reradiate the heat absorbed back into the atmosphere, into space and back onto the earth thus keeping it at the average temperature of 59°F (NASA). This average temperature and the interaction between the GHGs are maintained by the constant fluctuation in the levels of GHGs in the atmosphere, which is facilitated by weather activities and the growth of plants and trees. However, since the start of the industrial age the amount of GHGs emitted into the atmosphere has increased significantly due to the use of greater volumes of carbon rich fossil fuels that produce and emit much higher levels of carbon dioxide and other greenhouse gases, than wood and other earlier fuel sources. GHGs in the atmosphere by percentage as established by the NASA Climate Science Investigation Unit are as follows:

- Carbon Dioxide. 394 parts per million (ppm), 56.4 %
- Methane. 1.77 parts per million, 16.3%
- Nitrous Oxide. 0.32 parts per million
- Halocarbons. 1 part per billion, 11.6%
- Ozone. 10.2 %

According to NOAA and NASA, it is this increase in GHGs above the preindustrial age levels, caused by anthropogenic activities, that is causing greater amount of heat to be reflected back onto the earth, into the earth's atmosphere and consequently heating up the earth and causing climate change. It is therefore this amount of excess GHGs that must be reduced and properly managed to eliminate or mitigate the negative impacts of climate change. According to NOAA pre-industrial age carbon dioxide level in the atmosphere was 280 ppm and when first measure in 1958 these CO_2 levels were at 315 ppm (35 ppm above preindustrial level) and since that time CO_2 level has increased to 410 ppm in 2019. The levels of other GHGs in the atmosphere have also increased during this period but the levels of carbon dioxide are of greater concern due to the fact that it makes the greatest relative impact to the GHG effect and due to its much higher volume, carbon dioxide represents 81% of greenhouse gas emissions and it has a higher rate of increase (NOAA). According to the USEPA carbon dioxide represents 81% of GHGs emissions, methane 11%, Nitrous Oxide 6%, and Fluorinated Gases 3%.

According to the EESC (Columbia University) the relative contributions of the Anthropogenic Greenhouse Effect are as follows:

- Carbon Dioxide 60%
- Methane 15%
- Nitrous Oxide 5%

- Halocarbons 12
- Tropospheric Ozone 8 %

Trees and Carbon Sequestration

Carbon dioxide in the atmosphere is a natural resource for the growth and development of all plants, making all plants a natural sink for atmospheric carbon dioxide and under normal circumstances high levels of carbon dioxide in the atmosphere should mean that there are more plant food ingredients available to grow more trees and consequently that more trees will grow to continuously remove more carbon dioxide from the atmosphere. However, trees do a lot more than just remove carbon dioxide from the atmosphere as they also process it through photosynthesis and then absorb it to use in the process of growing and consequently become a long-term storehouse for excess carbon in the biosphere. The process for removing and storing carbon in trees is performed in two major steps, capturing and processing as described in Chapter 3 under photosynthesis. The chemical formulation is as follows:

- $6CO_2 + 12\,H_2O + photons\ of\ light = C_6H_{12}O_6 + 6O_2 + 6H_2O$
  Carbon Dioxide + Water + Light Energy = Glucose + Oxygen + Water

In the physical process the plant cells utilize chlorophyl, water, nutrients and sunlight to convert carbon dioxide, a gas, to glucose and starch (sugars), a solid state, that is very important to plant growth and these glucose and starches are stored in the leaves, stems, trunks, branches and roots of the plant. The sugars produced are utilized or stored as follows:

- The starch is stored in reproductive tissue such as flowers, fruits, nuts, pods and cone.

- Glucose is essential in respiration to help keep the tree alive.
- Cellulose, a sugar that is also manufactured by the tree, is very important for plant cell walls as it helps to maintain the tree structure and to keep it upright, wood is 40% cellulose.

Each tree has a relatively high carbon content, fifty percent (50%) of the tree's dry mass and this carbon is stored for the life of the tree and for the duration of time that the wood made from the tree lasts (Leys 2012). According to Leys (2012), carbon is stored in wood products as follows:

Item	Use	Storage Time (years)
1	House frame, flooring, roofing, doors and windows	100
2	Furniture	30
3	Rail Ties	30
4	Pallet and Paper	6

The carbon stored in trees and wood is only released when the tree dies and decays and when the wood from that tree is burned. Each tree, depending on the specie and size, can store fixed amount of carbon that may be calculated as follows:

- Carbon Dioxide (CO_2) sequestered per tree (kg) = Tree mass (kilogram of fresh biomass) x 65% (dry mass) x 50% (carbon) x 3.67 x 120%
- Tree mass(kg) = Volume of the tree (m^3) x Tree density(kg/m^3)
- Volume (m^3) = Tree height (m) x diameter^2(m^2) x 0.7854/3 (conical trees)
- Volume (m^3) = Tree height (m) x diameter^2(m^2) x 0.7854 (cylindrical trees)

This equation is based upon the following assumption:

- Water makes up 35% of the green mass of a tree
- The solid dry mass makes up the other 65%
- Half (50%) of the dry mass of a tree is carbon

- The roots which are below ground level, makes up 20% of the tree so multiplier of 120% is used.
- The carbon figure as obtained from calculations is multiplied by 3.67 to obtain the amount of carbon dioxide sequestered and stored.

With these equations, assumptions and information about carbon dioxide emissions, the amount of carbon that needs to be sequestered and stored by trees or a forest may be calculated thus giving an approximate number of trees or hectares of forest that could be required to put the carbon cycle in a particular environment back into balance or back to the pre-industrial levels.

Alternative Methods for Sequestering Carbon Dioxide

Tree, plants in general, are the most natural purpose-built elements to be used in the fight against climate change caused by excess carbon dioxide in the atmosphere, however, trees require land, vast amounts of lands to plant the number of trees that would be required to bring carbon dioxide levels down to 280 ppm, the pre-industrial revolution levels, that would ensure that the fuel driving the current climate change would be eliminated and the elimination of the fuel would decelerate the process of climate change. Unfortunately, in the current economic climate, it is thought that land provides better value in agriculture, commercial and residential real estate development, mining, timber and paper production than forests and the problem is compounded as even with a willingness to utilize more commercially profitable lands for afforestation and reforestation projects, the total amount of land required to grow the size forests to take up all of the excess carbon dioxide produced in the US is not available in the US and the same applies to other industrialized nations like China. According to the US Geological Survey (USGS) "Annual carbon emissions from burning fossil fuels in the US are about 1.6 gigatons (billion metric tons) whereas annual uptake is only 0.5 gigaton, resulting in a net release of 1.1 gigatons per year". The existing methods of carbon sequestration, terrestrial sequestration, is usually accomplished using forest and improved soil conservation practices that result in increased volumes of carbon storage from afforestation and reforestation projects and the reestablishment of wetlands and grasslands, which when combined with reduction in carbon emissions from all sources could produce the desired results of reducing CO_2 in the atmosphere. Unfortunately, while well designed and focused, most afforestation, reforestation, restoration of wetlands and grasslands projects do not create a significant impact as they only take up a small fraction of the excess carbon emissions, with the existing forests taking up the bulk (30%) or 0.5 gigatons (USGS). The current US forest coverage is 33.2% (FAO) of available lands, which is approximately 1,172,592 square miles or approximately 750,000,000 acres of land that is covered in forests. These 750 million acres have only taken up only 30% of total carbon emissions due to the burning of fossil fuels and it therefore means that if forest coverage is increased to the levels which existed in 1620, 46 % forest coverage, there would still not be sufficient forest to take up the balance of 1.1 gigatons of excess carbon dioxide on an annual basis. Based on the current amount being taken up by the 33.2% forest coverage, the total amounts of forested acres required to take up all the carbon dioxide emitted each year, if only terrestrial sequestration methods are used, would be approximately 2.5 billion acres which is more than all the land in the US, which consist of 2.26 billion acres. This reality clearly indicates that forests alone cannot resolve the problems associated with excess carbon dioxide within the atmosphere and that alternative methods of carbon sequestration and carbons reduction methods are urgently required.

Carbon Dioxide Capture and Storage (CCS)

"Carbon Dioxide (CO_2) capture and storage (CCS) is the capture and secure storage of carbon dioxide that would otherwise be emitted to the atmosphere" Herzog (2009). The technology for the capture and storage of carbon dioxide was developed and commercialized during the late 1970s and early 1980s, in the US for use in the oil industry, where the captured carbon dioxide could be injected into oil reservoirs to increase the mobility of the oil to facilitate an increase in the amount of oil that could be withdrawn from each reservoir. The increased withdrawal from each reservoir would increase overall productivity, reduce production cost and improve profitability of each operation and this development took place at a time when climate change was not a topic of concern. However, the technology lost its economic value when the price of oil fell during the 1980s and most oil companies stopped using it as it was thought to be too expensive.

CCS became very important again when climate change became a great concern around the globe with the recognition that the rising levels of carbon dioxide in the atmosphere, coming directly from agriculture, transportation, electrical power generation, industrial, manufacturing, institutional, residential and commercial facilities, was responsible for the warming of the environment and was consequently leading to changes in the climate, changes which will quite probable create significant negative impacts upon humans and the environment. In this environment, with its proven capacity to directly remove carbon dioxide from the atmosphere, CCS technology became very important again and new applications were developed for use wherever fossil fuel was used and fossil fuels provides 85 % of primary energy all around the globe, Herzog (2009). CCS gained greater prominence at the international level with the recognition of it capabilities as indicated by Edmonds (2008) and Herzog (2009) "preparations for the IPCC 5th Assessment Report have indicated that meeting low carbon stabilization limits is only possible with CCS". The major components of a CCS system are, capture, transport, injection and monitoring (Herzog 2009) and are as follows:

- Capture. Capture involves the separation of carbon dioxide from an effluent stream, such as the exhaust flow of a power plant, after which it is compressed into a liquid or supercritical state making it suitable for storage and transportation.
- Transport. Transport involves the movement of the carbon dioxide from its source to the point of storage. Transportation may be accomplished by one of several methods inclusive of trucking, railroad, shipping and by pipeline, with the most economical method being by depending on the distance

between the point of extraction and the location of the site where the carbon dioxide is to be stored.

- Injection. Injection involves the depositing of the liquid carbon dioxide into selected geological storage area. These selected storage areas may include depleted oil and gas reservoirs, deep oceans and ocean sediments.

- Monitoring. Monitoring involves the continuous monitoring of storage areas to ensure that the carbon dioxide placed into storage is not leaking out from the geologic formations back into the atmosphere.

Carbon Capture

The very first step in the process of sequestering carbon is to capture it, an activity that was naturally performed by the leaves of plants and trees an activity that these leaves were perfectly evolved to accomplish, however, as previously stated plants and trees do not have the required capacity to sequester all the excess carbon dioxide in the atmosphere and therefore mechanical means as described above were developed to meet the needs. The mechanical systems designed to perform this task is still a work in progress as many designs have been tried so far with varying degrees of success and according to a PG&E Whitepaper (2018) some systems already exist which remove carbon dioxide (CO_2) continually as a concentrated stream, but many systems inclusive of those used in many power generation, manufacturing and industrial facilities, still need further development or require modifications to their systems to meet their specific carbon dioxide capture and concentration needs based on the level of carbon dioxide concentration and the number and types of non-carbon dioxide elements inclusive of acids, particulates and oxygen, in the fuel or exhaust stream. The design or redesign may be based on one of four methods of carbon capture which includes oxyfuel carbon capture, pre-combustion carbon capture or post-combustion carbon and direct air capture (DAC).

- Oxyfuel Carbon Capture. This method is based on the combustion of fossil fuels in pure oxygen to produce rich carbon dioxide which can be separated from the other elements in the exhaust stream by condensation of steam and other gases, and filtering for solids as each gas has a different boiling point. This process has not been commercialized due the problems associated with high combustion temperatures and the high cost associated with eliminating nitrogen.

- Pre-Combustion Carbon Capture. In this method the fossil fuel is gasified to produce a 'syngas' consisting of carbon monoxide (CO) and Hydrogen (H_2) after which a second reaction converts the carbon monoxide into carbon dioxide (CO_2) followed by the separation of carbon dioxide from the hydrogen by a physical solvent. The separated hydrogen may then be used in an integrated gasification combined cycle (IGCC) electricity generating power plant.

- Post-Combustion Carbon Capture. In this method chemical solvents are used to separate carbon dioxide from the exhaust or flue gas stream and it is currently the most adaptable method available for use in retrofitting most existing plants.

- Direct Air Capture. In this method carbon dioxide is captured directly from ambient air when it is directed to flow through a chemical sorbent that is designed to remove carbon dioxide only from the ambient air. The captured carbon dioxide may then be sent directly to a permanent geological storage as a concentrated stream or be reused as required (Socolow 2011). Large scaled up version of DAC systems are potential mitigation tools for managing climate related risks associated with the high carbon dioxide content of the atmosphere.

Long-term Storage

Carbon is naturally stored in the ocean, rocks, soil, carbon minerals, plants and animal life, however, most attempts to increase the amount of carbon stored has been focused on increasing forest coverage, a method that has been recognized as being inadequate, by the IPCC, to meet the current carbon storage needs and this acknowledgement forced a shift to utilizing some of the other natural sinks. The most significant alternatives carbon storage methods identified to date are related to geologic locations inclusive of oil and gas reservoirs, deep saline formations, deep oceans, ocean sediments, un-mineable coal beds, basalt formations and new carbon minerals, as shown in Fig. 4.5 above. The IPCC's Special Report on Carbon Dioxide Capture and Storage indicates that "available evidence suggests that, it is likely that there is a technical potential of at least 2000 $GtCO_2$ of capacity in geological formations" and that 2000 $GtCO_2$ represents two orders of magnitude greater than total worldwide annual CO_2 emissions. However, according to Herzog the estimates produced by the US Department of Energy (DOE) indicates that the US and Canada has oil and gas reservoir capacity of $82GtCO_2$ and deep saline formations of 940-3400 $GtCO_2$ much higher than the IPCC estimate. This knowledge makes geologic locations the next best alternative to trees, however, there is still the need to develop the appropriate technologies to facilitate the capture and transportation of carbon dioxide, a process which has already started.

Alternative Uses of Carbon Dioxide

The main aim of all carbon sequestration activities is the capturing and securing in long-term storages all excess carbon in the atmosphere to ensure balance in the biosphere, however, captured carbon dioxide has many potential and practical uses. Carbon dioxide has been successfully used in many applications and has the potential to be used in many other applications inclusive of Food Processing, Refrigeration, Agriculture, Paper Processing, the creation of alternative fuels, additive to concrete for use in the construction industry, the creation of minerals, crude oil recovery, fracking and the creation of new fibers. According to Gilani (2017) other uses of carbon dioxide also includes:

- Industrial Applications. According to the IPCC Special Report on Carbon Dioxide Capture and Storage, carbon dioxide gas is involved in the production of refrigeration systems, welding systems, water treatment processes and carbonated beverages.

- Chemical and Pharmaceutical Applications. Carbon dioxide is used to make urea, methanol, inorganic and organic carbonates, polyurethanes and sodium salicylate, polymers and plastics.
- Electronics applications. Circuit board assembly and preparation of clean surfaces in the manufacture of semiconductors.
- Oil industry. Enhanced oil recovery (EOR) is a technology for increasing the quantity of crude oil extracted from fields.
- Agriculture. The potential for an application in agriculture where carbon dioxide waste could be combined with landfill methane and waste straw to form a soil enriching fertilizer.
- Refrigeration. Carbon dioxide has been used as the refrigerant in large industrial refrigeration and air conditioning systems, however, there is a longstanding problem associated with leakage from refrigeration and air conditioning systems which risk sending back a large amount of carbon dioxide directly back into the atmosphere. Carbon dioxide, however, has an advantage over most current refrigerants as it has a lower global warming potential than many current refrigerants and one major disadvantage as it can be unwieldly to use due to the large compression ratios required to produce required temperatures which tend to makes carbon dioxide refrigeration systems quite large and bulky.
- Minerals. Carbon dioxide can be used to create carbon rich minerals such as magnesite which has the capacity to store large amount of carbon in a crystalline form. Unfortunately, while requiring low energy input, the volume of magnesite required to store annual carbon dioxide output, 62 billion metric tons is exorbitant, makes the magnesite unrealistic at this time.

Destruction of Forests

Forests have been destroyed on all continents of planet Earth for the same reasons:

- Basic Survival – Providing basic food and shelter for humans.
- Economic – Growth of urban society and making money.
- Natural Events – Disease, fire, lightening, storms and flooding.

Basic Survival

Historically, humans in every corner of the globe have had the need to clear lands for the propagation of crops, essential foods which provide some of the basic nutritional requirements for human survival and in clearing lands for survival many stands of old-growth, ancient trees and many other species of very valuable plants that can never be replaced have been destroyed. The methods of clearance used by early humans were also quite destructive as the trees were chopped down, stumps uprooted and the grass, shrubs and other organic debris on the forest floor such as leaves and decomposed organic matter burned and the burning of all of these components while providing some benefits also destroyed microbes and animals essential for soil renewal making it much harder for trees and other plants to regrow in the cleared area. Early humans usually cleared just enough land to plant crops to meet their immediate seasonal needs and in so doing did much less damage to the environment than later agricultural practices that was built upon producing crops for immediate use, long-term use and for sale to create wealth as occurred in ancient Mesopotamia, the Indus Valley and the Egyptian civilizations that were built upon agriculture. This practice of creating wealth through agriculture could indicate that the agricultural practices that were less profit oriented such as that of the native tribes in places like Australia, New Zealand, Papua New Guinea, and the Americas did much less damage to the environment than the European migrants that would later occupy the land and build European style economies, where the approach to agricultural production was vastly different, more far reaching and mostly based upon commercial farming and the sale of surplus crops by small farmers.

According to Bronaugh (2012) natives of the Americas did significant damage to the environment as "By about 1000 BP (before the present) significant areas of forests were converted to intensive agriculture use for maize, squash and beans", however, he also made it clear that while the Natives Americans destroyed forest for survival purposes the approach of the Europeans were quite different as to them "Paramount was the near-universal perspective that forests were either a threat that hid enemies, an obstacle to settlement, a resource to be converted to profit or all the above" Bronaugh (2012), and this thinking and approach lead the Europeans with their steel axes and saws, much better tools than those that any Native American ever had at that time, to do a lot more damage than the Native Americans ever could. The growing European immigrant populations, which was said to have doubled every 20-30 years, saw the clearing of all forests from most lowland and coastal areas of the eastern US by 1850. These immigrants not only destroyed forests by their agricultural and construction practices but also by bringing non-native species of trees with diseases from Europe that negatively impacted native species such as the North American chestnut which was destroyed by the chestnut blight fungus accidentally imported from Europe. This, chestnut blight fungus, completely destroyed the north American chestnut population in 40 years, from its initial importation in 1900. Other species of trees were also affected and destroyed by imported pathogens and fungi such as the white pine blister rust, the Dutch Elm disease, the sudden oak death syndrome, the emerald ash borer and woolly adelgid among other tree diseases. The problems of imported species were also amplified when non-native species of trees inclusive of the tamarisk, Russian olive and cajeput along with many other invasive species, also started displacing many native species.

Economics Factors

Early agricultural production initially provided crops for consumption by the immediate family that were directly involved in the production process only, however, as societies grew and the division of labor became the established way of doing business, farming families started producing excess crops that were intended for trading and later sales to acquire material or monetary gain that would allow the family to acquire the things that they could not produce themselves. The demand for agricultural products grew with growing populations, urbanization and further societal changes that saw fewer individuals engaged in agricultural production and this growing demand allowed farming to become more profitable with the possibility to create great economic wealth. With the high demand for agricultural products, especially high value goods, and the possibility to accumulate great wealth from producing, reaping, processing and selling things like wheat, corn, rice, fruits and nuts, timber and forest products, many individuals and countries yielded to the desire for maximizing the profits that could be made from planting high value native and non-native crops without giving due consideration to the negative impacts that expanded production, especially of these non-native species of plants could have upon their environment, new or old, native flora and fauna and water supplies.

The intense farming of basic crops has been demonstrated over time, in many locations across the globe, to negatively impact forests, water supply, human and animal habitats and the environment in general. The negative impact of agriculture become much worst with widescale planting of non-native crops and trees as these plants were not evolved to produce in their new environment, did not develop any resistance to the pest in the new environment and may demand more water than most plants in the new environment does. Therefore, the planting of nonnative crops were more likely to require higher fertilizer usage, more pesticides and the withdrawal of greater volumes of water from local resources and consequently create many more environmental problems. The problems associated with expanding the planting of non-native species of crops has been demonstrated by a case in California, where a non-native almond tree has been planted for its high value and the success of this crop has been so great that California is currently the largest producer of almonds in the world, producing approximately eighty two percent of all almonds consumed worldwide, "Almond's economic impact and employment comprise a substantial part of the total economic activity and jobs in the economy of the Central Valley and especially the rural regions" Sumner et al (2015) with the projected impact for 2014 been $21.5 billion and 104,000 jobs.

These almonds require very large quantities of water, 1.1 gallon per almond (Philpott and Lurie 2015), and "accounts for close to 10% of California annual agricultural water use or more than what the entire population of Los Angeles and San Francisco use in a year". In the most severe droughts this high almond demand for water has sometimes led to excessive withdrawals from groundwater aquifers and surface water sources thereby reducing the amount of water available for human consumption and for maintaining aquifers and surface water sources at required minimum levels to ensure the environmental viability of other species. The negative impact of excessive water consumption water to produce almonds have already been showing up in California as under severe drought conditions, low water levels in streams and rivers have led to the decimation of endangered species like the King Salmon in Northern California Klamath River (Hamblin, 2014) and other aquatic species of flora and fauna. The over pumping of water from aquifers, during droughts, to meet the almond's demands for high volumes of water can also lead to collapse of the aquifer and adjacent lands as has been the experience in California. Unfortunately, the world demand for almonds, the new superfood, is only getting higher and until a more drought resistant almond plant or an almond plant that can produce more nuts than the current species using the same volume of water has been developed, their negative impact on the environment will continue. These non-native almonds have also negatively impacted native birds and insects inclusive of pollinating species such as bees and butterflies and other native animal species that have depended on and built symbiotic relationships with the displaced native trees and plants. The eventual outcome is that these species will be lost or have their numbers significantly reduced as their native habitats and food sources have been destroyed.

Almond is, however, only one of many such non-native crops that has been adopted by places like California for their great economic impact but which have also negatively impacted the environment and some of these other crops includes palm oil, sugarcane, coffee, corn, wheat, coca, potatoes, rice and many other such commercial crops that were adopted from their natural environment and planted in cleared forest in many new locations around the world. Another very good example of the planting of high value nonnative crops is the Oil Palm now widely planted in Malaysia for its highly valued palm oil, whose commercial value is so high that the Malaysian government and people are willing to destroy much of their native forests, inclusive of flora and fauna, to optimize their production output and boost the palm oil's economic value to their economy. This expansion in production has required and will continue to require the clearing of larger swaths of native forests to plant many more acres of oil palm in order to achieve the desired palm oil crop economic returns, however, this expansion has led to forest degradation, deforestation and associated negative impacts as reported by the Barthel et al (2018) "There is clear evidence that the expansion of oil palm cultivation has resulted in deforestation, biodiversity loss and net greenhouse gas (GHG) emissions". These cases clearly highlight the making of profits at the expense of the environment, a practice that is never environmentally sustainable.

Natural Pestilence

The natural pestilence of greatest concern to the survival of trees would be diseases and pests, fires that consume plants and trees inclusive of seedlings and seeds, complete or partial submergence in fresh or salt water and brine intrusion that would interrupt the proper functioning of the natural anatomical systems that are essential to the growth and development of plants and trees.

Diseases and Pests

Trees, like all living things are impacted by the many elements that make up of the natural environmental and ecological systems that they were nurtured and developed in over long periods of time, as these many elements in the many different locations usually help to form and shape the character of each species of trees. These elements usually determine the type of fruit or nut that a tree produces, the type of leaves, the height of the tree, how often it sheds leaves and almost every other characteristic that is particular to each specie. These environmental and ecological elements also have the ability to determine how well a tree performs, the volume of leaves, fruits and nuts produced, the color, shape, smell and taste of the fruits and nuts, but more importantly they can also determine the lifespan of the tree and the elements that the specie is susceptible to. This lifespan is determined by the resistance and tolerance, if any, that the immune system of each species of plant had developed to the many elements, inclusive of insects, bacteria, chemicals and physical conditions that makes up the locale in which that species of tree was developed and nurtured. Every geographical location on the earth evolved over time to develop and retain location specific elements that determine the quality and quantity of elements that make up the environmental and ecological systems based on climatic conditions, height above sea level, type and chemical make-up of soil, the availability and quality of water, the quantity and quality of the other species, plants and animals, that a particular specie of tree shared common space with. All of these elements help to determine the genetic make-up of each species of trees and even variations within the same species of trees, as the same species of trees developed and nurtured in different environments could have different reactions to a common event. All trees have two known groups of natural elements to which they are susceptible and which can have life changing impacts on their lifespan and these two groups consist of insects and plant pathogen or bacteria which usually attack trees when they are in adverse environmental conditions or when they are under stress. According to Nix (2019) "There are over 30 common tree diseases that contribute to the health and death of most trees in the United States" and there are also 22 common insect pests that are responsible for most insect damage to trees.

Tree Diseases

In line with their different environmental and ecological nurturing and development, all tree species are not negatively impacted by the same common tree diseases, as each species will have developed different levels of immunity to resist or tolerate each of the known tree diseases. The common tree diseases highlighted by Nix (2019) are as follows:

- American Chestnut Blight. This is a fungus that attacks hardwood trees and has been responsible for the decimation of American Chestnut trees as a commercial crop. The fungus is widespread and continues to survive as a non-lethal species with no known cure.
- Armillaria Root Rot. These are fungi that attacks many species of plants inclusive of hardwood and softwood trees, shrubs and vines across the continental US and it attacks trees in all conditions of health.
- Anthracnose and Leaf Spot Diseases. These are fungal diseases that tend to attack hardwood trees in spring as cool rainy weather creates the perfect conditions for the spores to spread.
- Annosus Root Rot. This is a fungal disease caused by the Fomes Annosus fungus which attacks softwood trees, particularly freshly cut stump surfaces.
- Aspen Canker. This disease is caused by a fungus called Cytospora Canker, that attacks the quaking aspen specie that have been stressed by one of many events inclusive of drought, extreme heat or cold and mechanical damages.

- Bacterial Wetwood. This disease is caused by numerous bacteria that infects inner sapwood and outer heartwood of hardwood trees however, it is not fatal to the trees but is considered to be a chronic disease.
- Beech Bark Disease. This disease is primarily caused by the Nectria Coccinea var. faginata fungi that attacks, kills or impairs hardwood trees such as the American Beech.
- Brown Spot in Longleaf Pine. This disease is caused by the scirrhia acicola fungus that attacks conifers and causes retardation and death in longleaf pines.
- Canker Rot. This disease is caused by the Canker Rot fungi that attacks hardwood trees inclusive of red oaks, white oaks, hickory and honey locust. The fungi attack and decay the sapwood three feet above and below the point of penetration, decays the heartwood and kills the cambium.
- Comandra Blister Rust. This disease is caused by the Cronartium Comandrae Pk. fungus that attacks conifers, grows on the inner bark of conifers but requires the assistance of a flowering plant to spread.
- Diploda Blight of Pines. This disease is caused by the Diploda Pinea fungus that attacks conifers killing current-year shoots, branches and ultimately the entire tree.
- Dogwood Anthracnose. This disease is caused by the anthracnose fungus, Discula Sp., that attacks dogwood trees during the cool spring or fall weather conditions.
- Dothistroma Needle Blight. This disease is caused by the Dothistroma pini Hulbary fungus that attack conifers, infecting and destroying pine needles.
- Dutch Elm Disease. This disease is caused by three species of the ascomycete fungi that attacks hardwood trees such as the American Elm by blocking it vascular tissues and preventing the movement of water which is essential to life of a tree.
- Dwarf Mistletoe. These are small, leafless, parasitic flowering plants, Arceuthobium Sp., that kills by slowly robbing the host tree of food and water, these host trees are usually conifers, mainly ponderosa and lodgepole pines, causing the retardation

of growth, reduced seed production and poor wood quality, which eventually leads to the death of the tree.

- Elytroderma Needle Cast. This disease is caused by the Elytroderma Deformas fungus which attacks and kills the foliage of susceptible pine trees, it however, seldom causes the death of the tree.
- Fire Blight. This disease is caused by the plant pathogenic bacterium, erwinia amylovora, that affects apples and pear trees and other members of the Rosaceae family of trees.
- Fusiform Rust. This disease is caused by the fungus Cronatiium quercuum f. sp. that attacks conifers such as loblolly pine and slash pine causing rust galls or cankers on the main stems and or branches of trees and usually leads to poor quality wood and deformed and broken branches in young trees.
- Laminated Root Rot. This disease is caused by the Phellinus Sulphurascens fungus and it attacks and kills conifers inclusive of Douglas-Fir and Grand Fir.
- Littleleaf Disease. This disease is caused by a combination of factors inclusive of the Phytophthora cinnamoni Rands fungus, Low soil nitrogen, poor internal soil drainage, microscopic roundworms called nematodes and species of the fungal genus Pythium. The disease attacks conifers and is especially dangerous to the shortleaf pine.
- Lucidus Root and Butt Rot. This disease is caused by the Ganoderma Lucidus fungus that attacks hardwood trees inclusive of oaks, maples, hackberry, ash, sweetgum, locust, elm, mimosa and willow. The attack usually leads to the decline and eventual death of the host trees.
- Mistletoe (Phoradendron). These are parasite of conifers, hardwoods and shrubs and kills tree by robbing their water and food sources.
- Oak Wilt – This disease is caused by the non-native Bretziella fagacearum fungus which is quite invasive and deadly to all species of oaks found in Minnesota, USA. The fungus attacks the carrying vessels of the oak trees and eventually kills them.

- Powdery Mildew. This disease is caused by several genera of fungi, such as the Golovinomyce cichoracearum, and is an obligate parasite requiring live tissues to live on and attacks all type of trees.
- Scleroderris Canker. This disease is caused by the Gremmeniella abietina fungus that attacks several species of pines, either in the European or North American strains of the disease. All species of pines are susceptible to the European strain especially the hard pines, while the Douglas-fir and all species of firs, spruce, larch and hemlock have varying degrees of susceptibility. The following trees are infected by the North American strain Scotch, red and jack pines in the US and western white pine, lodgepole pine, white and black spruce in Canada.
- Sooty Mold. This disease is caused by genera of sooty mold fungi inclusive of Aethaloderma, Capnodium, Cladosporium, Euantenneria, Scorias and Trichomerium. The Sooty Mold grows on leaves, stems and twigs of plants, but does no harm to the plant hosts.
- Sudden Oak Death. This disease is caused by a fungus-like plant pathogen Phytophthoria ramorum and the disease kills some oak species and has had devastating effects on coastal oaks in California and Oregon.
- Thousand Cankers Disease. This disease is caused by the disease causing Geosmithia fungus, whose spores are carried by the walnut twig beetle that attacks the trunks and branches of the black walnut tree.
- Verticillium Wilt. This disease is caused by the soil-borne Verticillium dahliae fungus that can affect 350 species of trees and plants including deciduous trees, vegetables, berries and flowers and the affected plants usually die as there is no fungicide.
- White Pine Blister Rust. This disease is caused by the Cronartium ribicola fungus or White Pine Blister Rust fungus. This fungus creates cankers on trunks and branches of trees and kills young trees, while mature trees can last for many years.

Insect Pests

Insects and trees have shared a very long and sometimes mutually beneficial relationship over many millennia, with the trees providing food and shelter for the insects and the insects providing pollination and pest control services for the trees, however, sometimes the relationships get crossed and trees end up with the wrong insects, insects whose affinity for the tree is more predatorial than helper and protector, and the end result is usually that the insect ends up impairing the trees and making them susceptible to plant diseases. According to Nix (2019) there are 22 common insect pests that usually do great harm to trees and these insect pests are as follows:

- Aphids. Aphids are very small, one tenth of an inch, insects that are usually one of several colors, green, black, brown, reddish brown and gray. These insects harm plants in two ways, sucking sap from shoots and leaves thereby weakening the plant and injecting their saliva into the plant thereby infecting the plant with any disease that they may have picked up elsewhere. Aphids are asexual and have the ability to multiply rapidly and quickly infect many plants in a short period of time. Their secretions, 'honeydew' also provide the base for a secondary disease the sooty mold fungus to insect plants.
- Asian Longhorn Beetles (ALB). ALB are harmful to trees as the mature insects lay their eggs in cracks or opening in the bark of a tree and the larvae produced from these eggs later bore deep into the wood of the tree to form a 'feeding gallery'. This feeding gallery disrupts the vascular functioning of the tree which weakens and eventually destroys the tree.
- Balsam Woody Adelgid. These are small, soft-bodied, invasive species of aphids that feed exclusively on conifers, inclusive of hemlocks and firs and they are usually named based on the specific plants that they feed on, names such as the Hemlock Wooly Adelgid and the Balsam Wooly Adelgid.
- Black Turpentine Beetle. This insect is usually found along the US eastern seaboard, New Hampshire to Florida and also from

West Virginia to Texas and these insects usually attack southern pines especially those that have been stressed by the production of lumber, turpentine, rosin and lumber.

- Douglas-fir Bark Beetle (Dendroctonus pseudosugae). This insect is native to the region between Southern Canada and Northern Mexico and poses the greatest danger to mature Douglas-firs in the Western North America.
- Douglas-fir Tussock Moth (DFTM). This insect is most destructive when it is in the form of a caterpillar that feeds on the needles of Douglas-fir, spruce and true firs. The damage done to the trees usually start at the top and spread downward during severe breakouts and the stress caused by the damage usually exposes the infected trees to diseases that could destroy the tree.
- Eastern Pine Shoot Borer. This is a small moth that infest various conifers, especially the young plants, and the damage caused by their feeding on the young plants can alter quite negatively the branch architecture of the infected tree as it matures. This insect natural habitat is Eastern Canada and sections of the US starting in New England south to Virginia and west to Minnesota.
- Emerald Ash Borer. This is an invasive species of exotic beetles, that is half inch long with a metallic green color and originally from Asia that was introduced in the US sometime in the 1990s. The mature beetle, which feeds on the foliage of the ash tree, does relatively little damage to the plant, however, its feeds on the inner bark of the plant and this activity affects the ability of the plant to transport water and nutrients, which will consequently lead to the death of the tree.
- Fall Webworm. This insect is a bright white moth with a hairy body, that lays it eggs on the underside of leaves of ornamental trees, shrubs and several agricultural crops. This insect is native to North America but has spread to Europe and Asia, where it has become an invasive species. The fall webworm usually does damage during its larval stage when it has the capacity to defoliate the host plant.

- Forest Tent Caterpillar. This is the larvae of the nocturnal forest tent tan moth that deposits it eggs in gray cylindrical masses around small twigs. The larvae emerge from the eggs in the middle of May, around the same time that the young leaves of aspen and other hardwood trees begin to appear and complete their transition by the middle of July and in the two-month period of larval growth the caterpillars can defoliated aspen and other hardwood trees. Under normal conditions this defoliation will not kill the tree unless it is continued for four seasons or under stressed conditions such as drought or mechanical damage.
- Gypsy Moth. This insect, both Asian and Europeans strains, are not natives of North America, however the European strain is now a voracious invasive species that is doing great harm to forests in North America. The larvae of this moth feeds on over three hundred species of trees and can destroy as much as1 million acres of trees per year or more.
- Hemlock Wooly Adelgid (HWA). This an aphid-like insect, that is native to Asia and is currently decimating hemlocks in the Eastern US and the Carolinas and they damage trees by feeding on the stored starches, which they access after the young HWAs permanently attach themselves at the base of the conifer needles, this feeding robs the twigs and small branches of required nutrients killing them which eventually leads to the death of the tree in four to ten years.
- Ips Beetle. These are small, one eighth to three eighths long, reddish brown to black native bark beetles that attacks spruce or pine trees that are dying or have been stressed by drought, fire or wind damaged.
- Mountain Pine Beetle. These are native Colorado bark beetles that attack mostly ponderosa, lodgepole, Scotch and limber pines and these insects damage host trees by boring into their bark where their activities disrupt the flow of water and nutrient to the crown that can lead to the death of the tree in one year.
- Nantucket Pine Tip Moth. This insect is a small reddish-brown silver-marked tortricid moth that produces yellowish brown

larvae that feeds on new shoots of various pines that eventually leads to the death of the tree.

- Pales Weevil. This is a relatively large insect that is 6-10 mm long, it is black to dark reddish brown in color, with small patches yellow-white scales on its head and wings. This insect feed on the terminal shoots of eastern white pine, Douglas -fir, and true firs, chewing off the bark down to wood and eventually killing the shoot and consequently the plant if the process continues.

- Hard and Soft Scales Insects. These are small inconspicuous insects that utilize different systems of external protection, one hard and one soft, that feed by sucking their nutrient from trees and shrubs by using their piercing sucking mouths. These activities negatively impact the vitality of the plant as it produces the initial reaction is changing colors and wilting of the leaves followed by the death of the affected areas and eventually the whole plant.

- Shade Tree Borers. This group include a number of insects that develop underneath the bark of woody plants that are stressed, dying or recently felled.

- Southern Pine Beetle. This insect is one of the most destructive enemies of pines in Southern US, Mexico and Central America. It attacks all southern yellow pines inclusive of loblolly, shortleaf, Virginia, pond and pitch pines and is closely associated with Ips and Black Turpentine beetles.

- Spruce Budworm. These insects are large, 24-26 mm gray moths that lay their eggs on the needles of Balsam fir, preferred, white, red and black spruce, larch, pine and western hemlock. The larvae from these eggs emerge in spring prior to the expansion of the balsam fir buds and feed on the terminal branch tips. The eating of these tips will usually produce a loss of foliage and an extensive loss of foliage over 5-7 successive years will lead to the death of the tree, however, the tree has the capacity to recover from fewer successive years of defoliation.

- Western Pine Beetle. This is an aggressive bark beetle that attack and kill ponderosa and Coulter pines that are stressed or have been weakened by drought, overstocking, over age, wind damage fire or disease. The female beetle bores through the bark of the tree into the phloem where it establishes a residence and lays her eggs, which later produces larvae that also feeds on the phloem and bores even deeper into the tree. The initial bore by the female beetle also initiates a fungal infection that grows into the water carrying passages blocking the flow of water and nutrients and the combination of the fungus and the damage done to the phloem by the beetles feeding on them kills the tree.

- White Pine Weevil. This is a small rust colored insect that is 4-6 mm long, that destroys eastern white pine in North America.

Fire

Nature at regular intervals uses natural fires, spontaneous combustion, lightening or meteorites, to renew life in forests by removing understory growth, dead leaves, branches or other impediment to the growth and development of trees in a forest and the fire may also directly help with some new growth as the seeds from some plants, such as the Lodgepole pine, needs fire before they can be released from their casing to facilitate germination and growth. These natural fires also help other members of the forest ecological system inclusive of birds, insects, rodents, snakes, deer and other large mammals that usually find their food on the forest floor, by opening up new access paths to food, prey, water and other essential items. According to the scientists from the Pacific Northwest Research Station "Fire is a part of the forest ecosystem and its effects have been well documented in the scientific literature". The beneficial effects of forest fire include but are not limited to plant regeneration, soil functions improvements, nutrient cycling, habitat revitalization, disease control, predator prey dynamics, biological diversity and vegetation development, all of which are shaped by a natural fire regime. There are also some negative impacts due to natural forest fires as indicated by San-Miguel (2019):

- Causes environmental degradation which leads to desertification in many locations around the world.
- Wild fires have been responsible for an increasing loss of human lives, crop losses and consequent economic losses in many regions of the world.

Each forest location or region has a particular frequency at which natural fires occur called the "fire return intervals" and these intervals may range anywhere from 5-30 years (Sierra Forest Legacy) depending on location or region. Over time these fires ensure the development of plants and trees that are well adjusted and resilient to the effects of fire and according to some scientists these natural forest fires do not appear to have a negative impact upon the growth of trees (Ladrach 2009). However, changes in the established natural fire return intervals can have significant negative impact upon a forest ecosystem, especially when the fires become much more frequent and there is not enough time for the regeneration or regrowth of new trees, shrubs and grass. The changes also occur when the fires are caused by humans and are as a result of a planned fire to control undergrowth, accidents or deliberate arson to destroy forest and score political points, as has been the case in many of the recent California's fires, the negative impact upon the forest is usually overwhelming and can lead to the complete destruction of forests. In many places around the globe, inclusive of places such as Alaska and Indonesia (2015), Canada, California and Portugal (2016), Chile, Canada, Australia, South Africa, California and Europe (2017), California and Europe (2018) and California, Europe and Australia (2019) we have begun to see more frequent and more fierce forest fires that bear the mark of the phenomena of climate change, however, while most scientific bodies agrees that warmer temperatures and lower humidity set the stage for these forest fires, they have not yet established a direct relationship between forest fires and climate change (USGS). In fact, what has been established is that most of the recent fires in California and Australia were either deliberately set by humans or the failure of overhead electrical power lines. One report from SFGate established that 12 Northern California wildfires were sparked by PG&E's power lines (Alexander 2018).

Salt Intrusion

While all trees share the very basics of roots, woody stem, limbs, branches, twigs and leaves and use photosynthesis to produce their source of energy, they are not all the same as they vary greatly in many ways inclusive of how much water, salt or other chemical they can tolerate or even the type of soil and atmospheric condition, that best suits each tree species. Tree species evolved in different areas and conditions around the world inclusive of high mountains, river valleys, plains, coastal regions, salt marshes, freshwater marshes, swamps and different climatic conditions and all of these different conditions help to determine certain characteristic of each tree species. In alignment with this fact, some trees such as the coconut tree and other coastal plants inclusive of the Atlantic White Cedar and the Southern Magnolia can withstand much higher levels of brine, in water and in the air, than most other plants and the same applies to the trees that live in Georgia's salt marshes inclusive of the red cedar, wax myrtle, saw palmetto, yaupon holly, yuca and cactus. The trees and plants in the Florida Everglades and other wetland areas of the continental USA, while sharing some similar characteristics are also all unique and will react differently based upon the locale in which they evolved or developed. Some of the special trees and plants in these special areas include the bald cypresses, oaks, water tupelo, green ash, black ash, red maple and eastern white cedar to name only a few. These species of trees mentioned developed over time a tolerance for different chemical, physical, biological, climatic and environmental conditions and performs best when planted in locations that are native to them. Experience has shown that when attempts are made to transplant or relocate trees to conditions, other than their native conditions, they will not perform as well, when compared to their performance in their native conditions. Thus, a tropical tree will not do well in a temperate climate, without special treatment, and similarly temperate climate trees will not do well in tropical conditions. The same applies to the introduction of substances such as sodium chloride or other salts to trees that have not developed a resilience or survival mechanism against such substances and the addition of such substances could lead to the terminal failure off these trees, depending on the level of tolerance that each tree developed over time.

The effects of salt intrusion remain the same irrespective of the means by which the salt is introduced to the roots, leaves or barks of the trees or plants and some of the possible ways of introduction include:

- Higher than normal tides or storm surges
- The subsidence of formerly dry land into water
- Saltwater intrusion into fresh water coastal or inland aquifers,
- Manual application
- Runoff from roads that are salted during the winter months.

In coastal regions where sea water levels are already rising due to climate change, salt intrusion has caused much damage to agricultural production in many areas of the world, where formerly productive lands have been lost due to higher-than-normal salt levels, too much water and marsh migration. The loss of land, due to the salt and water intrusions, usually has a deleterious effect on farming operations as they will directly lead to a reduction in output of the affected land area, a commensurate loss in production and consequently a loss in profitability of operations. Along with these losses that will be suffered by agricultural production, rising sea levels will also cause the destruction of coastal forests that did not develop a high tolerance for high levels of salts or high levels of water.

The prevention of salt intrusion is therefore very important for the survival of many species of plants, as salts greatly impacts the very mechanism by which plants perform their most important functions, pulling water and nutrients from the soil for the completion of the process of photosynthesis, the process by which the plant grows and live. Salts affect trees and plants in two ways, osmosis influence and specific ion toxicity. All plants use the process of osmosis to transfer water from the soil into its roots and the osmosis process is based on the principle of transference of water from areas of lower concentration to areas of higher concentration and during normal operations the level of concentration within the plant roots are usually higher that the level of concentration within the soil thereby allowing water to flow into the plant roots and up into the plant. The addition of salts or other compounds that would affect the concentration level within the soil, making the concentration in the soil greater than in the roots, which would ultimately stop the osmosis process and the natural and required flow of water into the plant. To compensate for the change in concentration levels within the soil relative to the plant each plant would synthesize organic compounds inclusive of plant sugars and organic acids to restore the required levels of internal concentration and thereby restoring the required flow of water and nutrients, however, this compensation process would require the utilization of energy needed by the plant to continue its growth and development and could lead to the retardation and stunting of the growth of the plant, with gradual degradation leading to the death of the plant. In the case of specific ion toxicity, which occurs when trees absorb the toxic ions of certain salts, inclusive of chlorine, boron and sodium that are present in the soil, through its roots into the stem and leaves where it is stored or when they are absorbed through leaves and barks from salt thrown on the plant. Many of these salts which occur naturally in the soil, are toxic to trees and the absorbing of their ions by the tree will lead to failure and probable death of the tree as it will cause the leaves on the tree to die and without leaves the process of photosynthesis which keeps the tree alive cannot be performed.

Flooding

All plants will survive best in the conditions that they evolved in and any change, including excessive amount of water, can thwart the growth of the plant or over time can completely destroy the plant, except in the cases where the plants evolved to survive in excessive amount of water such as can be found in salt marshes, freshwater marshes or in swamps. Therefore, all activities that could cause flooding inclusive of the creation of dams, the failure of dams, storm surges, extremely high levels of precipitation that cause overflow of river banks, ponds and lakes, which can create large areas of ponding, can negatively affect a plant's ability to function. According to Iles and Gleason (2008) there are many reasons why flooding kills trees, inclusive of the following:

- The flooding of the area tends to soften the soil and weaken the hold of the roots within the soil which will make the tree liable to falling over from wind and or water currents.
- Strong currents and soil particles suspended in the flood waters can also negatively impact the tree as they will erode the soil from around the base of the tree exposing the roots to dehydration and mechanical damage, thereby making the tree susceptible to forces of the wind, insect and bacterial infestation.
- The length of time that trees are subject to flooding is also very important as most tree can withstand short periods of flooding during the growing season, however, if the flooding is continuous or reoccurs frequently the soil may become overly saturated and serious damage may be done to the tree as flood waters and silting reduces the flow of oxygen to the soil and the roots and this usually results in growth inhibition and damage to the tree. The deposition of silt or sand as thick as three inches can be quite injurious especially to recently planted trees.
- The soil and flood waters usually contain a fair amount of natural and other chemicals from agriculture and automotive use, which when combined in stagnant water or waterlogged soil can react to produce chemicals such as hydrogen sulfide and alcohols that may be injurious to trees and other plants in the vicinity. These two specific chemicals, hydrogen sulfide and alcohols, will cause harm to the roots of a tree and create significant long-term damage that could shorten the life of the tree. Long-term flooding can also lead to the death and decay of a large portion of a tree's root system and the eventual death of the tree.
- Many species of trees can survive many months of flooding so long as their canopies are not flooded but if the canopies are covered or even partially inundated in flood waters the death of the tree could occur in less than a month. Some conifers are so sensitive that if their lower branches are submersed beneath the flood waters they will die within a few days.
- All trees are susceptible to harm from flooding however, over-mature and very young trees are more sensitive to the adverse effects of flooding than strong mature trees.

- Vigorous healthy trees will better withstand extended flooding than trees that were under stress prior to the flooding event and stressed trees will die much quicker after a flood event.
- Different species of trees have different levels of tolerance to flooding and flood sensitive trees that are unable to grow new adventitious roots quickly after a flooding event, may die quickly.
- Flood tolerant trees usually survive a flood in an active or a dormant condition or they may generate new roots, adventitious roots, from the root collar or trunk near the water surface.
- Flooded trees are stressed and weakened, and they tend to become vulnerable to attacks from opportunistic disease-causing fungi and insects. Water molds, Phytopthora and Pythium, tend to attack trees only when the soil is saturated or nearly saturated. These fungal spores swim through the soil water to attack the tree and the result of this fungal attack is to cause the roots or the crown of the tree to first turn brown and then become wet and decayed. A second group of fungi will then attack the branches and trunks causing cankers on the stressed tree which will also lead to death. Canker fungi are considered to be 'secondary attackers' because they attack only trees that are weakened by an event or other disease.
- Water molds and canker fungi causes greater damage to flood tolerant tree species that are planted in poorly drained clay soil or on sites that are subjected to flooding for prolonged periods of time.
- All trees develop an immune system that allows them to defend themselves from attacks both internally and externally, however, floods, droughts and premature defoliation damages the tree's defense mechanisms and this damage triggers a biochemical response that releases carbohydrates, sugars and other nutrients which appear to invite insects and fungal pathogens to attack the tree.
- Phloem borers and wood borers are 'secondary insect' attackers of major concern.

The flooding of tree in general usually occurs as the result of one of many precipitation events, however, quite often the flooding occurs as a result of deliberate human action, such as may occur during wars to prevent the enemy from benefitting from planted crops or to deny the enemy access to good landing sites. The deliberate flooding of trees also occurs when the energy that water can produce is deemed to be of far greater value than the continued existence of trees is a particular area and due to the potential energy that can accumulate in elevated bodies of water, millions of trees have been destroyed, on a global scale, to produce what is considered to be sustainable electrical power from hydropower. Hydropower plants require the creation of huge dams supported by huge lakes or reservoirs, the creation of which usually require the flooding thousands of acres of land. A few of the major hydropower projects around the world that have destroyed significant amounts of trees includes:

- The Hoover Dam in the US. This dam was completed in 1935 and forms a part of a large complex that generates electrical power, controls river flooding and supplies irrigation water to California, Arizona and Nevada. The complex consists of the dam, the power plant and accessories and a reservoir, Lake Mead, which supplies the required water to the power plant. Lake Meade is a manmade lake that is 120 miles long and covers a total area of approximately 250 square miles and can hold approximately 8-10 trillion gallons of water.
- The Aswan Dam in Egypt. This dam was completed in 1970 and forms part of a large complex that generates electrical power, controls river flooding and supplies irrigation water to Egypt and Sudan. The complex consists of the dam, the power plant and accessories and a reservoir, Lake Nasser, which supplies the required water to the power plant. Lake Nasser is a manmade lake that is 300 miles long by 10 miles wide covering an area of 3000 square miles and can hold approximately 45 trillion gallons of water. The Aswan Dam can hold much more water than the Hoover Dam and the Three Gorges Dam combined (Chao et al 2008; Arthur et al 2010).

- The Three Gorges Dam in China. This dam was completed in 2006 and forms part of a large complex that generates electrical power, controls river flooding and supplies irrigation water to different regions of China. The complex consisted of the dam, power plant and accessories and a reservoir, the Three Gorges Reservoir Region (TGRR), which supplies the water to the power plant. The reservoir is manmade and is approximately 373 miles long and covering an area of approximately 2240 square miles with a capacity of approximately 11 trillion gallons of water (Gleik 2013).
- The Itaipu Dam in Brazil. This dam is a joint project between Brazil and Paraguay, was completed in 1982 and forms a part of a complex that generates electrical power, controls river flooding and supplies irrigation water for farming for the benefit of both countries. The complex consists of the dam, power plant and accessories and the reservoir which supplies water to the power plant. The reservoir is manmade and is approximately 106 miles long with a surface area of 521 square miles with a capacity of approximately 8 trillion gallons.
- The Alqueva Dam in Portugal. This dam was completed in 2002 and forms a part of a complex that generates electrical power, controls river flooding and provides irrigation water for farming, for the Alentejo region of Portugal. The complex consists of the dam, power plant and the artificial lake which provides water to the power plant. The artificial lake, the largest in Europe, was approximately 52 miles long, with a surface area of approximately 97 square miles and a capacity of approximately 1 trillion gallons of water.

These hydropower plants are a small sample of the thousands of such hydropower/irrigation projects completed around the world in the last 100 or more years and all of them have similar effects on the surrounding environment inclusive of the destruction of millions of trees, by submergence when the reservoir is filled or by logging prior to filling up. The smallest of the mentioned projects, the Alqueva Dam, is said to have required the destruction of a million trees as reported "in February 2001 the clearing and deforestation of the area to be submerged by the Alqueva Dam started, involving the cutting of 1 million trees" (Platform for Sustainable Development 2005). Many environmental and civil society groups, including the Civil Society Organization, have concluded that dams destroy forests, even trees that are far away from the dam site, based on the effect that dams have on the hydrological systems.

Most energy producing hydropower plants have also negatively impact many other elements of the environment and local ecologies as have happened in many locations where the life and breeding cycles of many aquatic flora and fauna have been disrupted or completely destroyed leading to the loss of many species. The damming of the rivers has also negatively impacted many land mammals that were totally dependent upon the river for a source of food and water, many land plants that formerly grew along the wet banks of rivers and the livelihood of many humans who plied their many trades upon rivers. Most importantly damming rivers also disrupt the hydrological cycles and thereby can cause damage way beyond the immediate location of the dam and the section of the river that was dammed.

Weather Events

Weather event such as hurricanes, tornadoes and any related wind events may also have devastating negative impacts on forests as they could lead to the toppling and destruction of large acreages of trees in a single event or a series of events within a relatively short period of time, as could happen during hurricane season each year when there can be ten or more very active hurricanes starting from June and continuing through to the end of November. All hurricanes are usually a combination of heavy rains and high winds, a combination that can be quite harmful to trees as the high volume of precipitation could weaken the soil around the roots of the tree and the heavy wind could topple it and if a location is impacted by a series of hurricanes over a period of months the results could be quite devasting. Possible harm to trees from hurricane events could also be caused by wind damage such as the breaking of limbs and branches that would leave the damaged, distressed tree exposed to insects and bacterial diseases infestation.

6

Land Use Patterns Across the World

All across the globe fragmented and degraded forests and lands dried out by exposure to sunlight can be found at many locations that were abandoned by ancient communities and civilizations, leaving a distinct pattern of neglect caused by human hands, a pattern that is still being repeated in modern times. This pattern of neglect of forests and trees created over so many millennia raises the question about how ancient humans viewed and were educated about the relevance of trees, the proper place of trees in the scheme of life, and the place of trees in the overall existence of all animal life on the planet. The historical standard rationale for the destruction of forest and tree inclusive of clear cutting for agricultural purposes, cutting trees to create timber for the constructing of residential and other facilities, getting fuel wood for heating and cooking and creating open land for animal grazing, has been that all of these activities were very important factors in human life and the development of civilizations all across the planet. However, while the utilization of forests and trees in these ways was of great importance to human survival and growth since the first appearance of humans, questions must be asked and inquiries made into how efficiently early humans, first, and current humans have used and are using lands for agricultural, crop and grazing, forests for timber and fuel wood purposes, how efficiently humans have used the forest stocks that humans found on the planet and how these forests were and are being misused in so many areas of human life. We therefore need to examine and audit how we use land for agriculture, forest, grazing, dwellings, recreation, education and healthcare and then follow up with a comparative analysis of the amounts of lands that are dedicated to each sector and use this to see the importance that we place on forests, apart from the trees that we plant for fruits, nuts, timber and forest products.

For such an analysis we shall look at one country from each continent and the countries chosen are those with the largest populations on each continent and shall include USA, Brazil, Germany, China, Nigeria and Australia.

Land Use in the USA

The United States of America (USA) is a part of the North American continent which it shares with Canada and Mexico on a large landmass with great variations in climate, land forms, endemic species and human populations. The USA's portion of the continent consist of:

- 3,531,905 square miles or 2,260, 419,200 acres of land.
- Population of approximately 330,000,000 with 82 % (2018) living in urban centers. (World Bank).
- Two great mountain ranges, the Rocky Mountains in the West and the Appalachian Mountains in the east, along with other significant mountains.
- The Great Plains and Central Lowlands across the middle.
- The coastal plains along the Atlantic, Pacific and Gulf Coasts
- Many large rivers, the two largest being the Missouri and the Mississippi both of which are approximately 2600 and 2500 miles long respectively.
- The lands to the west of the Rocky Mountains
- Four deserts inclusive of the Chihuahuan Desert, 139,769 square miles, The Great Basin Desert (190,000 square miles), the Mohave Desert (47,877 square miles) and the Sonoran Desert (100,000 square miles).

According to the USDA and Bloomberg, land in the lower 48 states of the US is used as follows:

- Pasture and Range Lands – 654 million acres
- Forest Lands – 538.6 million acres
- Crop Lands – 391.5 million acres
- Special Use – 168.6 million acres
- Miscellaneous 68.9 million acres
- Urban – 69.4 million acres

According to the USDA, Forest Services (2001) at the start of European colonization in 1630 forest occupied 46% of all US land while today forests only occupies 33% of US lands, approximately 70% of the original land coverage.

Brazil

Brazil is located on the South American Continent which it shares with thirteen other countries inclusive of Colombia, Venezuela, Guyana, Suriname, French Guiana, Ecuador, Peru, Bolivia, Uruguay, Paraguay, Argentina and Chile, on a large landmass with great variations in climate, land forms, flora and fauna and human population. The Brazilian portion of the continent is as follows:

- 3,287,597 square miles or 2,104,062,080 acres of land
- Population of approximately 210,000,000 with 87 % living in urban centers (World Bank).
- Many mountains inclusive of the largest, Serra do Espinhaco, and the three tallest ones Tumucumaque, Imeri and Pararaima.
- The biggest tropical rainforest in the world –Amazonia
- The largest river in South America, The Amazon River, which starts in Peru and also runs through Colombia, Ecuador, Bolivia, and Venezuela. The Amazon River is 4000 miles long and has the largest drainage system and basin area in the world.
- Great Savanah grass lands.

Land usage in Brazil has been changing constantly over the last 100 years as more tropical rainforests are destroyed to facilitate agriculture, animal grazing and mining. According to the Brazilian government agencies, land use in 2011 are as follows:

- Forests (Woodlands) 48%
- Indigenous Land 12%
- Grass Lands 19%
- Crops Lands 7%
- Other 10%
- Urban and Water 4%

Since the colonization of Brazil by Portugal, forest coverage in some areas has been reduced by as much as 87% and according to the University of East Anglia "Once mighty Atlantic Forest are 'empty' after 500 years of over-exploitation". While all areas in Brazil are not like this, it is symptomatic of what the overall outcome could be if the current rate of exploitation is not reduced in a timely manner.

Germany

Germany is located in western Europe and is a part of the larger European continent, which it shares with many other nations inclusive of France, Spain, Portugal, Nederland, Belgium, Poland Denmark, Norway, Sweden, Finland, Lithuania, Latvia, Estonia, Ukraine, Russia, Czech Republic, Slovakia, Slovenia, Serbia, Bosnia Herzegovina, Albania, Croatia, Hungary, Romania, Italy, Greece, Luxembourg, Monaco, Switzerland, Austria, Hungary, Bulgaria, Montenegro, Kosovo, North Macedonia, Ireland and Cyprus. The German portion of the continent is as follows:

- Approximately 137,846 square miles or 88,221,440 acres of land.
- A population of approximately 83 million with 77% living in urban centers (World Bank).

- Several mountains inclusive of the Bavarian Alps with its highest point being Zugspitze at 9718 feet and the Ore Mountains which are the highest mountains in Germany.
- Many large rivers inclusive of the Rhine, Elbe, Wesser and Danube Rivers, which are some of the largest rivers in western Europe.
- Vast North European Plains

According to government agencies land use is as shown below:

- Agriculture inclusive of crops and grazing utilizes 51.66% or 45,597,929 acres of land.
- Forest occupies - 30.59 % or 26,998582 acres of land.
- Urban activities – 7% or 6,181, 422 acres of land.
- Transportation Infrastructure -5.06 % or 4,463,537 acres of land.

According to studies done at the University of Plymouth (2018), pollen analysis from one thousand sites has indicated that more than two thirds of central and northern Europe were once covered by trees. This coverage was however significantly reduced due to the growing demand for more land for agricultural to support a growing population, more wood for the construction of shelter and more wood for heating and cooking all of which caused the depletion of even more forests and the situation became much worse with the birth of the industrial revolution that demanded humongous sources of energy. All of these competing demands lead to a depletion of forests across Europe and created an energy crisis which was according to Elwell, due to the fact that "Many parts of Western Europe had achieved a kind of saturation with humankind by the 14th century". This shortage of timber in Europe lead to the development of the earliest schools of thought for how to sustainably use forest and forest products as presented by Hans Carl von Carlowitz in his book "Sylvicultura Oeconomica" (1713).

China

China is located on the southeastern portion of the great Asian landmass, which it shares with the Russian Federation, India, Bangladesh, Nepal, Pakistan, Bhutan, Afghanistan, Iran, Iraq, Saudi Arabia, Turkey, Turkmenistan, Kyrgyzstan, Kazakhstan, Mongolia, Laos, Vietnam, North Korea, South Korea, Burma, Malaysia, Thailand, Singapore, Cambodia, Uzbekistan, Tajikistan, Azerbaijan, Syria, Israel, Lebanon, Jordan, UAE, Yemen, Oman, Qatar, Kuwait and Bahrain. The Chinese portion of the Asian Continent consist of:

- 3,710,000 square miles or 2,374,400,000 acres of land.
- A population of 1.4 billion, 59 percent of whom live in urban centers (World Bank)
- Several great mountains inclusive of the Himalayan Mountain Range on its southwest border with India, Kunlun Shan, Altun Shan, Tien Shan, Da Hinggan Ling and Xiao Hinggan Ling mountains.
- Some of the largest rivers in the world inclusive of the Yangtze-3900 miles (third longest in the world), the Mekong - 2703 miles and the Yellow Rivers 3395 miles (sixth longest river in the world).
- Great plains in the middle and on the coasts.
- Two large deserts, the Taklamakan Desert -123,550 square miles and the Gobi Desert 500,000 square miles (Britannica)

According to the China Statistical Yearbook (2010) Land use in China is as follows:

- Agricultural crop lands – 12.7 % or 301,548,800 acres of land.
- Forests – 19 %, projected to be 23% by 2020 (UN), or 451,136,000 acres of land.
- Grass Lands 41.7% or 990,124,800 acres of land.
- Tea and Fruit Orchards – 1.4% or 33,241,600 acres of land.
- Water bodies – 1.8% or 42,739,200 acres of land
- Other Uses – 23.5 % or 557,984,000 acres of land

According to the Encyclopedia Britannica (2020) up to fifty percent of the current Chinese land mass may have been covered with forests in its early history which is a far cry from the current 21% land coverage.

Nigeria

Nigeria is located on the western coast of the African continent, a great land mass with great variations in landforms, flora, fauna and human population. Nigeria shares this great continent with many other nations inclusive of Western Sahara, Mauritania, Algeria, Morocco, Tunisia, Senegal, Niger, Mali, Chad, Guinea, Guinea Bissau, Ivory Coast, Sierra Leone, Liberia, Benin, Togo, Gambia, Ghana, Burkina Faso, Libya, Egypt, Sudan, South Sudan, Eritrea, Ethiopia, Somalia, Kenya, Tanzania, Uganda, Cameroon, Gabon, Central African Republic, Congo, Democratic Republic of Congo, Angola, Namibia, Botswana, Zambia, Zimbabwe, Mozambique, South Africa, Lethoso and Swaziland. The Nigerian portion of the continent contains the following:

- Land area 356,668 square miles or 228,267,520 acres of land.
- Population approximately 195 million with 50% living in urban centers (World Bank)
- Several mountains three of which are Chappal Wadi the highest peak at approximately 7936 feet, Tsaunin Kwaiki the second highest peak at approximately 7740 feet and the Kumari the third highest peak at approximately 7480 feet (Media Nigeria)
- Nigeria has many rivers flowing through it, some from outside of the country and some from inside and the most important of these rivers are the Niger River which at 2613 miles in the third longest river in Africa, the Benue River, which flows into the Niger, 870 miles and the Kaduna River 344 miles. These great rivers and the lesser ones provide the country with significant sources of fresh water for human consumption, industry and agriculture.

- Vast savanna made up of three zone, the Guinea forest savanna mosaic, the Sudan Savanna and the Sahel Savanna.
- The Sahel is an arid zone where land degradation and desertification is occurring and represents a significant area of concern for Nigeria.

Nigeria Land Use

According to the government agencies land use in Nigeria is as follows:

- Arable land 38.4 % of total land available or 87,654,728 acres
- Permanent Crops 7.4 % of total available land or 16,891,800 acres
- Forest 9.0% of total available land or 20,544,077 acres
- Other use 45.2% of total land available or 103,176,919 acres.

In 1897, just before the beginning of British colonial rule in 1900, Nigeria had approximately 150 million acres of forest, 65.71 percent land coverage, but by 1997, 100 year later, most of it, approximately 124 million acres were gone leaving approximately 26 million acres. (Carty 1992; Mfon et al. 2014)

Australia

Australia is located between the Indian Ocean and the Pacific Ocean and is the smallest of all continents and is remotely located away from all of the other major landmasses and this isolation has fostered the development of entire species of flora and fauna that is quite unique to Australia. The Australian landmass, however, developed landforms similar to the other continents inclusive of mountains, plains, river, creeks/streams and lakes giving Australia regular land features. The following are the main features:

- 2,967, 909 square miles or 1,899,461,760 acres of land
- Population – 26.41 million with 86 % of the population living in urban areas (World Bank)

- Several significant mountains inclusive of the Great Dividing Range that is 2175 miles long, the third longest mountain range in the world, the Australian Alps with a highest peak, Munt Kosciuszko that is 7310 feet, Hammersley Range, the Darling Range and several other mountainous regions.
- Many productive river systems inclusive of the Murrumbidgee River- 928 miles, Darling River -966 miles, Lachlan River- 837 miles, Copper Creek- 696 miles, Finders Rivers- 628 miles and the Diamantina River- 588 miles.
- Australia has ten deserts with the four major deserts being the Great Victoria Desert- 134,653 square miles, the Great Sandy Desert- 110,036 square miles, the Tanami Desert- 71,236 square miles and the Gibson Desert- 60,232 square miles.

According to the Australian Collaborative Land Use Management Program land use in Australia is as shown on the pie chart above and is as follows:

- Nature Conservation – 7% or 132,962323 acres of land
- Other Protected Areas including Indigenous use – 15% 0r 284,919,264 acres of land.
- Minimal Use - 15% or 284,919,264 acres of land.
- Livestock Grazing – 54% or 1,025,709,350 acres of land.
- Forestry - 2 % or 37,989,235 acres of land.
- Dryland Agriculture – 4% 0r 75,978,470 acres of land.
- Irrigated Agriculture – 0.2% or 3,798,924 acres of land.
- Intensive Animal and Plant Production 0.02% or 379,892 acres of land
- Intensive use (mainly urban) 0.2% or 3,798,924 acres of land.
- Rural Residential – 0.2 % or 3,798,924 acres of land
- Waste and Mining -0.02% 0r 379,892 acres of land
- Water -2% or 37,989,235 acres of land.

Australian Land Use Historical Data

According to Bradshaw (Flannery 1998; Rasmussen et al. 2011; Bradshaw 2012) the continent of Australia was occupied by the

Aboriginal peoples for at least 75,000 years prior to the arrival of Europeans and their agricultural practices and their use of wood in one form or the other, had negative modifying impacts upon the ancient Australian forests. However, going back 75,000 years in time to establish a working baseline is not feasible and in order to create a baseline from which to work, it is important to establish a point in history from which to select data and the point selected is the start of European colonization in 1788. Several writers have indicated that "It has been estimated that approximately 30% of Australia's land mass was covered by 'forest' at the time of the first European colonization in the late 18th century" (Bradshaw 2012 & Barson et al., 2000) The rest of the land was covered by "shrubland" – 40%, open woodland- 22%, grassland -7% and unvegetated areas -1% and these numbers were significantly modified over time since 1788.

Comparison of Land Use by the 6 Chosen Nations

Country	Size (sq. miles.)	Population	Urban Population	Rural Population	Forest	Crops	Grazing	Special	Agri land use acres per person
Australia	2,967,909	26.41mil.	86 %	14%	2%	4.2%	54%	37%	41.86
Brazil	3,287,597	210 mil.	87%	13%	48%	7%	19%	26%	2.6
China	3,710,000	1.4 bil.	59%	41%	19%	14.1%	41.7	25.5%	0.946
Germany	137,846	83 mil.	77%	23%	30.59%	37.2%[1]	14.46%	17.75%	0.549
Nigeria	356,668	195 mil.	50%	50%	9%	45.8%	33.3%★	12.5 %	0,926
USA	3,531,905	330 mil.	82%	18%	28.4%	20.72%	34.62%	16.24%	3.79

Table 6.1 Comparison of Land Use in the Chosen Six Major Nations.

Notes.

Some of the data as shown in table 6.1 have varied since the date of the information shown.

- "Special" in the table covers uses inclusive Miscellaneous, Urban, Transportation and other Designated Special Uses
- China's forest coverage is said to be up to 21 % as of 2020
- The data from the German Federal Agency indicates that 51.66 % of land was used for agriculture without any indication of

grazing or crop areas. The division shown 37.2% crop & 14.46% grazing was done based on CIA World Factbook.

- The data for the US only covers the lower 48.

Comparative Analysis of Land Use in the Six Selected Nations

1. Only two of the selected nations, Germany and Brazil have more forested lands than the lands dedicated to grazing and Germany has the lowest percentage of land dedicated grazing which could indicate that Germans consume much less red meat than all of the other nations in the table.

2. Australia dedicates more land per person for agriculture than all of the other five nations which could indicate that most of their agricultural products is for export or that their agriculture was very inefficient, however, this latter does not appear to be the case.

3. Australia with the smallest population dedicates more lands for grazing, 1,602670.86 square miles, than all the countries with much larger populations and land masses, which could indicate that most of the meat produced from their grazing animals are not intended for Australian consumption but for export.

4. China with the biggest population by far, dedicates less land, 1,547,070 square miles, to grazing than Australia 1,602,670 square miles, even with a population that is 53 times larger than Australia's and may point more efficient use of grazing land in China.

5. The nations with the largest amounts of grazing lands are also the nations with large deserts and large areas that are at risks of becoming deserts, which clearly points to the problems associated with overgrazing, which is known to cause desertification.

6. Germany's 0.546 acres per person could indicate the most efficient use of agricultural lands.

7. Nigeria dedicates a larger percentage of its land to agriculture than the other five nations and could indicate an overdependence on agriculture for employment and GDP and could be tied into

the fact that 50% of its population still lived in rural areas, the highest among the six nations, and this high percentage of rural population could automatically dictate its land use policy and be an indicator of the level of development in the country.

8. China has the second largest percentage of its population (41%) living in rural areas, a rural population that is exceeded only by India the second largest population in the world. This large rural population would also indicate a large farming population and maybe reflected in the China's employment numbers and a high contribution of agriculture to China's GDP. This large rural population also speaks to the level of development in this very rich nation or could indicate a very large divide in the nation.

7

Agriculture

Agriculture may be defined as a human endeavor for the preparation of land, planting and nurturing of seeds and plants, reaping and storage of the end products and the nurturing of animals, for food, fiber, shelter, medicines, fuels and many other uses. The practice of agriculture has ensured a relatively constant supply of food resources that has been critical for the growth, development, health and welfare of the human population for many millennia since the tapering off of the hunter-gatherer period of human development and it continues to provide sustenance into the 21st century and beyond as life in a modern world with large human populations would not be possible without agriculture in one form or the other. Agriculture's most basic requirement is good arable land on which to plant crops, good grasslands for the grazing of many species and breeds of domesticated animals and lands for the storage and processing of crops, historically land for processing and storage was only for grains, nuts and other crops that had long shelf life.

The decision of where to plant the first crops may have been very easy for that very first farmer, as a crop had to be planted in a location that showed that it could support plant life and where better, than a forest full of trees and plants of every species, to plant some of the very same or in the vast open grasslands where the tall grasses like wheat, barley, oats, corn, rice, wild rice, sorghum, millet and the many other edible grass seeds grew or along the banks of rivers that had their high annual deposits of rich silt on flatlands. This thinking, without the scientific base that we have today, proved to be quite accurate as the soils in forests had grown rich from millennia of plant and animal waste decomposition, the soil in the grasslands and on the banks of the rivers which are enriched on an annual basis by nutrient rich silt, proved to be great places for planting crops, as shown by the earliest civilizations along the Amazon, Mississippi, Indus, Tigris, Yangzte, Euphrates and Nile Rivers. The second important thing that ancient people learned, probably through trial and error, was that plants needed a lot of sunlight or they would not produce at their highest levels and that while the soil of the forest was great, the forest cover prevented full sunlight from reaching most plants in their understories and therefore prevented the full development of most plants planted under the forest cover. This second understanding created the need to remove trees and associated understory plants to make the way clear for the planting of crops that had become important in the diets of early humans.

The combined knowledge of soil conditions and the need for sunlight led to the clearing of lands for agricultural purposes, a practice which has grown continuously over time and continues in modern times even now when the values of trees have taken on more importance with the recognition of their ability to preserve the environment and reduce the effects of climate change. In many places the trees were permanently removed, stumps and roots, and the land farmed on a continuous and permanent basis, while in many other places the land was only partially cleared to be used for only short periods of time after which the land would be allowed to rest for a period of time before being used again. This second method usually referred to as slash-and-burn or slash and mulch is usually practiced by small itinerant farmers practicing subsistence farming to ensure the survival of their family units, while the other method is practiced by large farm holdings. According to Pollini (2014) "Slash-and-burn agriculture typically refers to land uses where a cropping period is usually rotated with a fallow period that is long enough to enable the growing of dense woody vegetation and where the biomass is eliminated from the plot by cutting, slashing and burning it, prior to the next cultivation cycle". This fallow period can last anywhere from 3-25 years to ensure the regrowth of woody material that provides the required energy for the removing, by burning of weeds, pests and diseases from the selected plot of land and to supply the land with the nitrate rich ash from the plants. According to Stief (2019) the practice of slash–and–burn agriculture is usually done in the following steps:

- Field preparation. Cutting down the vegetation in a plot of land and leaving in place undisturbed any plant or tree that provide food and timber.
- Drying time. The chopped vegetation is allowed to dry which will make it easier to burn when required, which was usually just before seasonal rains.
- Burning. The dried vegetation is burned to eliminate weeds, pest and vermin, and any unhealthy bacteria that may have occupied the plot of land and the ash from the burnt vegetation is spread over the soil to add needed nutrient.
- Planting. The crop is planted in the ashes left behinds.
- Fallow period. The land is used until it loses its fertility after which it is allowed to rest or lay fallows for between 3-25 year depending on the availability of land and during this period woody and herbaceous plants are allowed to grow to provide biomass for the next time that that plot of land will be used.

In modern societies slash–and–burn agriculture is usually the form of agriculture practiced by landless people, people without title of ownership and therefore only temporary users of the land with or without the permission of the owners or in many cases the government. This temporary status ensure that the users can never lay legal claim to the lands and can therefore be required to move on at regular intervals without doing permanent damage to the property and allowing the land to rest. However, while this practice may appear to be harsh, it provides significant benefits to the landowners and to the people using the land as it gives the owners of the unused lands the ability to monitor and keep control of their property and provides the users with the opportunity to provide food for their families and also to earn an income. According to the FAO approximately seven percent of the world's population, 200-500 million people provide food for themselves in this manner.

The main problems associated with slash-and-burn agriculture are as follows:

- Deforestation. Where forests lands, public or private, are used by a large population of people for slash-and-burn agriculture the practice can lead to fragmentation of forests followed by forest degradation and eventually deforestation as less time is usually allowed for plants to regrow and permanent trees and many other species of plants are lost over time. The problems associated become more severe with growing populations and with increasing poverty due to the many changes that occur in most modern economies.

- Erosion. The loss of vegetation and the loss of the soil adhesion, caused by the heat from the burns, may cause the soil to become dried out and more fragmented thus making it much easier for it to be eroded by water and wind.

- Nutrient Loss. With overused lands, even with regular moves, the field may lose all of its fertility and become unable to support plant life which could cause the field to dry out and eventually lead to desertification.

- Biodiversity Loss – The clearing and burning of lands over any period of time will automatically lead to the loss of biodiversity as the farmer must remove all other plants that may interfere with the growth and development of their selected crop. The animals naturally associated with that piece of land will also have learned to avoid it due to the initial danger of fire and later by the farmers intent on keeping their plants and products safe from damage by all forms of animals especially those that may also enjoy the crops that was planted.

The problems associated with slash-and-burn agriculture is also associated with all forms of agriculture as permanent farms utilize some of the same practices and create some of the very same problems and in many instances even more problems depending on the technology and methods of agriculture used. According to the United States Geological Survey (USGS) there are many significant environmental and social problems associated with the general practice of agriculture, all around the globe, and some of these problems include desertification, deforestation, forest fragmentation and degradation, changes in the hydrologic cycle, the introduction of toxic chemicals, nutrients and pathogens, the reduction and alteration of wildlife habitat and the introduction of invasive species of plants and animals(USGS, 2007). Some of the specific problems in the US highlighted by the USGS includes:

- Approximately 50% of the land in the contiguous 48 states has been converted into farmland for crops, pastures and ranges (Lubowski and others 2006; USGS 2007)
- Approximately 50% of original wetlands in the contiguous 48 states were modified and used as farmlands up to 2004 (Claasen 2004)
- From the arrival of the Europeans until 1954, nearly 42 percent of all wetlands were drained and filled and later used for settlement and agriculture.
- Most of the forests, prairie and wetland areas in the Midwestern and Great Plains states were converted to farmlands or were negatively affected by the agricultural production of the European immigrants.
- The growth of intensive agricultural production created a need to artificially replenish the fertility of the soil, and this was achieved by the use of chemicals called fertilizers. The use of these chemicals to rapidly increase fertility had many unintended consequences inclusive of negatively impacting both surface and ground water sources upon which both humans and animals depended for potable water.
- The growth of intensive large-scale agriculture also demanded quicker and more effective methods of handling both plant and insect pests which lead to the creation of a whole new range of chemicals called pesticides and herbicides that were all designed

to quickly eliminate insect pest, vermin and troublesome weeds. These new chemicals also had many unintended consequences that includes contaminating water supplies, destroying animals, destroying aquatic plants and animals, poisoning humans and killing the pollinators upon which agriculture depends.

- Intensive large-scale agriculture also demanded bigger and faster growing animals for human consumption which led to the development and use of antibiotics and hormones in farm animals, to achieve the desired end results with many negative unintended consequences. The use of antibiotic and hormones in farm animals intended for human consumption has led to significant health problems in the human population.

- The intensive large-scale breeding of cattle to meet the great US demand for beef has also led to the greater amounts of animal fecal matter, pathogens, antibiotics and hormones entering surface and groundwater sources, all of which has the potential to harm humans, land-based flora and fauna and aquatic flora and fauna, all of which consume the water and the aquatic flora and fauna products.

These problems are not unique to the US as they also occur in every developed and developing nations around the globe as all nations are focused on producing more agricultural food products faster to meet the nutritional demands of their growing human populations. Unfortunately, many developing nations, large and small, fall into some of the very same traps that the US has fallen into, as most of them pattern their agricultural activities after the practices and achievements of the US and other developed nations agricultural industries, all of whom are also copying the practices of each other.

The social problems created by agriculture are, however, not limited to the health problems that it has created for the human population and the environment but extends to how it can and has disrupted the lives of many people across the globe in it attempts to obtain and utilize its most precious resource, land. No other agricultural resource has the same value as land and even with the greatest improvements in the efficiency of agricultural production created by new technology, the elimination of waste and the elimination of all of negative inputs that have harmed humans and the environment, there is one resource that will still be of primary importance to agriculture for many years to come and this resource become more important each day with a growing human populations, this resource is good arable land and it is limited in supply which places a relatively high premium on it. According to Gilbert (2016) this resource is now fueling a new 'land grab' by the international financial forces of the world as there is currently taking place great growth in 'Land Investments' particularly by developed nations in developing nations, which has given rise to frequent international references to new 'land grabbing'. This current 'land grab' while similar to the old 'land grab' by European nations, is now being driven by the marketization of land for its potential use in agriculture and the production of food, for profit, to feed a fast-growing world population and by conservationists seeking to preserve land, flora and fauna. The problems associated with all such 'land grabs', past and present, are how they will affect the people at the very bottom of the economic ladder, which in many developing nations are the indigenous people, whose hold on the land that they have lived on for many millennia has become quite tenuous as they do not have "legal titles" to these lands. Gilbert (2016) indicates that "This 'global land rush' is very often negatively impacting indigenous people who are seeing a dramatic loss of access to their own lands and territories". This is not a new phenomenon as earlier land grabs saw the indigenous peoples of Africa, Australia, New Zealand and the Americas losing all of their lands to Europeans and according to Laltaika and Askew (2018) of the UN, this phenomenon is again raising its ugly head in Africa "However, powerful transnational corporations and conservation organizations- both typically aligned with local political and economic elites – were already identified in 2003 WGIP report as a threat to indigenous lands resources and livelihoods". Fois and Machado (2018) also confirmed that these same negative forces are also at work in Brazil (Americas) taking away the lands of the indigenous people "During our research we also visited families who had been evicted from reoccupied areas due to agribusiness expansion and are now left with no land. Squeezed between sugar cane, soy and corn plantations, they were ousted to the side of the road." This is happening even though the Brazilian Federal Constitution guaranteed the rights of its indigenous people to occupy their lands in 1988 (Fois and Machado 2018).

Agricultural Land Use

The amount of land used in agriculture in each of the nations examined is usually a function of the size of the population, arable land available, the amount of natural rainfall received each year and the availability of irrigation water and systems, however, sometimes when a country is rich in land, with a relatively small populations it utilizes its land wealth to build its economy through the export of agricultural and other products that can be obtained from the land inclusive of timber and minerals. Using the sample of six nations, Australia, Brazil, China, Germany, Nigeria and the USA, the amount of land in agriculture is as follows:

- Australia with a population of 26.41 million (World Bank) utilizes approximately 1 billion acres of land for livestock and 80 million acres for crops for total of 1.08 billion acres of land in agriculture representing approximately 57 percent of total Australian lands (Australian Collaborative Land Use Management Program {ACLUMP}).
- Brazil with a population of 210 million (World Bank) utilizes approximately 400 million acres of land for grazing and approximately 150 million acres for crops for a total of 550 million acres which represents approximately 26 percent of total Brazilian lands. (IBGE 2011, MMA&IBRAF2011, ICONE)
- China with a population of 1.4 billion (World Bank) utilizes approximately 990 million acres of land for livestock and 335 million acres of land for crops for a total of 1.325 billion acres which represent approximately 56 percent of all Chinese lands (China Statistical Yearbook 2010)
- Germany with a population 83 million (World Bank) utilizes approximately 46 million acres of land for grazing and crops which represents 51.66 percent of total German lands. (German Federal Agency for Nature Conservation)

MICHAEL GRAHAM MSc.

- Nigeria with a population of 195 million (World Bank) utilizes 105 million acres of land for agriculture which represents approximately 46 percent of total Nigerian lands (Nigeria FAO STAT)
- US with a population of 330 million (World Bank) utilizes 654 million acres of land for grazing and 392 million acres of land for crops for a total of 1.046 billion acres representing approximately 55.34 percent of total US lands in the lower 48 states (Bloomberg)

Comparative Agricultural Production Stats

Agricultural production around the world fluctuates based on demands, availability of water supplies and the availability of arable lands. The agriculture production of some of the major crops and meats are shown on the tables below.

Rank	Country	Annual Production 2018 (metric tonnes)
1	China	2,400,000
2	Australia	700,000
3	New Zealand	400,000
4	Turkey	350,000
5	Iran	300,000

Table 7.1 Top Sheep Meat Producing Nations 2018. Source: ABS, FAO 2018.

Rank	Country	% World Production
1	China	39
2	India	9
3	Pakistan	6
4	Nigeria	4
5	Bangladesh	4
6	Australia	1
7	Other	38

Table 7.2 Top Goat Meat Producing Nations 2017. Source FAO and Meat & Livestock Australia.

Rank	Country	Annual Production (metric tonnes)
1	USA	18,290,000
2	Brazil	13,600,000
3	China	12,700,000
4	India	4,200,000
5	Russia	3,750,000
6	Mexico	3,270,000
7	Argentina	2,100,000
8	Turkey	1,900,000
9	Thailand	1,780,000
10	Indonesia	1,640,000

Table 7.3 Top Chicken Producing Nations.
Source: WhichCountry.com

Rank	Country	Annual Production (million metric tonnes)
1	USA	12,515
2	Brazil	10,310
3	European Union	7,800
4	China	6,900
5	India	4,150
6	Argentina	3,085
7	Australia	2,065
8	Mexico	1,840

Table 7.4 Top Beef and Veal Producing Nations
(million metric tons). Source: Statista

Rank	Country	Annual Production (thousand metric tonnes)
1	China	54,650
2	European Union	24,050
3	USA	12,166
4	Brazil	3,675
5	Russia	3,050
6	Vietnam	2,800
7	Canada	2,015
8	Philippines	1,600
9	South Korea	1,321
10	Mexico	1,305

Table 7.5 Top 10 Pork Producing Nations. Source: USDA

Rank	Country	Annual Production (metric tonnes)
1	China	76,150,000
2	Indonesia	20,880,000
3	India	9,600,000
4	Vietnam	6,330,000
5	US	5,410,000
6	Myanmar	5,050,00
7	Japan	4,770,000
8	Philippines	4,690,000
9	Russia	4,400,000
10	Chile	3,820,000

Table 7.6 Top Fishing and Aquaculture Producing
Nations. Source: WorldAtlas.Com

Rank	Country	Annual Production (million metric tonnes)
1	Brazil	124
2	USA	96.79
3	Argentina	51
4	China	18.1
5	Paraguay	9.9
6	India	9.3
7	Canada	6

Table 7.7 Top Soybean Producing Countries. Source: WorldAtlas.com

Rank	Country	Annual Production (metric tonnes)
1	Canada	21,328,000
2	China	13,274,010
3	India	7,917,000
4	France	5,200,000
5	Australia	4,313,730
6	Germany	4,275,600
7	Poland	2,697,265
8	Ukraine	2,194,790
9	United Kingdom	2,167,000
10	Romania	1,673,330

Table 7.8 Top Rapeseed Producing Nations. Source WorldAtlas.com

Rank	Country	Annual Production (metric tonnes)
1	India	890,000
2	China	626,000
3	Nigeria	580,000
4	Myanmar	540,000
5	Tanzania	420,000

Table 7.9 Top Sesame Producing Nations (2017)
Source: FAO &WorldAtlas.Com

Rank	Country	Annual Production (metric tonnes)
1	Indonesia	36,000,000
2	Malaysia	21,000,000
3	Thailand	2,200,000
4	Colombia	1,320,000
5	Nigeria	970,000
6	Others	58,800,000

Table 7.10 Top Oil Palm Producing Nations (2018). Source: FAO & WorldAtlas.com

Rank	Country	Annual Production (1000 metric tonnes)
1	US	384,778
2	China	219,554
3	Brazil	86,500
4	European Union	60,309
5	Argentina	36,500
6	Ukraine	28,000
7	Mexico	26,000
8	India	24,500
9	Russia	15,500
10	Canada	13,200

Table 7.11 The Top Corn Producing Nations. Source: USDA and Maps of World

Rank	Country	Annual Production (metric tonnes)
1	China	134,340,630
2	India	98,510,000
3	Russian Federation	85,863,132
4	US	47,370,880
5	France	36,924,938
6	Australia	31,818,744
7	Canada	29,984,200
8	Pakistan	26,674,000
9	Ukraine	26,208,980
10	Germany	24,481,600

Table 7.12 Top Wheat Producing Nations. Source: WorldAtlas.com

Rank	Country	Annual Production (million metric tonnes)
1	European Union	56.34
2	Russia	16.6
3	Others	9.68
4	Canada	8.4
5	Ukraine	7.4
6	Turkey	7.4
7	Australia	7.3
8	Argentina	4.5
9	Kazakhstan	4.2
10	US	3.33

Table 7. 13 Top Barley Producing Nations (million metric tons). Source: Statista

Rank	Country	Annual Production (1000 metric tonnes)
1	European Union	6,256
2	Russia	1,914
3	Belarus	650
4	Ukraine	396
5	Turkey	320
6	Canada	235
7	US	214
8	Argentina	100
9	Australia	30
10	Kazakhstan	23

Fig. 7.14 Top Rye Producing Nations (1000 metric tons) Source: Statista

Rank	Country	Annual Production (metric tonnes)
1	India	10,910,000
2	Nigeria	5,000,000
3	Niger	2,955,000
4	China	1,620,000
5	Mali	1,152,331
6	Burkina Faso	1,109,000
7	Sudan	1,090,000
8	Ethiopia	807,056
9	Chad	582,000
10	Senegal	572,155

Table 7.15 Top 10 Millet Producing Nations. Source: WorldAtlas.Com

Rank	Country	Annual Production (million metric tonnes)
1	US	11.5
2	India	7.5
3	Nigeria	7.4
4	Mexico	6.1
5	Sudan	4.4
6	Sudan (former)	3.7
7	China	3.1
8	Argentina	2.9
9	Ethiopia	2.2
10	Australia	1.9

Table 7.16 Top 10 Sorghum Producing Nations.
Source: FAOSTAT &WorldAtlas.com

Rank	Country	Annual Production (1000 metric tonnes)
1	Russia	4,027
2	Canada	2,680
3	Poland	1,439
4	Finland	1,159
5	Australia	1,050
6	United States	929
7	Spain	799
8	United Kingdom	784
9	Sweden	776
10	Germany	668

Table 7.17 Top Oat Producing Nations. Source: WorldAtlas.Com

Rank	Country	Annual Production (metric tonnes)
1	China	206,507,400
2	India	157,200,000
3	Indonesia	70,846,465
4	Bangladesh	52,325,620
5	Vietnam	44,974,206
6	Thailand	32,620,160
7	Myanmar	26,423,340
8	Philippines	18,967,826
9	Brazil	12,175,602
10	Japan	10,549,000

Table 7.18 Top Rice Producing Nations. Source: FAOSTAT

Rank	Country	Annual Production (metric tonnes)
1	China	99,205,580
2	India	48,605,000
3	Russia	29,589,976
4	Ukraine	22,208,220
5	US	20,017,350
6	Germany	11,720,000
7	Bangladesh	10,215,957
8	Poland	9,171,733
9	Netherlands	7,391,881
10	France	7,342,203

Table 7.19 Top Potato Producing Nations. Source: WorldAtlas.com

Rank	Country	Annual Production (metric tonnes)
1	China	70,963,630
2	Nigeria	3,478,270
3	Tanzania	3,345,170
4	Ethiopia	2,701,599
5	Indonesia	2,382,658
6	Uganda	1,863,000
7	Vietnam	1,401,000
8	US	1,346,910
9	India	1,087,880
10	Rwanda	1,080,780

Table 7.20 Top Sweet Potato Producing Nations.
Source: FAO & WorldAtlas.com.

Rank	Country	Annual Production (metric tonnes)
1	Nigeria	38,000,000
2	Ghana	6,638,867
3	Cote d' Ivoire	5,674,696
4	Benin	2,739,088
5	Togo	864,408
6	Cameroon	520,000
7	Central African Republic	460,000
8	Chad	420,000
9	Colombia	361,034
10	Papua New Guinea	345,000

Table 7.21 Top 10 Yam Producing Nations (2012). Source: FAO

Rank	Country	Annual Production (metric tonnes)
1	Nigeria	52,403,455
2	Brazil	25,349,088
3	Indonesia	24,009,624
4	Thailand	21,912,416
5	DRC	15,569,138
6	Angola	14,333,509
7	Ghana	14,240,867
8	Mozambique	10,093,619
9	Vietnam	9,897,912
10	India	8,076,000

Table 7.22 Top 10 Cassava Producing Nations.
Source: FAO & Worldlistsmania.Com

Rank	Country	Annual Production (metric tonnes)
1	China	554,290,000
2	India	127,140,000
3	US	32,620,000
4	Turkey	24,930,000
5	Russia	16,410,000
6	Nigeria	16,380,000
7	Vietnam	15,730,000
8	Mexico	15,520,000
9	Egypt	15,250,000
10	Iran	14,700,000

Fig. 7.23 Top 10 Vegetable Producing Nations (2017) Source: Statista

Rank	Country	Annual Production (metric tonnes)
1	India	23,240,790
2	Canada	8,715,161
3	Myanmar	7,053,336
4	China	5,005,181
5	Russia	4,264,829
6	Australia	4,123,606
7	Nigeria	3,475,988
8	Brazil	3,045,872
9	US	2,941,372
10	Ethiopia	2,922,922

Table 7.24 Top 10 Pulse (Peas and Beans) Producing Nations. Source: FAOSTAT

Rank	Country	Annual Production (metric tonnes)
1	China	240,750,000
2	India	98,720,000
3	Brazil	40,050,000
4	US	26,020,000
5	Turkey	23,600,000
6	Mexico	22,770,000
7	Indonesia	20,440,000
8	Spain	19,330,000
9	Iran	18,900,000
10	Italy	18,010,000

Fig. 7.25 Top 10 Fruit Producing Countries (million metric tons) 2018. Source: Statista

Rank	Country	Annual Production (metric tonnes)
1	Brazil	2,592,000
2	Vietnam	1,650,000
3	Colombia	810,000
4	Indonesia	660,000
5	Ethiopia	384,000
6	Honduras	348,000
7	India	348,000
8	Uganda	288,000
9	Mexico	234,000
10	Guatemala	204,000

Table 7. 26 Top 10 Coffee Producing
Nations. Source: WorldAtlas.Com

Rank	Country	Annual Production (metric tonnes)
1	Cote d'Ivoire	1,448,993
2	Ghana	835,466
3	Indonesia	777,500
4	Nigeria	367,000
5	Cameroon	275,000
6	Brazil	256,186
7	Ecuador	128,446
8	Mexico	82,000
9	Peru	71,175
10	Dominican Republic	68,021

Table 7. 27 Top Cocoa Producing Nations. Source: WorldAtlas.com

Rank	Country	Annual Production (tons)
1	China	2,000,000 (over)
2	India	1,200,000
3	Kenya	432,400
4	Sri Lanka	340,230
5	Vietnam	214,300
6	Turkey	212,400
7	Iran	160,000
8	Indonesia	148,100
9	Argentina	103,000
10	Japan	84,800

Table 7.28 Top Tea Producing Nations. Source: WorldAtlas.Com

A review of the agricultural production highlighted in the many tables above will show production in the selected six nations as follows.

Australia

Australia while having a relatively small population, 26.41 million, and a relatively large landmass, approximately 1.9 billion acres, has built its economy based on the land available through agriculture and many other endeavors inclusive of mining and timber production. In the area of agriculture, it produces and exports many crops inclusive of wheat, rye, oats, sorghum, pulse, sheep meat, goatmeat, beef and veal, rapeseed, rice, corn, soybeans, cotton seed, cotton lint and sunflower seed and became a world top ten producers in the following areas:

- Sheep meat. The second largest producer in the world behind China.
- Goatmeat. The sixth largest producer in the world behind China, India, Pakistan, Nigeria and Bangladesh.
- Beef and Veal. The seventh largest producers in the world behind US, Brazil, EU, China, India and Argentina.
- Rapeseed. The fifth largest producer in the world behind Canada, China, India and France,

- Wheat. The sixth largest producer in the world behind China, India, Russian Federation, US and France.
- Rye. The eighth largest producer in the world behind EU, Russian Federation, Belarus, Ukraine, Turkey, Canada, US and Argentina.
- Sorghum. The tenth largest producer in the world behind, US, India, Nigeria, Mexico, Sudan, South Sudan, China, Argentina and Ethiopia.
- Oats. The fifth largest producer in the world behind Russia, Canada, Poland and Finland.
- Pulse. The sixth largest producer in the world behind India, Canada, Myanmar, China and the Russian Federation.
- Cotton. The eighth largest producers of cotton in the world behind China, India, US, Pakistan, Brazil, Uzbekistan and Turkey.

Australia's agricultural production is quite significant on the world stage based on the size of its population and the amount of land dedicated to agriculture, approximately one billion acres to livestock and 80 million acres to crop (ACLUMP), however, the impact on world livestock production could be greater based upon the amount of land used compared to other countries. Australia's total agricultural production contributes 2.1 % of its 2019 Gross Domestic Product (GDP) (World Bank 2019).

Brazil

Brazil is the largest nation in South America and one of the largest in the world, with a population of approximately 210 million (World Bank) and a land mass of approximately 2.1 billion acres and they are using agriculture as one of their main tools to lift themselves to first world economic status, however, in this process it has earned the wrath of its indigenous people, people all around the world and environmentalists, as more agriculture requires the destruction of more forest, the displacement of more indigenous people and the loss of habitat to many species. Their main agricultural products include coffee, soybean, wheat, rice, corn, sugarcane, cocoa, citrus and beef given in order of importance, with products like poultry, banana, millet, sorghum, tobacco, cotton, and cassava following in no fixed order. Brazilian impact on trade in agricultural goods has grown significantly over the years with it gaining leadership in production and exports in several important sectors inclusive of:

- Coffee. The largest producer and exporter in the world
- Soybean. The largest producer and exporter in the world
- Sugarcane. The largest producer and exporter in the world
- Fruits. The third largest producers of fruits behind China and India
- Pulse. The eighth largest producer in the world behind India, Canada, Myanmar, China, Russian Federation, Australia and Nigeria.
- Rice. The ninth largest producer of rice behind China, India, Indonesia, Bangladesh, Vietnam, Thailand, Myanmar and Philippines.
- Corn. The third largest producer of corn in the world behind the US and China.
- Beef and Veal. The second largest producer in the world behind the US.
- Chicken Meat. The second largest producer in the world behind the US
- Cocoa. The sixth largest cocoa producer in the world behind Cote d'Ivoire, Ghana, Indonesia, Nigeria and Cameroon.
- Pork. The fourth largest producer in the world behind China, Eu and US.
- Cotton. The fifth largest producer of cotton in the world behind China, India, US and Pakistan.

Brazil's agriculture is still growing and can achieve much more than it has to date, however, it may pay a very high humanitarian and environmental price in achieving the much larger production numbers. Agriculture is one of the main drivers of the economy in Brazil and it is responsible for 4.4 % of Brazil's GDP (World Bank 2019).

China

China is currently the world's most populous nation, approximately 1.4 billion (World Bank), and has land mass of approximately 2.4 billion acres of which it uses 990 million acres for livestock and 335 million acres for crops (China Yearbook 2010) which it utilizes to feed its population and also to earn income from exports. China's agricultural activities have had significant effects upon the environment as it currently struggles with desertification and other related environmental problems in order to produce sufficient crops and protein to feed its growing population. The main crops produced in China are rice, wheat, corn, soybeans and tubers followed by cotton, peanuts, rapeseed, sesame, sugarcane, tea, tobacco, mulberry and fruits. China's agriculture outproduces the world in many significant categories inclusive of:

- Vegetables. By far the largest producer of vegetables in the world.
- Fruits. By far the largest producers of fruits in the world.
- Sweet Potato. The largest producers of sweet potatoes in the world by far.
- Potato. The largest producer of potatoes in the world by far.
- Rice. The largest producers in the world by far
- Wheat. The largest producers in the world by far.
- Goatmeat. The largest producer in the world by far
- Sheep meat. The largest producer in the world by far
- Fish and Aquaculture. The largest producer of fish and aquaculture products in the world.
- Pork. The largest producer of pork in the world by far.
- Cotton. The largest cotton producer in the world
- Chicken. The third largest producer in the world behind the US and Brazil
- Beef and Veal. The fourth largest producers in the world behind US, Brazil and European Union.
- Corn. The second largest producer in the world behind the US
- Rapeseed. The second largest producer in the world behind Canada
- Soybean. The fourth largest producer in the world behind Brazil, US and Argentina.

- Millet. The fourth largest producer of millet in the world
- Sorghum. The seventh largest producer of Sorghum in the world
- Pulse. The fourth largest producer of pulse in 2017 (FAOSTAT) and should be the largest at this time.

China, from all the data gathered, is the most productive agricultural nation on the planet and with its population of 1.4 billion and growing, it will need to produce even more in the future, however, with its current problems with existing deserts and desertification it needs to find more efficient means of producing at and above the current levels and it is also quite likely that China will overtake all nations in the categories that it does not already lead such as chicken, beef and veal, pulses and corn. Agriculture plays a very critical role in China's economy and according to the World Bank agriculture contributes 7.1 percent to China's growing GDP.

Germany

Germany with a population of 83 million (World Bank) is the most populous nation in the European Union and it uses approximately 52% of its 88,221,440 acres landmass (German Federal Agency for Nature Conservation 2016) for agriculture, crops and grazing for animals, which is utilized to feed Germany and the wider European Union population. The main products of German agriculture are wheat, barley, maize, rye, triticale, oat, canola, potato, milk, beef, pork, poultry, cabbage and sugar beets. The country is a world level producer in the following categories:

- Potato. The sixth largest producer of potato behind China, India, Russian Federation, Ukraine and the US
- Rapeseed. The sixth largest producer behind Canada, China, India, France and Australia.
- Oat. The tenth largest producer behind the Russian Federation, Canada, Poland, Finland, Australian, US, Spain, UK and Sweden.
- Wheat. The tenth largest producer behind China, India, Russian Federation, US, France, Australia, Canada, Pakistan and Ukraine.

Germany is also a top producer in the EU and helps to make the EU the leader in several significant areas inclusive of:

- Barley. The largest producer in the world
- Pork. The second largest producer in the world behind China
- Beef and Veal. The third largest producer in the world behind the US and Brazil
- Corn. The fourth largest producer in the world behind US, China and Brazil.

Agricultural production is currently responsible for 0.8% of Germany's GDP and the German economy is currently one of the strongest in the European Union and supported by its strong scientific underpinnings in research and development it is very possible for Germany and European Union to further increase their agricultural output while reducing the amount of land used and their impact upon the environment.

Nigeria

Nigeria with a population of 195 million (World Bank) is the most populous nation in Africa and it uses approximately 105 million acres or 46% of its landmass (FAOSTAT) to produce agricultural products that it uses to feed it population and to earn income from exports. The main crops planted in Nigeria includes yams, cassava, sweet potatoes, pulse, millet, sorghum, corn, cocoa, tropical fruits, vegetables, rice, peanuts, cashew nuts, sesame, soybean, kola nut, oil palm, cotton, tobacco, sugarcane and animal husbandry for cattle, sheep, goats, pork, poultry and fish. The country is a world level producer in the following areas:

- Yams. The largest producer in the world
- Cassava. The largest producer in the world
- Sweet potato. The second largest producer in the world
- Millet. The second largest producer in the world behind India.
- Cocoa. The fourth largest producer in the world behind Cote d'Ivoire, Ghana and Indonesia.

- Goatmeat. The fourth largest producer in the world behind China, India and Pakistan.
- Vegetable. The sixth largest producer in the world behind China, India, US, Turkey and the Russian Federation.
- Pulse. The seventh largest producer in the world behind India, Canada, Myanmar, China, Russian Federation and Australia.
- Sorghum. The third largest producer in the world, behind US and India
- Sesame. The third largest producer in the world behind India and China.
- Oil Palm. The fifth largest producer in the world,

Nigeria with a large population is one of the largest agricultural producers in the world as shown by the above numbers and according to the World Bank agriculture is responsible for 21.9% of Nigeria's GDP. While Nigeria produces vast quantities of agricultural products, it also imports a vast amount as well, as it imports 60 % of the fish, 60% of the rice, 50 % of the beef, 50% of the mutton, 50 % of the goatmeat and 50% of the pork that it consumes (FAO in Nigeria) Unfortunately, unless efficiency is significantly improved any increase in production could lead to further degradation of forest and deforestation, which is already at crisis levels in the Sahel. Nigeria like all nations with large population need to invest more in agricultural research with an aim to increase their output while utilizing less land, fertilizers and pesticides.

US

The United States of America has a population of approximately 330 million (World Bank) and occupies a landmass of approximately 2.26 billion acres of land of which it utilizes 1.045 billion acres, (approximately 46 percent) for agriculture, 391.5 million acres for crops and 654 million acres for pasture and range for grazing animals. According to the USDA the US plants a variety of crops inclusive of corn, wheat, barley, oats, rye, sorghum, triticale, millet, amaranth, rice, buckwheat, soybean, rapeseed, flax, sunflower seed, peanut, pulse, potato, sweet potato, vegetables, fruits, tree nuts, cotton, tobacco and many other minor crops along with animal husbandry for cattle, sheep, goats, pigs, poultry, fish and wild game. The US is a world leading producer in many areas inclusive of:

- Beef and Veal. The largest producer of beef and veal in the world
- Poultry. The largest producer of chicken meat in the world
- Corn. The largest producer of corn in the world
- Sorghum. The largest producer of sorghum in the world.
- Soybean. The second largest producer in the world alternating with Brazil.
- Pork. The third largest producer in the world behind China and the EU
- Vegetables. The third largest producer in the world behind China and India.
- Fruits. The fourth largest producer in the world behind China, India and Brazil.
- Wheat. The fourth largest producer in the world behind China, India and the Russian Federation.
- Fish and aquaculture. The fifth largest producer in the world behind China, Indonesia, India and Vietnam.
- Potato. The fifth largest producer in the world behind China, India, Russian Federation and Ukraine.
- Oat. The sixth largest producer in the world behind the Russian Federation, Canada, Poland, Finland, and Australia.
- Rye. The seventh largest producer in the world behind the EU, Russian Federation, Belarus, Ukraine, Turkey, and Canada.
- Sweet Potato. The eighth largest producer in the world behind China, Nigeria, Tanzania, Ethiopia, Indonesia, Uganda and Vietnam.
- Pulse. The ninth leading producer in the world behind India, Canada, Myanmar, China, Russian Federation, Australia, Nigeria and Brazil.
- Barley. The tenth largest producer in the world behind the EU, Russian Federation, Other, Canada, Ukraine, Turkey, Australia, Argentina and Kazakhstan.

The US is one of the largest producers, exporters and importer of agricultural goods and service in the world and according to the World Bank, agriculture contributes 0.9 % to the GDP of the world's largest economy. The US is also one of the leading nations in the field of agricultural research and development and has introduced several crops that were genetically modified that would produce more, had the ability to better resist different environmental conditions inclusive of drought, insect and bacterial pests and other features that could make these crops more efficient to use in some of the more difficult regions of the world and in general, improve agricultural efficiency. The US also needs to use its great scientific capacity to reduce agriculture's impact on the environment both in the Us and internationally.

Data Review

The data collected and presented clearly highlights the level of agricultural production in the six nations highlighted and the importance of agriculture to these nations both socially and economically, as while some nations are more dependent on agriculture than the others, (agriculture contributes approximately 22% of Nigeria's GDP, while only 0.8% of Germany's), meeting the nutritional needs of their nations and earning export dollars is vitally important to the existence and stability of each nation.

CHAPTER

8

Timber

Trees, in the form of wood, have played a major role in all phases of human life and development inclusive as a source of energy, for the construction of shelter, for the construction of infrastructure such as bridges and later rail lines. As a source of energy, wood was used for cooking and heating, since the first humans learned to make fire and this use of wood continued unabated with growing human populations through many millennia and the use became more intensive with the coming of the industrial age. The industrial age was built upon steam as a motive force fueled first by burning wood followed later by coal, oil, nuclear energy and much later by gas. However, at the start of the Industrial Age most early steam generating plants and steam engines used wood as the only source of energy and the use of wood to generate steam spread across a wide filed inclusive of steam engines used on ships, trains, residential, commercial, institutional and industrial facilities and this growing use of wood saw the destruction of extensive swaths of forests and subsequently the loss of many animal species with the loss of their habitat and this destruction affected all countries that had started on the road to industrialization. The destruction of trees got much worse with the growth of rail services as a major source of transportation including its expansion across the continental North America, South

America, Europe and Asia, Africa and Australia as along with the use of wood as a fuel, timber was also the material of choice to construct the major rail infrastructure such as rail ties, bridges, tunnels and even train cabins. The explosion in the exploitation of forests brought on by the industrial age was, however, not limited to energy production, construction, transportation and manufacturing, as there was also an explosion in use of paper for the production of the newspapers, books, packaging material and sanitary paper for human use and trees were the most basic ingredient in the manufacture of pulp and paper and the growth of the printing industries developed to become a major spoke in the wheel of all major economies.

Prior to arrival of the European immigrants and the start of the industrial revolution the American continents were rich in trees and many other natural resources that had laid dormant for many millennia, however, after the arrival of the immigrants these resources were not to last much longer as within 200 years these resources were used to make the former colonies new nations, independent of Britain, Spain, France and Portugal, and in another 100 years these resources were used up to make a few people of the continents financially very wealthy, leaving the countries and continents much poorer environmentally as trees and other natural resources were reaped on an industrial scale without any consideration given to destruction of the habitat of many species of flora and fauna that were indigenous to the continents and little or no effort was made to replant trees or repair the damaged ecological systems for the benefit of humans in the future. The amount of timber reaped, in the US alone, in 1840 grew from one billion square feet to 46 billion square feet in 1904 and according to Bronaugh (2012) by 1920 more than two thirds of American forests had been reaped at least once and it was only the Pacific Ocean that forced the timber industry in the US to start a replanting program. Without the Pacific Ocean, early environmentalists such as John Muir and later laws designed to preserve some lasting evidence of the great abundance in flora and fauna that the European immigrants first found upon their arrival at the shores of the North American continent, the continent would probably be treeless, due to "economic activities" or best-case scenario looked like the almost treeless lands of Europe that most of the immigrants were running from in the first place.

Trees have provided great economic value to the economies of human societies inclusive of hunter-gatherers, early organized societies and civilizations, the middle ages, the Enlightenment, through the Industrial Age and continuing into the 21st century and has consequently affected the economies of Africa, Asia, Europe, Australia, New Zealand and the Americas and there is great hope that trees will continue to do so way into the foreseeable future with the main areas of focus being timber production, fruit production, pharmaceutical production and paper production.

Timber Production

According to the Food and Agricultural Organization (FAO) the categories of timber produced and consumed around the world includes industrial roundwood, wood pellets, sawn wood, wood-based panels, pulp for paper, recovered paper, paper and paperboard and wood fuel and the biggest producers and consumers of these products are as shown below.

Rank	Country	Annual Production 2012 (cubic meter)
1	US	320,729,000
2	Canada	151,151,106
3	Brazil	146,804,000
4	China	144,035,300
5	Russian Federation	136,375,000
6	Sweden	63,000,000
7	Indonesia	62,605,500
8	India	45,957,000
9	Finland	44,614,134
10	Germany	42,862,602

Table 8.1 Top Industrial Roundwood Producing Nations 2012. Source: FAOSTAT and FRA, 2010.

More recent data for industrial roundwood production shows the top countries as follows:

1. US – 18% of world production
2. Russian Federation – 11% of world production
3. China – 9% of world production
4. Brazil – 8% of world production
5. Canada – 7% of world production
6. Indonesia – 4 % of world production
7. Sweden – 3% of world production
8. Finland – 3% of world production
9. Germany – 3% of world production
10. India – 3% of world production

Rank	Country	Annual Production (1000 tons)
1	China	99,300
2	US	75,083
3	Japan	26,627
4	Germany	22,698
5	Canada	12,112
6	South Korea	11,492
7	Finland	11,329
8	Sweden	11,298
9	Brazil	10,159
10	Indonesia	10035

Table 8.2 Top Pulp and Paper Producing Nations. Source: WorldAtlas.Com

Rank	Country	% World Annual Production
1	US	20
2	Canada	8
3	Vietnam	7
4	Germany	6
5	Sweden	5
6	Russia Federation	5
7	Latvia	4
8	France	4
9	Austria	4
10	Estonia	3

Table 8.3 Top Wood Pellet Producing Nations. Source: FAO

Fuelwood Production
According to the FAO more recent data shows the following:

1. India – utilizes 16% of total world wood fuel production
2. China -utilizes 8% of total world wood fuel production
3. Brazil – utilizes 6% of total world production
4. Ethiopia – utilizes 6% of total world production
5. Democratic Republic of the Congo -utilizes 4% of total world production
6. US – utilizes 4% of world production

The Economics of Timber and Forest Products

The Food and Agricultural Organization (FAO) State of the World's Forests (2009) Report indicates that the forestry industry contributed approximately one percent (1%) of global value added in 2006, which based on today' global economy would be worth approximately one percent of $85.911 trillion (World Bank 2018), which would make the contribution of timber and timber products production and sales approximately $850 billion dollars annually. The World's Richest Countries site indicated that the 2017 value of export trade in timber products was $136.9 billion and the trade in forest products impacts the economic life of most countries in very significant ways such as indicated by data on Canada, one of the world largest timber products producer and exporter.

In 2008 Canada was the world's largest exporter of forest products, exporting $30.1billion worth of timber and forest products which represented 1.9% of Canada's GDP (2008). This activity generated 273,700 direct jobs and 422,000 indirect and induced jobs. The Canadian data is only used as an example of the impact of forest products on the economy of producing nations, of which there are many, with the economic impact being lesser or greater based on the size of the economy, the size and utilization of the forest resources and the stage of development of the country's economy. Forest products are produced, utilized in and exported from all continents inclusive of Africa, Asia, Europe, North America, Oceana and South America. According the World Richest Countries site the largest exporters of timber in 2017 from each continent are as follows:

Africa

The continent of Africa exported US 3.4 billion of timber products as shown in the table below.

Rank	Country	Annual Export Sales (million US $)
1	Cameroon	611.9
2	South Africa	534.5
3	Gabon	488.4
4	Congo	380.6
5	Equatorial Guinea	283.3
6	Ghana	203.9
7	Cote d'Ivoire	116.8
8	Gambia	98.9
9	Swaziland	91.5
10	DRC	72.5

Table 8. Top Timber Exporting African Nations.
Source: World Richest Nations Site

Asia

The continent of Asia exported US $31 billion of timber products as shown in the table below.

Rank	Country	Annual Export Sales (million US$)
1	China	13,700
2	Indonesia	4,000
3	Malaysia	3500
4	Thailand	2900
5	Vietnam	2700
6	Philippines	1400
7	Turkey	764
8	India	308.4
9	Japan	291.3
10	Myanmar	291.2

Table 8. Top Timber Exporting Asian Nations.
Source: World Richest Countries Site.

European Union

The European Union as a block sold US$52.2 billion of timber products as shown in the table below.

Rank	Country	Annual Export Sales (million US $)
1	Germany	9,000
2	Austria	5100
3	Poland	4300
4	Sweden	4100
5	Finland	3200
6	France	2790
7	Belgium	2750
8	Czech Republic	2200
9	Latvia	2140
10	Italy	2060

Table 8. Top Timber Exporting European Nations.
Source: World's Richest Nation site

Latin America and Caribbean

Latin America and the Caribbean exported US$7.2 billion of timber products as shown in the table below.

Rank	Country	Annual Export Sale (million US $)
1	Brazil	2800
2	Chile	2200
3	Uruguay	944.6
4	Ecuador	344.1
5	Argentina	124.8
6	Peru	117.2
7	Guatemala	108.9
8	Costa Rico	82.1
9	Paraguay	68.21
10	Panama	68.18

Table 8. Top Timber Exporting Latin American and Caribbean Nations. Source:

Middle East Region

The Middle East region exported US$233 million of timber products as shown in the table below.

Rank	Country	Annual Export Sales (million US $)
1	United Arab Emirates	113.1
2	Saudi Arabia	45.1
3	Oman	23.3
4	Bahrain	18
5	Lebanon	10.3
6	Israel	9.9
7	Jordan	7.4
8	Kuwait	3.5
9	Iran	1.3
10	Syria	0.485

Table 8. Top Timber Exporting Middle Eastern Nations. Source:

North America

North America exported $24.3 billion worth of timber products from the following countries:

- Canada US$14.1 billion
- USA US$9.7 billion
- Mexico US$463.6 million

The information shown above and FAO indicates that timber contributes over US $850 Billion annually to the world's GDP, clearly highlighting the economic benefits of timber on a worldwide basis and it also clearly highlights that even the most environmentally conscious nations, treat trees as a commodity to be cut, sawed, used and shipped according to the economic benefits attached to them. Based on this data the trade in timber and other forest products is vital to the economies of many countries as it provides business in local trade, exports, millions of jobs and taxes for the governments of countries with large forest resources and businesses. The monetary values, as indicated are quite significant, however, trees provide even greater value from the environmental services that they provide such as clean air, habitat for various species, stable soils, clean and adequate water resources, healthy populations and the sequestration of carbon, which is vitally important if the world is to overcome the major crisis of modern times, climate change.

Mining

"Mining is a significant driver of deforestation" Siqueira et al., (2020). In general every significant mining activity requires the clearing of primary or secondary forests for direct mining activities and also for the installation of necessary infrastructure to facilitate access to the location and removal of the ore. The infrastructural works usually includes roads, rail service, access for heavy duty machinery, warehouses and repair shops, transportation facilities, staff facilities, utilities and general services. Unfortunately, the creation of access roads and the installation of the road infrastructure and accessories for mining purposes also provides direct access to forests for unrelated economic activities as the forest has now been opened up for interested third parties to have direct access to, legal or illegal, the forest and forest products and thereby increasing the chances of forest fragmentation, degradation, deforestation, loss of species and extinction of flora and fauna. The extraction of metals or other minerals usually require some amount of land clearing especially where the metal or mineral is located in forests, as indicated by Priyadarshi (2009) about iron mining in the state of Jharkhand, India, "Today uncontrolled mining for iron ore both legal and illegal is destroying not just the forest, but also the wildlife, apart from the livelihoods of the local tribal communities". According to

Global Forest Atlas (Yale School of Forestry and Environmental Studies) the extraction of minerals has a similar negative impact upon the environment "Oil, gas and mineral extraction account for an estimated 7% of global deforestation in the subtropics with increasing exploration and development taking place in the Amazon and Congo basins".

Historically, the most common set of metals, gems and minerals that were and are actively mined in countries all around the world includes gold, silver, iron, lead, alumina, copper, zinc, coal, oil, gas, gems stones, the radioactive metals, such as uranium, and the new exotic metals that are extremely important in the telecommunications and computer industries. The mining of gold, silver, diamonds, iron and copper are activities that are thousands of years old and was carried on by ancient peoples and has been responsible for the degradation of forests for thousands of years. We shall examine four of the main metals inclusive of iron, aluminum, gold and copper.

Iron

Iron (Fe) the most common metallic element found in the universe is also the most widely used metal in all spheres of human life due to it high strength, durability, ability to be formed into any shape, ability to mix well with other elements to form various alloys to perform varying high strength and high temperature functions. Steel, one of the most basic alloys of iron is widely used in the construction of bridges, building (from single story facilities to tallest buildings in the world), all modes of transportation machines inclusive of bicycles, bikes, automobiles, ships, rail, air transportation and space travel, household items inclusive of refrigerators, stoves, dishwashers, clothe washers and dryers, heating and cooling systems, pot and pans, knives, forks and spoons, in general iron alloyed products can be found everywhere.

Iron is usually found in one of several iron ores inclusive of magnetite, hematite, siderite and limonite and can usually be found everywhere on planet earth, however, the largest accumulations are to be located in banded sedimentary formations, which form the bulk of iron ore worldwide. The sedimentary rock formations are formed from chemical reactions between iron and oxygen in marine and fresh water locations, with the original deposits forming right after the first plant organisms started making oxygen in the process of photosynthesis and releasing it into water (King 2009).

Iron ore deposits are usually found on the sea floor or in regions with large water resources such as lake, swamps, bogs and rivers, in such as places like the Lake Superior Region in the USA where iron ore was first discovered in the US, on the Marquette Range, Upper Peninsula Michigan, by a US Deputy Surveyor, William Burt in 1844(Burt 1994). Iron ore is usually located very close to the surface or in pockets deep underground, up to 2000 feet in depth (Williams 2005) where greater effort is required to access, remove and transport it to a processing facility and this ore usually comes in the form of one of several compounds inclusive of Magnetite, Hematite, Goethite, Siderite, Taconite, Jaspilite and Limonite. The removal of ore from the soil is usually done using two basic mining techniques, Surface Mining and Underground Mining or Subsurface Mining, with the majority of the mining activities utilizing Surface Mining based on the depth of the ore and this surface mining technique is usually described as open pit or open cut pit mining. The five basic steps in any mining activity includes Exploration and Evaluation works, Mine-site Design and Planning, Construction of Required Works, Production, Closure and Reclamation of Site. The specific steps in open pit/open cut mining includes the following (Satyendra 2014):

- Stripping the overburden which includes surface vegetation, soil and rocks.
- Creation of benches to facilitate drilling, blasting and removal of ore
- Transportation of ore out of the pit to processing areas and facilities.
- Processing the ore which includes crushing and washing of the ore.
- Sending ore to smelting plant.

Underground and subsurface mining follow the same five basic steps however, the design and construction of underground mining systems would be much more involved with greater emphasis place on safety systems to ensure workers health and safety beneath the surface. The works would include, vent/air shafts, elevators for human and material transportation, pumping stations to prevent flooding and environmental health and safety systems inclusive of fire protection systems.

The main considerations in the design of the Mine-Sites involve the creating access to locate the mine, creating access to the site for humans and machines, locating required processing plants, locating mine wastes dumping/storage areas, locating utilities for the site, locating transportation hub and servicing facilities and assessing the environmental impact of mining operations on the site. According to Priyadarshi (2009), discussing the impact of iron mining on the environment in India, the damages incurred are more than just loss of forest as it affects customs and culture within local tribes. The destruction of forests or other surface vegetation is of course the first step required in the mining of iron ore which causes significant negative impacts inclusive of the loss of wildlife, damage to the ecosystems, impairment of the hydrologic systems, the fragmentation and degradation of the forests, impacts which are considered to be only "collateral damaged" in the quest to extract the target ore. The mining of iron also causes other significant environmental damage inclusive of destruction of land and surface features, accelerated soil erosion, sedimentation of water bodies, surface and groundwater, and the generation of mining wastes in the form of overburden and toxic tailings (Williams 2005 and Goudie 2000). Sedimentation becomes more acute with the removal of limonite from swamps, bogs and stream banks and the sinking of subsurface mines which quite often pollute groundwater sources (Williams 2005).

In the early days of the iron industry the forest of Europe and continental USA were seen as inexhaustible storehouses of energy in the form of charcoal, to be utilized for the smelting of iron ore (Williams 2005 and Cox et al., 1985) and this view along with the actions taken by the 'great industrialists' of the time led to the destruction of much forests on both sides of the Atlantic Ocean. During that era Britain was said to have suffered from a serious shortage of wood in the sixteenth and seventeenth centuries which was thought to be cause in part by their iron industry (Williams 2005 and Perlin 1989). One British arboriculturist, John Evelyn, was quoted as saying that it would be better for the people of Britain to make their iron in the American colonies than to exhaust their forests stock at home in Britain "Twere better to purchase all of our iron out of America, than to exhaust our woods at home". (Williams 2005; Whitney 1994).

The use of charcoal, dehydrated wood, as a fuel for the iron industry extended well into 1945 and this continued use fostered the further destruction of great swaths of forests in the great iron producing centers of Michigan and Pennsylvania, even though the use of anthracite coal, starting in1830s, and coke, starting in 1850s, as alternative sources of energy had long commenced (Williams 2005; Schallenberg 1975, 1981; Tarr 1994). This continued usage of charcoal was said to be based on the fact that charcoal produced a better iron for certain applications. Charcoal was an essential input in the processing of iron and to ensure a continuous supply of it the large producers of iron acquired extremely large tracts of forests that would be cleared just to make charcoal. "The Charcoal Iron Industry had many impacts on the nations lands and waters, but probably the most obvious was the industry's effect on forests" (Williams 2005). When carefully examined it could be said that mining, specifically open pit mining did relatively little harm to the environment, as the area cleared is usually relatively small, usually a few square miles that would only require the destruction relatively small volumes of trees, plants and forest ecosystems during land clearance and that the greatest damaged was done by smelting where charcoal was the fuel of choice for smelting the iron ore and according the Williams (2005) even this amount of wood used for charcoal was very small, less than1 percent of fire wood used in US at the time. While small comparatively, the mass destruction of trees and plants to provide fuel for the iron industry, would have contributed to the degradation and fragmentation of forests, the destruction of plant and animal habitat and the creation of a certain attitude towards forests that would eventually see American forest coverage reduced from 46 % to less than 20 %, which caused the extinction of many plants and animal species.

The pattern of using charcoal as energy in the modern era for smelting iron, was started by ancient Nubian civilizations (Marks 2010), followed by Europeans many centuries later and was to expand beyond North America into the other regions of the world colonized by the British such as Australia, a former British colony and today the largest producer of iron ore in the world. Australia was first located by Europeans by British ship Captain James Cook in 1770 and colonized by 1788 by the British government, irrespective of the fact that the land was owned and occupied by a large group of aboriginal people native to the land for over 50,000 years prior to the arrival of Europeans (Macintyre 2009). This island continent was rich in mineral wealth inclusive of iron, aluminum, gold, copper, tin, lead, zinc, uranium nickel, tungsten, rutile (Titanium) oil and natural gas. According to Geoscience Australia, iron was the first metal discovered in Australia by the Europeans and several efforts was made to get the iron industry going using charcoal as the required source of energy, however, all early efforts failed and the industry was only later established with discovery of coal in 1797 (Australian Bureau of Statistics 2012) and this coal later served as the energy source of choice for the Australian Iron industry. According to the Canadian Encyclopedia, another former British colony, charcoal was used for smelting steel in the Canadian iron industry from 1822 to the late 19th century when coal fired blast furnaces were replaced by more efficient coke fired furnaces.

From the above it can be seen that the mining and more so the processing of iron ore was responsible for the destruction of much forests on the European mainland, Britain/England, India, North America and Australia.

Aluminum

Aluminum ore, bauxite, the most widely used source of the world's aluminum, occurs as a rock in one of several color variations, reddish-brown, white, tan and tan-yellow and usually contains the aluminum minerals gibbsite, boehmite and diaspore (Minerals Education Coalition). Bauxite ore is one of the most abundant ore in the earth and can be found in many tropical and subtropical, or formerly tropical or subtropical, regions around the world inclusive of places like Australia, Brazil, Canada, China, Europe, Guinea, Guyana, Jamaica, Russia and USA. Bauxite is typically located beneath overburden, top soil and vegetation of up to 10 meters thick and in unusual cases up to 70 meters thick, and is usually found in pockets of 4- 6 meters thick and can be mined using either open cast mining or underground mining methods. Approximately 85-90 % of all bauxite mined around the world is mined using open cast mining which utilize backhoes, bucketwheel excavators, bulldozers, draglines, power shovels, and scrapers in the pit and the ore is usually transported to a processing plant or storage areas using special heavy-duty trucks, rail, conveyors and overhead cable cars. From the storage areas the ore can be sent to a processing plant that is in close proximity or transported by rail or ship to processing plants that are much further away.

Bauxite Mining in Jamaica

Jamaica is an archipelagic nation in the Caribbean that is located at latitude 18° 15' N, Longitude 77° 20' W in close proximity to Cuba, 90 miles to the north, the Island of Hispaniola (Haiti and Dominican Republic), 120 miles to the northeast. The main island is approximately 150 miles at its longest points, east to west, and 52 miles at it widest points, north to south and cover an area of 4244 square miles with many mountain ranges with the Blue Mountains having the highest peak at approximately 7400 feet above sea level. The main island is surrounded by many islands and cays on both the northern and southern coasts, with the largest set of islands and cays located in the Pedro Banks off the southern coast and the combined the main island and cays give the country a total exclusive economic zone of 99,667 square miles. The island is rich in natural mineral deposits inclusive of bauxite, copper, nickel, gold, silver, platinum, rare earth metals, limestone, gypsum, marble, silica, sand, gravel, clay and salt. (National Environmental Protection Agency-NEPA). Limestone, Gypsum, Silica, Sand, Gravel and Clay are all mined and used locally in the manufacturing of cement and the construction industry, while bauxite, gold and limestone are mined for export, with bauxite producing 5-10% of Jamaica's GDP (Jamaica Bauxite Institute), the lion share of Jamaica's mineral earnings for many decades. According to Jamaica Bauxite Institute (JBI) the mining and shipment of bauxite commenced in

1952, however, the existence of the ore on the island was known since 1869 and explorations to locate and determine quantities available began in the 1940s. The production of bauxite in Jamaica ramped up quite quickly from 1952 – 1957 a period which saw the country producing 5 million tons of bauxite annually and made Jamaica the leading producer of bauxite in the world a position that it only lost to Australia, a much larger nation with much larger bauxite reserves, in 1971(JBI). Jamaica's bauxite ore exist in a series of deposits across the middle of the island, east to west, with the largest deposits located in the parishes of St. Ann, Manchester, St. Elizabeth and Trelawny and smaller deposits in Clarendon, St. Catherine, St. James and Portland, which when combined gives Jamaica a total proven bauxite reserves that exceed 2.5 billion tons with processable reserves of approximately 1.5 billion tons (JBI). With the many changes which have occurred over the last 50 years Jamaica's position is the bauxite producing world has been significantly changed with an explosion in the demand for and production of bauxite across the globe. The numbers below show the current world bauxite production as of 2018(JBI) are as:

Rank	Country	Annual Production (million tons)
1	Australia	75
2	China	70
3	Guinea	50
4	Brazil	27
5	India	24
6	Jamaica	10

Table 9. Top Bauxite Producing Nations 2018.
Source: Jamaica Bauxite Institute.

Jamaica was also ranked 6th in the world in the area of alumina production in 2018, producing 2.5 million tons, behind the top three producers China 72 million tons, Australia 19 million tons, Brazil 7.9 million tons.

Bauxite is mined in Jamaica and around the world using opencast or open-pit mining (World Aluminum 2018), which requires the removal of vegetation, top soil, and overburden before the ore can be accessed and in many cases the removal of vegetation includes the removal of virgin natural forest, in Jamaica's case dry limestone forests, leading to fragmentation of forest, forest degradation and deforestation. The steps in bauxite mining as recommended by World Aluminum (World Aluminum 2018) are as follows:

- Clear ore site of vegetation and recover any useful timber for future use
- Collect the seeds, seedlings and cuttings of plants that will be required for the revegetation of the location after mining is completed as required.
- Remove top soil (and sometime subsoil) for use in rehabilitation for future or immediate use in rehabilitation of mined out lands, stockpile if there is no immediate need.
- Remove the overburden, the layer between the top soil and the bauxite ore.
- Break up the bauxite using methods such as ripping with very large bulldozers or in some cases, drilling and blasting.
- Once the bauxite is broken up transport it in trucks or rail wagons or conveyors or overhead cables to a beneficiation plant or to a stockpile.
- Transport the bauxite to an alumina refinery when required.
- Rehabilitate the mined-out lands after the completion of mining activities.

Bauxite mining in Jamaica has over the last 68 years provided great business opportunities, great direct jobs and many downstream jobs for a large section of the Jamaican population and has provided billions of US currency to support the programs of the Jamaican government inclusive of the funding education up to the tertiary level, health service through an established systems of hospitals and clinics, roadworks across the island, transportations systems in a few municipalities and national security through the national constabulary force and the military, however, bauxite mining has also helped to create a major problem that could one day make void all the positive benefits they have provided over a very long period of time. This problem is called deforestation and according to Johansson (2003) "In Jamaica, bauxite mining is considered to be one of the most significant reasons behind deforestation". Jamaica has since 1952 assigned mining licenses to several multinational companies to mine particular sections of the island using the opencast or open-pit method of mining which requires the clearing of top soils and vegetation from the selected site prior to the removal of the overburden and the commencement of mining operations and according to Neufville (2019), one company Alcan, estimates that they have cleared up to100 hectares of land each year for 48 years for a total of 4800 hectares over that period. These 4800 hectares does not include the land cleared by the other companies over the same period and the company, Alcan, states that the greatest damage done to forests in Jamaica is not from mining but from the opening of access roads through forests for use in mining activities that has given direct access to the forest resources to the general public thus allowing all and sundry to illicitly reap timber and other forest products. As recommended by World Aluminum and required by Jamaican law (Neufville 2019) all bauxite companies are required to return the land to a "productive state" which under Jamaican regulation only requires filling of the large holes and laying down 38 centimeters of top soil, which to date, is only suitable for the construction of houses, small garden plots and pasture lands, not the original forest that covered the land. Both the government of Jamaica and the Alcan company recognize the problems associated with the level of restoration being done compared to the internationally required restoration of forests, however, the agreements signed between the government and the companies and the local regulations in place do not require the companies to restore forests. Thus, in the "land of wood and water" annual drought is a regular occurrence and the regulating authorities appear to have no answer and according to Neufville (2019) over the last thirty years annual rainfall has been decreased by a minimum of 20% and droughts are much longer and much harsher. It also appears that not much consideration was given to the length of time required, from the removal of the vegetation to the full regrowth of the natural forests, and amount of rainfall that would be lost leading to much downstream damage in agriculture, potable water resources, natural flora and fauna and the aesthetic value of our natural environment.

The only conclusion that could be drawn from this Jamaican experience is that while bauxite mining has directly impacted approximately 150,000 acres (JBI has not answered my request for information on the amount lands mined out since 1952 and the amount restored to original condition) of land by the several mining companies over a 68 years period. This acreage includes mined lands, the roads and other infrastructures that was built by the mining companies to access and process the bauxite ore and the forest lands that were damaged by the bauxite infrastructure which inadvertently facilitated access deep into the natural forests in Jamaica and caused even greater levels of forest fragmentation, degradation and deforestation, probably up to 20 times greater than the damage done by mining alone. The Executive Summary of Red Dirt 2020 produced by the Jamaica Environmental Trust (JET) indicates that Geologist Arthur Geddes estimated that by 1990 bauxite mining had already caused extensive damage to Jamaica's natural ecology on at least 60,000 acres of land which when extrapolated, given increased production over the last 31 years, approximately 150,000 acres of land could have been extensively damaged by 2021.

Gold Mining

Gold is the preeminent precious metal that has been a driver of world economic systems from ancient times going back many millennia and has played a prominent role in all ancient civilization inclusive of Sub-Saharan Africa, North Africa, Mesopotamians, Egyptians, Indians, Greeks, Babylonians, Persians, Native Americans, Incas, Aztecs, Mayans and the Jewish people of the bible. All of these civilizations highly valued gold and used it where the highest honor was demanded such as making household vessels for royal families, crowns for the heads of Kings and or Queens, as jewelry for the very wealthy and royal families, in their temples to honor their gods, and with the Egyptians as capstones for the pyramids at Giza and burial ornaments for the god kings. This place of honor was maintained throughout the ages and gold became even more important when it was first given monetary value and today it still maintains its place in a modern economy where it has become the safest financial instrument in which to invest. The rationale behind this very long historical valuation of gold is quite uncertain, as it has been in use long before most metals inclusive of copper, iron and steel which have all found much wider use, except when considered for its relative scarcity compared to these more abundant and useful metals.

Gold can be found everywhere on the planet Earth in varying quantities from very minute to vast amounts, and in various locations on all major land masses, small islands, in sea water, in rivers and streams, on mountains or in valleys at or near the surface or deep underground and it can be recovered by one of several gold mining methods inclusive of panning, sluicing, dredging, rocker box, hard rock mining and by product gold mining (World Gold Council). The top ten producers of gold are China, Australia, Russia, USA, Canada, Indonesia, Peru, South Africa, Mexico and Ghana (US Global Investors 2018).

Panning for Gold

Panning for gold is one of the simplest and least invasive ways to mine for it and it is normally done for placer deposits of gold, which are concentrations of loose gold that can be found in the sediments of riverbeds and beaches. In this method of mining, the miner uses a wide shallow pan, 12-18 inches diameter, a dish-like container to pick up quantities of silt, gravel and rocks from the riverbed and using a swirling motion and shaking which separates the gold from the other particle, with the gold going to the bottom due to its much higher density (Geology In). The investments for this method of mining are usually small and can be done by almost anyone but it is not suitable for large commercial size operations except in situations where labor is very cheap, the gold is in vast quantities and is very easy to access. The level of environmental damage is relatively small, but not negligible as the bed of streams and rivers may be harmed.

Sluicing

Sluicing is the use of a "sluice box" in a river or stream to separate gold from rock, gravel and sand, by placing a specially designed box in the direction of flow of a river or stream, loading the material to be separated at the front of the box manually, removing large rocks and debris by hand and allowing the flow of the stream to wash away the lighter colored sand and gravel, leaving the black sand and gold in the box. The sluice box is usually installed in the flow of water with a downhill tilt of 1" to 1-2 feet and will facilitate the faster movement of water through the box and improve the separation capacity. Standard modern sluice boxes come in sizes varying from 54 – 24 inches long x 12-14 inches wide, internally, x 4 inches deep and is built with riffles at the bottom, to catch the black sand and gold, and are usually constructed from wood, aluminum and plastic. These sluice boxes are meant for small scale non-commercial size operations and cause relatively small environmental damage to rivers and streams, but much more than panning.

Rocker Boxes

Rocker boxes are designed to separate gold from sand, gravel and rocks and sorts the material using a screen, an apron and riffles with riffles on the floor of box. The boxes are usually built into three distinct sections, body or sluice box, Screen and apron which are assembled together to form the boxes which have typical dimensions of 24-60 inches long x 12-15 inches wide by 6 – 24 inches deep, with screens 16-20 inches square with ½ inch holes. The material of construction is usually wood - body, metal -screen and cloth – apron. Rocker boxes are designed for small non-commercial sized operations, but much larger sized mechanized boxes are built for commercial operations. The larger size facilitates processing much larger volumes of material and using much larger volumes of water and are therefore more likely to cause much more damage to rivers, streams, aquatic flora and fauna and affect the lives of humans and animals which depend on these sources of water.

Dredging

Dredging involves utilizing a suction device to lift material from river beds or sea floor onto a mechanized rocker box or sluice box which is located on a boat or pontoon to separate gold from sand, gravel and rocks. The size of the hose, suction device and pontoon determine the amount of material that may be processed at any one time. Dredging may be used in small or commercial operations. The use of dredging equipment has a greater capacity to do harm to the environment, aquatic flora and fauna.

All of the above, panning, sluice box, rocker box and dredging are all methods designed for recovering placer deposits of gold only and were mainly used in the very early days of gold mining and by small operation or hobby miners today. These methods had limited to minor effects upon the environment except where the rocker box and dredging processes have been commercialized to process very large volumes of water and gravel, the movement of which adversely affect rivers and streams, and any aquatic life that may reside in them. The separating tools when combine with hydraulic mining techniques can and has created disastrous outcomes environmentally as high-pressure water is used to blast river banks and other sensitive areas to locate placer gold.

Hard Rock Mining

Hard rock mining, which is used to produce most of the world's gold, is usually done using two methods, Open Pit Mining and Underground Mining both of which have been previously described.

Gold Mining and Forests

Open pit mining as previous described requires the removal of vegetation, top soil and overburden above ore containing desired metals, and causes forest fragmentation, degradation and deforestation in all areas of the world in which it is practiced. The problems created are directly related to the mining activities, associated infrastructure and utilities created and installed to facilitate the mining process but which ultimately also facilitate other activities, unrelated to the mining activities, that lead to deforestation. In the case of gold mining the environmental and ecological problems created in the Guiana Shield area of South America (Guyana, Suriname, French Guiana and the Brazilian state of Amapa) provides great examples of the problems that gold mining can create.

The high price of gold on the world market has created significant environmental and ecological problems related to forest degradation, deforestation, contamination of freshwater supplies, loss of habitat and loss of species in the Guiana Shield region of South America. These problems, which blossomed in the last 21 years (1999-2020) are as a result of a combination of factors inclusive of the high price of gold on the world market, deep seated poverty, political instability, the incursion of Brazilian miners into the region due to the enforcement of land-use and tribal integrity laws (Hammond et al., 2007 and Rahm et al., 2015). According to Rahm et al., (2015) "Although gold mining is contributing to the economic development in the region in terms of revenues and jobs creation, it also has negative impacts on the forest, freshwater and biodiversity." The problems created are many inclusive of:

- The removal of top soil and vegetation to facilitate open pit hard rock mining.
- Fragmentation and degradation of virgin forest due to mining and mining related activities
- Deforestation to create new community living spaces and new agricultural land use.
- The use of mercury in the gold mining process, which is never recovered, and leads to the contamination of soil, air, water and the deterioration of human health.
- Uncontrollable illegal mining and forest clearing activities in this vast region.
- The creation of infrastructure to facilitate mining which also facilitate illegal activities that contribute to fragmentation and degradation of forest and deforestation.

- The influx of an ever-growing number of poor people into the region seeking to improve their economic status.
- The very slow recovery of forests and the poor quality of regrown coverage produced after gold mining.

According to Peterson and Heemskerk (2001) and Rahm et al., (2015) "Unlike areas in nearby old-growth forest, large parts of mined areas remain bare ground, grass and standing water." This clearly indicates that gold mining activities create permanent negative impacts upon forest, land and water and according to a 2010 study the negative impacts upon the forests, as seen from satellite photos, has grown three folds between 2001 and 2008 (Rahm et al., 2015). It was also discovered that most of the deforestation is being caused by small and medium sized operations, which could point to individuals, legal or illegal, doing their own thing, similar to the activities of subsistence farmers working to provide for their families and these activities are almost uncontrollable in countries and populations the size of Brazil, Guyana, Suriname and French Guiana combined, as the lure of free gold for the taking is almost unstoppable.

According to Holmes (2019) The top ten gold producing nations of 2018 are as follows:

Rank	Country	Annual Production 2018 (tons)
1	China	399.7
2	Australia	312.1
3	Russia	281.5
4	US	253.2
5	Canada	193
6	Indonesia	190
7	Peru	155.4
8	South Africa	123.5
9	Mexico	121.6
10	Ghana	101.8

Table 9. Top Gold Producing Nations 2018. Source: GFMA, Refinitiv, Thomson Reuters, US Gold Investor

Copper Mining

Copper is one of the most important metals in the modern world due to its properties as one of the best electrical and thermal conductors, its high malleability, ductility and tensile strength which allows it to be used in many applications inclusive of electrical power distribution, (industrial, commercial and residential) power generation systems, electrical motor drives, lighting systems, controls systems, computers, electronics, communication systems, heat exchangers in refrigeration, air conditioning and industrial processing plants, plumbing conduits, process vessels for cooking many products inclusive of pharmaceuticals and confectionaries, art and jewelry. Historically copper was the first metal mined and processed by humans and through the ages it has been used in many different ways inclusive of use as jewelry, art, in medicine, making weapons, tools, cooking vessels and many other household items.

Copper is the earliest metal that was mined and processed by ancient humans, from as early as 9000 BC, and has been used by ancient humans located in many different places, independently, all over the globe. This includes people in ancient Mesopotamia, where an ancient pendant was found that was dated to approximately 8700 BC, Africa where the Egyptians were known to have used copper tools to mine and cut the huge blocks of stones for the pyramids, starting around 5000 BC, the natives of the American continents discovered and used copper Stanley et al., (2015) and the Greeks also started using copper around 5000 BC followed much later by other European nations.

Copper Ore

Copper ore deposits are formed by the action of hot water, commonly associated with previous volcanic activity, and sediments which can be found on every land mass around the world. It can be located in the earth's crust as pure copper, however, more often than not it is found as a part of a composite mixture with other elements and is found as copper pyrites (Chalcopyrite), Chalocite or copper glance, Malachite Green, Azurite Blue, Bornite or peacock ore, Melaconite and other mixed copper ore. The concentration of copper in each of these ores is usually less than 1% and each type of ore requires different mining and processing steps to achieve the desired 99.99% pure copper, the purest metal in existence.

Top Copper Producing Nations

According to da Silva (2019) The top 10 copper producing nations are as shown in the table below.

Rank	Country	Annual Production (metric tons)
1	Chile	5,800,000
2	Peru	2,400,000
3	China	1,600,000
4	DRC	1,200,000
5	US	1,200,000
6	Australia	950,000
7	Zambia	870,000
8	Indonesia	789,000
9	Mexico	760,000
10	Russia	710,000

Table 9. Top Copper Producing Nations 2019. Source: Da Silva (2019)

As an essential metal that is used in almost every area of modern life, the production and sale of copper generates significant income for the mining and smelting companies and the countries that own the copper ore. According to the International Copper Study Group (ICSG) World Copper Factbook 2019, pages 21 and 36 the total amount of copper produced worldwide, in 2018, was 24.5 million tons, and the value, at the 2018 prices was approximately $6500/ ton, which should give a total value of the copper produced worldwide, in 2018, at 24.5 million times $6500.00 = $159,250,000,000.00 = $159.25 billion.

Mining Methods

The methods used for mining copper hard rock ore, are open pit mining and underground mining both of which create significant amount of damage to the environment inclusive of forest fragmentation, degradation, deforestation, contamination of water supply and contamination of the air.

Copper Mining in Panama

Copper mining in Panama was done using open pit mining of which the most basic requirement is the removal of vegetation and top soil, followed by the removal of overburden before the removal of the desired ore. According to the recommended guidelines for sustainable mining the last step in every mining activity after completion of mining is the restoration of the mined-out areas, however, from the pictures presented above no restoration of site has taken place at this location and the people within the affected communities are experiencing adverse conditions that did not exist prior to the commencement of mining within the locale. According to Arcia (2018) the problems being faced are as follows:

- The deforestation of the areas started with the mining of gold by one company, Petaquilla Gold, and has continued with the mining of copper by a separate company, Minera Panama, a subsidiary of a Canadian company, First Quantum Minerals.
- The objective of both companies was to extract metals, gold and copper from the Petaquilla Hills under one contract endorsed by Panama's National Assembly (Congress), Panama's legislative body.
- The activities of both companies have resulted in the destruction of a forest rich in regional biodiversity, the Mesoamerican Biological Corridor that connects seven Central American nations to southern Mexico.

- The contracts for mining cover an area of 13,000 hectares which directly influence three important watershed areas for the Petaquilla River, Caimito River and the San Juan River.
- The area being mined contained primary forest that were undisturbed until 2000.
- Satellite monitoring of the site records frequent alerts to forest deforestation activities.
- The climatic condition in the local has changed significantly over the 10year period of mining activities.
- The mining activities have severely affected agriculture within the community adjoining the forests. Some plants, such as the peach palm tree, are no longer producing fruits, as each year after flowering the flowers fall.
- Loss of water resources due to pollution of the local rivers
- The displacement and loss of local fauna including those insects required for pollination of plants. The proposed mining plans had called for the relocation of larger animals but not insects and bats which are very important to the ecology of the forest.

Data Review

In this chapter we have examined the mining activities of only four of the many important metals that are in high demands in all countries and economies around the world and the information highlighted and presented clearly indicates that mining is a major contributor, directly or indirectly to the fragmentation and degradation of forest and deforestation in many countries and the information also clearly shows that these mining activities are critical to the economies of the local partner nations, the multinational mining companies and the global economy in general.

CHAPTER

10

The Impact of Ancient Civilization on Forests and Trees

According to the Cambridge dictionary "civilization is human society with its well-developed social organizations or the culture and ways of life of a society" and ancient civilizations refers to the oldest known civilizations which were located in many different places across the globe. Some of these civilizations arose independently such as those in the Americas and Australia while others were significantly affected by their neighbors and include places such as Egypt, Nubia (Sudan), Mesopotamia, Persia and the Greek civilizations. Some of the earliest civilizations as highlighted by Smit (2019) include the following:

- The Australian Aboriginal Culture 50,000 BCE – Australia
- The Catalhoyuk Settlement 7500 -5700 BCE – Turkey
- Ayn Ghazal Civilization 7200 – 5000 BCE – Jordan
- The Jiahu Culture 7000-5700 BCE - China
- The Mesopotamian Civilizations 6500-539 BCE – Iraq, Syria and Turkey
- The Danubian Culture 5500 – 3500 BCE – Europe
- The Norte Chico Civilization 3000- 1800 BCE - Peru

- The Ancient Egyptian Civilization 3150 -30 BCE – Egypt
- The Ancient Greek Civilizations – 2700 – 479 BCE
- The Mayan Civilization 2600 BC- 900 AD – Belize, El Salvador, Guatemala, Honduras and Mexico.
- The Indus Valley Civilization – 2600- 1900 BCE – India and Pakistan.
- The Chinese Civilization 1600 – 1046 BCE

The foundation of all civilizations was based on the ability of people to feed themselves on a consistent basis and the ability to do so developed into the art and science that is today called agriculture, which involves the growing of different crops and animal husbandry. The preparation of land, planting, maintenance and reaping of crops and animal husbandry required the use of fertile land, water, tools, human and animal power and seed materials, all of which when combined in agriculture negatively impacted forests, rivers, lakes and grasslands.

The historical data presented will show that the activities of many ancient civilizations have severely degraded the forest and the environment in which they were located and that these degraded areas later became deserts and had the following characteristics:

- The places were the centers of intense agriculture and urban living.
- The civilizations occupied the same location for extended periods of time.
- Agriculture, inclusive of planting of crops and animal husbandry, not only fed the population but also built an empire.
- The culture of the people in these locations required the extensive use of trees for non-consumer and non-productive purposes, such as the creation of stone monuments and temples for religious and other purposes.
- The location had the predisposition to become a desert by having either an arid or semi-arid climatic disposition.
- Had a culture where religion played a very strong role in the society.

The locations to be considered shall include three ancient middle eastern civilizations, one eastern civilization and two cultures in the Americas and shall include of Egypt, Sudan, Mesopotamia, Indus Valley-India, Chaco Canyon, USA and the island of Rapa Nui, Chile.

Egypt

The pyramids of Egypt are among the biggest and most audacious stone monuments ever built anywhere in the ancient world and they do not have any equals with the exception of the great pyramid of Cholula in Mexico which is shorter than, but of a greater volume than the Great Pyramid of Giza (McCafferty 1996). The largest pyramids in Egypt are the three major pyramids at Giza and includes the Great Pyramid of Khufu, the Pyramid of Khafre and the Pyramid of Menkaure with the dimension of each pyramid and the time of construction according to Gadalla (2016) are as follows:

- Great Pyramid of Khufu (2551- 2528 BCE) - 756 feet x 756 feet x 480 feet high
- Second Pyramid of Khafre (2520- 2494BCE) – 708 x 708 x 471 feet high
- Third Pyramid of Menkaure (2494- 2472 BCE) – 357 x 357 x 218 feet high

The pyramid complex at Giza includes the three major pyramids, six queen pyramids, the Sphinx, several temples, one subsidiary pyramid, other tombs and other facilities as shown on Fig. 10.2 below. According to historical records the Great Pyramid of Khufu took anywhere from 20,000 – 100,000 men working three months per year for twenty years to complete (Herodotus- The Project Gutenberg Ebook 2006). Herodotus reported 100,00 men from local Egyptian sources and modern western archaeologists and writers sought to modify this number to what they considered a more reasonable number of 20,000 men, by their calculations. The construction effort required to build each of these great monuments would have caused extreme stress on the, forest, soil and environment, in the immediate vicinity of the site, along the road leading up to the site and at the location where the stones were mined. The vast majority of the stones for the Giza pyramids was taken from a quarry on the Giza plateau itself while small amounts were taken from Tura across the Nile and from Aswan (Gadalla 2016). The soil over which the large heavy blocks were transported for such a long time, 20 years, could become compacted and contaminated with tons of stone dust and particles that could reduce the capacity of the soil in the immediate vicinity of the pyramids to grow plants after the completion of the project. If the negative impacts are multiplied to include the over 100 pyramids, hundreds of temples and other ancient stone monuments built in Egypt, the millions of tons of stone taken from quarries and transported to the respective sites, the millions of feet trampling the soil, the roller and sledges drawn over the soil, twenty years for each major pyramid, over the full pyramid construction era of 1200 years, 2760 BCE (Djoser Step Pyramid) to the 1540 BCE (Pyramid of Ahmose) in the arid or semi-arid climate and locations on the western side of the Nile, one could clearly see the possibility of large volumes of trees and plants being destroyed and the gradual drying out of the soil in the vicinity leading to desertification, if the area was not already a treeless desert. However, when consideration is given to the many ways in which wood could have been used during this period and especially during the construction of the pyramids the possibility that deforestation in the areas could have been caused or accelerated by the construction of the pyramids and monuments appears to be reasonable. Wood was used for the following purposes during the construction of the pyramids:

- Cooking, baking and heating for 20,000 – 100,000 men and their families for three months each year over a twenty years period of time for each of the large pyramids and shorter periods of time for the smaller pyramids and monuments within the construction of pyramid era of 1200 years from 2760-1540 BCE.
- Heating hundreds of thousands of tons gypsum to make mortar for the construction of the pyramids and monuments over the 1200 years period.

- Heating copper ore to smelt copper and heating the metal produced to form cutting tools that were required to cut and shape the millions of stones, 1-2.3 million, for the large pyramids, used to construct the pyramids and monuments over the 1200 years period.

The demand for wood was so great that the from as early Pharaoh Sneferu's rule, Khufu's father, timber was imported from Lebanon for the construction of the pyramids which left the team of scientist from the David H Koch "Pyramid Radiocarbon Project" (Wenke et al 1984) to conclude that "..the construction of the pyramids marked a major depletion of Egypt's exploitable wood" and later that "The giant stone pyramids in the early Old Kingdom may mark a major consumption of Egypt's wood cover.."(Wenke et al.,1995). The conclusions drawn from the findings of these two research teams seem to confirm that the construction of Egypt's pyramids may have been responsible for the destruction of forests and consequently the drying out of the soil the regions which lead to the formation of dry deserts.

While the national life of Egypt may have had a heavy focus on the construction of monuments, temples and pyramids, the relatively large population 1.6 – 2million between 2500 -1250 BCE (Snape 2019) still needed to be fed and Egyptian agriculture with its heavy dependence upon the rich silt of the Nile River was more than capable of filling the role. The meals eaten by the wider Egyptian population was by necessity mostly vegetarian, as meat was relatively expensive and could only be afforded by the monarchy and the upper classes, and the basic crops planted to satisfy these needs included wheat, barley, flax, onions, cabbage, radish, turnips, lettuce, leeks, garlic, greens peas, beans, lentils, plums, melons, grapes, figs, dates, sesame, castor oil and later opium. The animal protein for those that could afford it came from cattle, sheep, lamb, goat, poultry, pigs, wild antelopes and fish, and "Fish was the most common food of the lower classes but considered unclean by many upper-class Egyptians" (Mark 2017). The growing of crops and the grazing of large herds of animals required the use of forests land and grasslands that would have further facilitated the problems associated with forest fragmentation, degradation, deforestation and desertification.

When combined, intense agriculture and the frenzied construction of pyramids, temples and monuments over a 1200 years period, 2760-1540 BCE, could have created the necessary conditions for the development of deserts as exists today in Egypt.

Sudan

Egypt shared its southern border with the nation of Nubia (Sudan) and had a long and tumultuous relationship with it, with Egypt conquering and ruling Nubia for an extensive period of four hundred years, 1500-1100 BCE, "With the rise of Thutmose I in Egypt Nubia was invaded and Kerma sacked around 1500 BCE" (Ross 2013) and Nubia (Sudan) conquering and governing Egypt for less than one hundred years 730-671 BCE. "In the year 730 BCE, a man by the name of Piye decided that the only way to save Egypt from itself was to invade it" (Draper 2008) and this man was the king of Nubia. This long relationship between Egypt and Nubia saw many cultural exchanges between both countries and peoples leading to Nubians adopting many Egyptian practices and cultural symbols inclusive of titles, religions and gods, and even burial customs. However, in this very long relationship there were and still are many points of dispute relating to the exact source of many shared cultural norms and these discussions are still in vogue today with Nubia's successor nation, Sudan, endeavoring to show the world that pyramids were in fact a Nubian creation and that they, Nubians, have built many more pyramids than the Egyptians. El-Behary (2017) noted, "The Sudanese Minister of information Ahmed Bilal Othman, claimed on Sunday that the Meroe pyramids of Sudan are 2000 years older than Egyptian pyramids" and the Sudanese government has taken this claim as high as the United Nations. The Nubian pyramids are, however, not in the same class as the great pyramids of Egypt as they are much smaller than most Egyptian pyramids, taking up much less space, requiring much less stones, mortar, wood, requiring fewer people to construct and a much shorter construction period. This use of less material, labor and shorter time to construct would automatically ensure that construction of Nubian pyramids had significantly less negative impact upon the environment than the Egyptian pyramids, however, this did not totally eliminate the negative impacts as they used the same materials and method of construction and therefore many Nubian trees and plants would have been destroyed in the process of constructing the Nubian pyramids, monuments and temples of which they also constructed many.

The economies of Ancient Nubian societies were fairly complex as they were built upon several industries inclusive of construction, mining and metallurgy, forestry and export of timber products, and agriculture inclusive of the planting, reaping and storage of crops and animal husbandry. These ancient Nubians were quite industrious and had developed over time several areas of economic specializations inclusive of gold and iron mining, the smelting of the gold and iron ores, the forging and fabricating iron and gold products, agriculture, crop propagation and animal husbandry, and forestry, for which they had also developed very strong markets among their neighbors to the north and many other nations as far away as India. These several Nubian industries placed significant pressure on their natural forests as these activities demanded the use of timber products, the clearing of forests for the planting of crops and animal husbandry and the clearing of forests for the construction of pyramids, temples, monuments and residential facilities. The demands were as follows:

- The mining and metallurgy industries required the stripping of vegetation, the use of timber to support mine construction, the use of timber as fuel for the smelting, forging and fabrication processes. According Marks (2010) "The iron industry, requiring enormous amounts of wood, led to deforestation of the surrounding lands while cattle grazing and agriculture destroyed fields and depleted soils".

- The Nubian construction industry required vast supplies of timber for the construction of their over two hundred pyramids, numerous temples and monuments, other public facilities and their residences. The pyramids, monuments and temples which used large volumes of mortar, would require the burning of large volumes of lime using the only fuel source available at the time, wood.

- Nubian trade in timber, first to the Egyptians followed by the Romans conquerors, required the logging of vast amounts of trees to fill their many orders for timber and also for the creation of the required transportation to deliver the timber.
- The agricultural activities required to feed the Nubians large population and for export required intensive crop planting and extensive animal husbandry and according to Omer (2008) the Nubians were more than able and capable as "unlike the Egyptians the Kushites extensively domesticated cattle and sheep", and all of these activities required the clearing of even more forests.

The Nubian nation was wealthy in many ways as they had significant natural resources inclusive of water, forests, good arable lands, mineral wealth and over time they developed a highly skilled population that were very industrious upon which they built several significant industries inclusive of agriculture, mining, forestry and a metallurgy. Nubia also had a ready market for most of their natural resources as they shared a border and a long historical relationship with a dominant, giant neighbor, Egypt, which had an insatiable appetite for Nubia's products. The many activities of this industrious nation, in the construction of large stone pyramids, temples and monuments, in a thriving mining and metallurgy industry, in intensive agriculture (intensive grazing by cattle, sheep, and in planting many crops), extensive trade in forestry products and minerals all led to the creation of conditions which have engulfed both Nubia and its giant neighbor in the largest dry desert on the planet.

Chaco Canyon

Chaco Canyon is an ancient abandoned community, located in the Four Corners area of New Mexico, Arizona, Utah and Colorado in the US, that was built by the ancient Pueblo Ancestral People of the region in an architectural style that was unique to the region, the country and the whole Americas. The design and layout of the buildings in the communities were elaborate, well laid out and included dwelling quarters for upper and lower classes citizens, religious centers for worship, food storage areas and other facilities. Unfortunately, after approximately 4 centuries of activity the city was abandoned by everyone and the site has long since laid in ruins.

History of Chaco Canyon

Chaco Canyon was the site and the center of a unique culture of early North America that commenced prior to or about 850 AD and lasted until about 1250 AD, (National Park Service, US Department of the Interior), when unknown forces caused most of the Ancestral Pueblo People to drift away from the location and to start new communities in other areas of New Mexico, Utah, Colorado and Arizona. During the 400 years of its existence (850 – 1250 Ad) the people built up an incredible culture based up trade, art, astronomy, religion, architecture and engineering that produced significant dwelling called "Great Houses", places of worship called Kivas, residences for the people at the lower levels of the community and a very good road network.

Some of the architectural and engineering achievements in Chaco Canyon include the construction of five story apartment buildings which could house up to 650 people, a feat unique to these people and quite possibly the largest buildings in North America up to the 1800s. According to Lekson (2006) "At the culmination of, about 1125, almost seven hundred rooms stacked four and perhaps five stories tall covered an area of about 0.8 ha". These large residences were call "Great Houses" and there were 15 such great houses spread over a fairly large area surrounded by 150 smaller "great houses", kivas and great kivas, hundreds of regular dwelling houses and a well-developed road network all of which pointed to a well ordered and developed, hierarchical society. However, even with what outwardly appeared to be a very strong community the Chaco Culture suddenly collapsed around 1250 with sections of the community moving in different directions to form new communities. According to Holloway (2014) "The long-held theory is that the downfall of Chaco Canyon culture occurred because of the poor land use and deforestation that took place to build the cities". However later researchers attempted to dispel this theory indicating that there was no scientific or archaeological data to substantiate this, however, these later researchers offered no theory for the cause of the collapse. Others, including Posey (2015) thinks that the failure may have been due to one of several social reasons inclusive of religious differences or changes, political differences and the growing gap between the haves and have-nots in Chaco Canyon society, once again there is no concrete evidence to support these ideas.

The only established facts are that a group of Native American people entered the Chaco Canyon and Four Corners area of the Southwest United States, around 850 AD and started a community that grew in numbers, knowledge and skills and that this depth in population numbers, knowledge and skills enabled them to build a great civilization and that at the peak of their power, around 1250 AD everyone packed their bags and walked away. The evidence left behind indicates that:

- They were good architects, engineers and builders.
- They understood and utilize a significant knowledge of astronomy.
- They had significant agricultural knowledge and skills.
- They were skilled artists.
- They were skilled in the trade of goods and services.
- They had a great understanding of logistics.
- They had significant knowledge of metallurgy.
- They had knowledge of and used precious stones in trading and the making of jewelry.

These ancient Pueblo People also left evidence that they had established a societal hierarchy, a religious system of worship and also that they knew how to use political and or moral power to organize and keep a large group of people together for an extended period of time (850-1250 AD), in a relatively small area. The evidence they left behind also clearly indicates that their society fell apart and that those who were still alive moved away to other parts of Arizona, Colorado,

Utah and New Mexico to establish different communities that are still in existence today.

The works done by this ancient civilization in Chaco Canyon are quite significant and were way ahead of any other such works in the Americas, however, the Four Corners and surrounding region paid a high environmental price with the destruction of forests to provide lumber for the creation of the buildings, the clearing of the lands for agriculture and the chopping of wood for fuel for the community for four hundred years. According to Guiterman et al (2015) "The iconic great houses of Chaco Canyon occupy nearly treeless landscapes and yet were some of the largest pre-Columbian structures in North America. This incongruity has sparked persistent debate over the origins of more than 240,000 trees used in construction". These 240,000 trees used on the great houses do not include the trees used for the construction of the other residences, storage areas, Great Kivas, Kivas or the trees used over the 300- 400 years existence of the community to provide heat for cooking and warmth during winter.

Chaco Canyon enjoyed varying climatic conditions throughout the year, harsh blistering hot temperatures and very dry summers, very cold winters, uncertain rainfall and very short growing seasons (Lekson 2016), these conditions however, did not prevent the residents of Chaco Canyon from growing crops for themselves, inclusive of maize, beans and squash. They also supplemented their vegetable diets with meat obtained from the hunting of wild game inclusive of rabbits, mule deer and pronghorn antelopes (Eaton 1985) and the importation of goods that they could not produce for themselves such as chocolate that they imported from Mexico and South America. According to the University of Cincinnati (2018) there was compelling evidence that the people in Chaco Canyon had the knowledge and technology to produce their own food. It also appears that even with the adverse conditions in the region, agriculture was fundamental to the establishment and growth of the population and the infrastructure of Chaco Canyon and the impact of agricultural activities on the environment would be similar to the effects of agriculture everywhere, especially with the growing population of the Canyon which varied from 1200 – 40,000 based on different reports.

Rapa Nui (Easter Island)

Rapa Nui is one of the most isolated islands in the world and it was first located by a group of Polynesian people who ventured out on the rough Pacific Ocean in their well-built sea crafts seeking a new place of peace, a place where they could bring up their families far away from the overcrowded conditions of their first homes without the strife that may have become a way of life in their old island homes. The place that they found was an island that was 2180 mile west of Chile, 4300 miles Southeast of Hawaii, 2000 miles east of Tahiti and 2700 mile north of Antarctica and was a paltry 65 square miles in total area. All information indicates that the first Polynesians arrived somewhere between 400 to 1200 AD and according to Mann et al., (2007) "What we know is that prior to the arrival of Polynesian farmers, much of Rapa Nui was covered with forest dominated by a now-extinct species of palm" (Flenley et al., 1991, Ortia 2000).

Rappa Nui is the top of a complex of underwater volcanoes, consisting of three volcanoes Terevaka, Poike and Rano Kau and most of the island was formed from the lava flow of the youngest volcano, Terevaka. The land mass consists of volcanic cones and lava flow surfaces, two natural lakes, one stream that runs on the surface and underground, one reed swamp and large areas that were covered by an extinct species of palm trees, several other trees species, shrub and grass. The island had also been the home to six species of endemic flightless(land) birds, 26 species of seabirds, herons, two types of rails, two types of parrots and barn owls (Charola 1994) mammals and insects, most of which were lost due to extinction. The mean temperature of the island was 21°C, with a high of 24°C in January and a low of 18°C in August (Strethen &Zillman 1984), with a mean annual precipitation of 1300-1350 mm. The arriving group of Polynesians consisted of approximately100 individuals led by their legendary King, Hotu Matu'a (Charola 1994) and they brought with them seeds, tubers, plants, pigs, dogs and chickens, of which only the chickens among the animals appeared to have survived. The new arrivals were farmers and they brought new crops from their home islands, crops that were new to Rapa Nui, and the farmers did the necessary clearing of the land to plant their imported crops, which would have consisted of potatoes, taro, yams, bananas, plantains, sugar cane and agave. The farmers also planted some new trees inclusive of paper mulberry, soapberry, Oceanian Rosewood and Sandalwood some of which did not survive and the farmers also developed inventive ways of ensuring the survival of the imported crops which had to survive strong winds, salty air and some amount of salt intrusion. The destruction of the native species and their replacement with non-native species may have had a significant negative impact upon the environment as over time all of the trees on the island had died, both native and the imported species.

This loss of trees is thought to have occurred as a result of the growing population which had grown from 100 to a possible high of 17,500 (Puleston 2017) at its peak and this growth in numbers would have required more houses, more land for agriculture and more trees for the construction of a new art form that the people of Rapa Nui developed after they had been living on the island for some time. The arrival of the Polynesians with their new crops and animals may have had severe negative impacts upon the environment of the island, however, the Polynesian population thrived in other areas as indicated by Charola (1994) "Nonetheless on Easter Island (Rapa Nui) spectacular advances were made, such as the development of a written language that had no parallel in the rest of the world and the creation of innumerable sculpted and architectural stone works of great size and quality". The creation of the sculpted and architectural stone works, while magnificent in appearance, may have had an overall negative impact on the environment as according to Charola (1994) the competition between different groups on the island saw the size of the sculpted stones, called moai, getting larger and larger, requiring even more effort and material to build, relocate and install.

The arrival of the first Europeans in 1722 (Clark 2000), a minimum of 500 hundred years after the arrival of the Polynesians, brought the existence of the people of Rapa Nui and their unique art, way of life and treeless island to the attention of the rest of the world. The Europeans noted that there were no large trees only small stunted ones and also noted that the people had no boats. This absence of large trees and boats suggested that through their agriculture, the planting of invasive species of plants, the arrival of new animals, home construction, art and the construction of their stone monuments, the people of Rapa Nui may have destroyed all of the large trees on the island over a period of 500-1300 years, however, many modern scientists now doubts that this happened (Than 2006) and have offered differing explanations including the presence of an extremely large population of rats that may have eaten the seeds of the palm trees, and were thus responsible for the loss of most of the trees from the island.

India

Rajasthan is the largest state of India and it is located in the northwest region and it is the home to 60% of India's largest desert, the Thar Desert or the Great Indian Desert that was the location of one of the main centers of the ancient Indus Valley Civilization. The main facts about the Indus Valley Civilization according to Mian are as follows:

- The Indus Valley Civilization was an ancient civilization that developed and grew along the banks of the Indus River in the North-Western region of subcontinental India and Pakistan.
- The Civilization existed from about 3000 -1300 BCE with the high point of it occurring from 2500-1750 BC with its earliest developments beginning in 7000 BCE.
- The Civilization included parts of Punjab, Sindh, Baluchistan, Gujrat, Rajasthan and the outer regions of Western Uttar Pradesh. It ran from as far north as Jammu, to as far South as the mouth of the River Narmada, went as far west as the Makran Coast of Balochistan and as far east as Meerut.
- Up to 1999 archaeologists had already uncovered more than one thousand and fifty-two cities (1052), which is an indication of the size of the population.
- The total area covered, approximately 1.26 million square kilometers, made the Indus Valley Civilization the largest of all ancient civilizations.

- This civilization had strong agricultural practices which produced two types of wheat and barley, rai, peas, sesamum, mustard, rice and cotton.
- They had also domesticated oxen, cattle, buffaloes, goat, sheep, pigs and used camels and donkeys as beast of burden and they kept pets, mostly dogs and cats, and had knowledge of Elephants and Rhinoceros.
- The surplus goods produced in the Indus Valley facilitated the development of both local and international trade with Mesopotamia and other places in that region of the world.
- The development of urban and city planning. The major cities uncovered to date show that they were laid out on grids which show a high level of planning.
- The Indus Valley development of writing with over four hundred distinct symbols.
- The development of mining and smelting of copper, lead and tin and the development of metallurgy inclusive of the developments of alloys such as bronze.

An examination of figures 10.13 and 10.14 clearly indicates that there is a very strong overlap between Thar, the Great Indian Desert and the location of the Indus Valley Civilization. The Indus Valley Civilization could have contributed to the creation of the desert in the region due to the following:

- The creation and establishment of more than 1052 ancient cities to house a large population, said to be 5 million at its peak. The buildings in these cities were constructed from burnt bricks and would have required large sources of heat, heat that could only have been produced from burning wood at that time.
- The establishment of large acreages in agriculture for planting crops and grazing animals to feed a large and growing population and for trading.
- The mining and smelting of copper, lead and tin that would have utilized large volumes of wood to provide necessary

infrastructure support for the mines and the heat energy for smelting the ores.

- The use of wood as fuel for domestic uses such as cooking and heating for the large population.
- The cutting of trees for sale as timber for many applications (Dani and Thapar 1996)

The clear cutting of vast acreages of land for agriculture, mining, metallurgy, the establishing of cities and villages and the daily cutting of wood to provide domestic fuel could have led to forest fragmentation, forest degradation, deforestation and the combination of all of these activities would have negatively impacted the hydrological cycle within the region resulting in long periods of drought and eventually the drying out of the soil followed by soil erosion and desertification. The high levels of activities in agriculture, mining, timber production and construction would have stressed the lands and forests of the region and could have led to desertification over the extended life (7000-1300 BC) of the civilization and beyond. According to Dani and Thapar (1996) "These three items- copper, cotton and timber appear to have been the mainstay of urban prosperity". The current conditions of the land in the Thar Desert indicates that it was previously forested as it still shows many trees still thriving even the desert conditions.

The later construction of numerous monuments, temples, large tombs and memorials, large fort cities, palaces, large homes and numerous residences, in states like Rajasthan, Dehli, New Dehli and other adjoining states, in both India and Pakistan, which are located within the boundaries of the old Indus Valley Civilization would have continued the pressure on the already stressed forest resources and increase the problems related to desertification.

Iraq (Mesopotamia)

Modern day Iraq is the home for some of the ancient Middle Eastern civilizations and is also part of the location that has been referred to in ancient history as the "Fertile Crescent" or called Mesopotamia, land between the rivers. This land gave rise to such ancient civilizations as

Sumer, Akkad, Babylon and Assyria, civilizations that were similar to those of Egypt and the Indus Valley, civilizations that were also built upon great rivers, similar to the Nile and the Indus, however in the case of Mesopotamia, there were two great rivers, the Tigris and the Euphrates Rivers, which provided the fertile top soil brought down by the rivers each year and laid the foundation for the agriculture growth that energized several great civilizations. These civilizations may have been the contemporaries of both the Egyptian and Indus Valley civilizations and probably functioned in a very similar pattern as they affected the environment in a similar manner and they all left extensive deserts in their wakes.

Deserts of Iraq

According to the Encyclopedia Britannica, Iraq has three deserts the Al-Jazirah Desert, the Western and Southern Deserts, that cover approximately 64,900 square miles and makes up two fifth of the Iraqi land mass.

Sumer

The land of Sumer consisted of the lower half of Mesopotamia with an area of approximately 10,000 square miles running from just north of Baghdad down to the Persian Gulf (Kramer 1963). The land was made by the annual silt deposits of the Tigris and Euphrates Rivers over thousands of years, which made it flat, treeless, with a dry and arid soil that may have remained quite unproductive without the intervention of the Sumerians whose tough mindedness made the difference as according to Kramer (1963) "But for the people that inhabited it, the Sumerians as they came to be known by the third millennium BCE, were endowed with an unusually creative intellect and a venturesome and resolute spirit". To best utilize the treeless, flat arid land through which two great rivers ran the Sumerians developed irrigation systems and agricultural practices over significant periods of time to make the land work for them. The irrigation systems saw them collecting and channeling the silt laden overflow water from the Tigris and Euphrates rivers into their fields and gardens to water the crops that would later grow their civilizations. The development of the irrigation systems was only one of the many very important things created by the Sumerians over the period of their civilization, 5000–1750 BCE (Mark 2011) "their history unfolds from approximately 5000 BCE to 1750 BCE" and some of these inventions are as follows:

- Utilization of river clay and mud to create essential utensils in the absence of trees
- Utilization of marsh reeds, tied together in bundles or plaited together and plastered with mud to construct shelters.
- The creation of brick molds for the shaping and baking of bricks that were used for construction of shelters and temples.
- The creation of other building systems such as arches, vaults and domes
- The creation of the plough for land preparation for agricultural purposes
- The creation of the potter wheel for making clay pottery
- The creation of the wagon wheel for the transportation of crops
- The development of metal joining methods such as riveting, soldering and brazing and metal working such as casting in copper and bronze.
- The development of sculptures in stone, engraving, inlays and writing in clay.
- The development of the cuneiform script.
- The development of early systems of governance, laws and law codes.
- The development of Sumerian sailing boats.

Sumerian Agriculture

Sumerian agriculture was enhanced by the development of irrigation systems, ploughs, chopping tools such as the pickaxe, sickles and the practices of drying and storing crops and according to van der Crabben (2011) "The main types of grains that were used for agriculture were wheat, barley, millet and emmer" and in addition to these main crops they also planted peas and beans, flax, sesame, olives and fruit crops such as figs, pomegranates, apples, muskmelons, dates and pistachio nuts. The Sumerians also domesticated a wide variety of animals inclusive of oxen, cattle, pigs, goats, sheep and donkeys, all of which they used for various purposes inclusive of the oxen for pulling the ploughs, the cattle and goats for milk and meat, pigs for meat and sheep for meat and wool.

The planting season in Sumer was in the spring and reaping occurred in the fall, when all crops, except those of shorter growth times, were reaped, processed by threshing, and stored away in appropriate vessels, ensuring that there was adequate food for the population until the next reaping cycles the following fall. The growth of these processes and the consistency with which they were done over time figured significantly in the growth of the Sumerian population and society and these successes led to the development of villages and towns, which consequently led to the need for systems of governance, laws for everyone to live by and the overall organization of the society.

Sumerian Religion

Religion played a major role in the life of all Sumerians and based upon the systems of belief and philosophies that the society developed, they also developed practices to please the deities that they considered to be important. In Sumer the deities consisted of as many as 3000 gods with a hierarchy which determined which ones were the most important and deserved greater adoration and each urban center had its own god or goddess. To ensure the safety of the society, in relations to the gods, a religious hierarchy was developed to ensure that the correct things were said and done to please the gods who governed in every area of the society. At the top of this religious hierarchy were the priest who was responsible for predictions, divinations, sacrifices, the creation and writing of the rules by which the population would live, the worship the important gods and the creation of necessary rituals required to gain favor or ask pardon from the gods. Some of the rules created by these Sumerian priests have been adopted over time by other people and groups and have been passed down through other religious systems of beliefs and philosophies, and are still used today in the governance of modern societies.

Many historians and philosophers have highlighted the similarity between Sumerian stories, such as the Epic of Gilgamesh and the Jewish biblical creation story and the rules created by Sumerian priests and the biblical ten commandments. According to Allen (2014) although there has been much debate about the issue, it was commonly accepted by many scholars that several parts of bible may have been influenced by other cultures inclusive of the Sumerian culture.

The role of the priests in Sumer later evolved over time to include that of government administrators and also educators for the Sumerian civilization, roles that gave order to the good governance of city states and empires and these roles also further elevated the importance of the priests in the Sumerian society. One of the major outcomes from the well-ordered Sumerian religion was the development of the places of worship, which the priestly class made the center of Sumerian life and these places of worship/temples were located at the center of their urban areas as each city was built around a grand place of worship called a ziggurat which was a part of a large multi building complex and the importance placed on the Ziggurats is reflected in the importance that Jews, Christians and Muslims later placed on their houses of worship. The architecture and style of the ziggurats are still being adopted and used for many other types of buildings in many different places in the world today inclusive of universities, hotels, state building, temples and many other uses in places like the USA, UK, Russia, Rumania and Iraq. The ancient ziggurats could be described as a pyramid with multi levels and a flat top, as shown in the Fig 10.22, and were some of the biggest monuments created in the Sumer and the later Mesopotamian civilizations.

Akkad

According to Mark (2011) "No one knows where the city of Akkad was located, how it rose to prominence or how precisely it fell", however, there can be no doubt that it existed or that the empire arising out of Akkad had an impact on the then known world as it became the center of the first great empires in world history and was led by a king by the name of Sargon the Great. Sargon during his reign (2334-2279BCE) unified Mesopotamia and along with the kings that followed for next the 142 years (2344- 2198 BCE) of the Akkadian empire, established systems that lead to growth and development in several important areas, inclusive of the arts, sciences, literature, agriculture and religion. Of these five areas of growth and development the two most likely to affect the environment negatively were agriculture and religion.

Akkadian Agriculture

Akkadian society, similar to its Sumerian predecessor, was totally dependent upon agriculture to provide all that was needed to keep their kingdom alive and thriving and it therefore had to develop trading and commerce to acquire things like essential material that was not available in Akkad for the construction of its temples and other monuments that had become an essential part of Sumerian and later Akkadian life. In general, agricultural operations took place in two main regions of the country, the Low Country and the Upper Country and it depended on two different sources of water for the growth of crops and of animals, with the Low Country (Southern Mesopotamia/Sumer) being totally dependent upon irrigation water from the Tigris and Euphrates Rivers, while the Upper Country (Northern Mesopotamia) completely depended on rainfall. Akkadian trade was built upon agricultural surpluses which were traded far and wide to earn silver and to exchange for timber, building stones and metal ores. The high level of production required to sustain significant trade would have required the use of significantly more land and water for agriculture than would have been required for domestic use alone and this intense use may have led to the environmental crisis that took place around 2200 BCE when a major drought devasted the region and caused life in the Upper Country to come to a standstill and forced the mass relocation of the entire Upper Country population to the Low Country. During this drought period several important things happened that would have negatively impacted Akkadian life (Gibbons 1993):

- Rainfall fell to 20 mm (less than 1 inch) per year in low country.
- Extreme drought and the collapse of agriculture in the upper country
- Flood levels in the Tigris and Euphrates fell approximately 5 feet (1.5 meters) below the flood levels of the previous 400 years (3000-2600) and by the Akkadian period the levels fell even lower to between 18 inches to three feet below the 2600 BC levels
- There were periods of high wind and dust (Whitehead and Yuter)
- Growing salinization of soils due to poor irrigation drainage which caused a reduction in wheat production in the southern part of the country and forced a transition to another crop, a more salt tolerant barley.
- By 2600 BC the population levels in the urban centers had reached their highest levels.
- The city of Akkad was abandoned soon after the completion of massive projects inclusive of a massive city wall, reconstruction of its temple and the reorganization of its grain production.
- One other project completed during this time was a 112 miles long wall that was built to keep out grazing animals.
- People did not return to the upper country for approximately 300 years

It should be noted that the problems encountered by Akkad in 2200 BC sounds very similar to events in the United States during the "Dust Bowl" crisis of the 1930s, however, the departure and absence from the affected locations in the US was not as long.

With the great importance of agriculture, the kings of Akkad made agricultural infrastructure their personal responsibilities and they ensured that sufficient land was made available for planting, that proper irrigation systems were built and maintained and that adequate storage facilities were available at all times. All agricultural and agricultural related activities were prioritized and formed a large part of the projects that kings would attend to each year.

Akkadian Religion

Akkadian religion basically followed the same pattern as the Sumerian religion with priests, places of worship in each city (ziggurats), cities with their own god or goddesses and a vast pantheon of gods with a set of major or more important gods. One of the observed differences between the Sumerian and Akkadian major gods were the names used, as the Akkadians changed the names of the major gods to suit their language and social differences. The roles of the priest also remained the same, performing religious services, making predictions and performing roles as government administrators and educators.

During the Akkadian dynasty there was significant growth in the size of the country as Sargon the Great conquered neighboring cities and regions up to the Mediterranean Sea, and consolidated all of the captured places into his empire. This growth in the size of the country and peoples would have automatically expanded the reach of the Akkadian economy and religion inclusive of its systems of belief and accompanying religious buildings and would have required the construction of new irrigations systems where required and new ziggurat complexes and monuments in each conquered city. Ziggurats, the central worship and government administration centers, were normally constructed from sun dried mud bricks which had a relative short life and these bricks would usually deteriorate leading to the collapse of some structures which triggered the response of the kings who had total responsibility for the construction and repairs of places of worship and all other significant buildings.

The growth of the Akkadian kingdom also saw the kings and their families increasing the size of their personal dwelling places and palaces and to fill this growing list of needs the kings would order the construction of new palaces and recreational facilities dedicated for the use of their families only. These new residences and palaces were usually built from material that had to be acquired through traded with other nations that were rich in stone and other building material that did not exist in Akkad and all such trades increased the pressure to produce more causing the deterioration and degradation of farming lands, rivers and the people actually doing the work of farming. These pressures also further increased the level of salinization that took place on most Mesopotamian farms due to irrigation drainage design problems.

Babylonian Empire 1792-1750 BCE

Babylon was a port town established on the banks of the Euphrates River by an ancient Akkadian-speaking people from the southern region of Mesopotamia, around 2300 BCE and though insignificant at the time, this town was destined to be the heart of one of the most famous and richest empires in ancient history, twice. Babylon remained relatively quiet and insignificant from the time of its founding in 2300 BCE until the arrival of the Amorites, an invading tribe from the region of modern-day Syria, which was located outside the boundaries of Mesopotamia, and these Amorites were led by an Amorite chieftain named Sumu-abum in 1894 BCE (Sasson1995). Sumu-abum later became the father of the first Babylonian dynasty, made his first tasks, after capturing and subduing the town, the strengthening the important infrastructures of the town inclusive of its temples, irrigation channels and walls. Sumu-abum's activities were later continued by his successors who over time slowly grew the boundaries of the town until it became a small kingdom city-state until the time of Hammurabi (1792- 1750 BCE), the third great grandson of Sumu-abum. The map shown in Figure 10.25 shows the size of Babylon at the beginning,1792 BC, and ending1750 BCE, of Hammurabi's reign. This map shows that Hammurabi greatly expand the boundaries of what was once Babylon a city state into a great empire that became known as Babylonia the new Empire. Hammurabi, was a great warrior, diplomat, administrator, lawgiver, builder of empire and buildings and he used all of his talents as shown below:

- Conquered significant territory from friends and neighbors as well as enemies
- Astutely managed the business of his enlarge realm.
- Wisely governed the affairs of his subjects in Babylonia
- Created, wrote and published new laws to ensure justice for all of his subjects

- Acted diplomatically to maintain relationships with his neighbors and friends whom he had not yet conquered.
- Constructed and repaired the important infrastructures of the new empire inclusive of city walls, irrigation systems and beautiful temples complexes throughout his new empire.

Hammurabi was as famous for his laws as he was for his many construction projects and according to Mark (2018) "A popular title applied to Hammurabi during his lifetime was *bani matim,* "builder of the land" because of the many building projects and canals he ordered constructed throughout the region". Unfortunately, the Empire built by Hammurabi did not last very long as it started going into decline right after his passing and shortly afterwards disappeared totally from history. The most enduring elements of Hammurabi's works were the laws that he created, wrote and published, as these laws later affected the living codes of many other civilizations and physically endured on steles that survived history, with one such stele being currently housed in one of the largest museums in the World. His most important construction works, however, did not last very long as they have long been destroyed due to natural weathering, wars and soil subsidence. It must be noted again that most ziggurats, protective walls and many government buildings created during that era, were made from sunbaked clay bricks.

After the fall of the Amorite dynasty, Babylon remained dormant for approximately one thousand plus years, after which another Babylonian empire arose and this second empire was led by another set of invaders called the Chaldeans, who also originated from outside of Mesopotamia and this new Babylon, referred to as Neo-Babylon in history, rose to be much greater than the first Babylon.

Babylon 626- 536 BCE

The empire of Babylonia, Old Babylon, was a consolidation of all the city states within Mesopotamia, going from the Persian gulf up to the borders of ancient Syria, while the new Babylonian Empire was much grander as it expanded well beyond the borders of Mesopotamia and covered almost the entire region, inclusive of portions of Egypt,

Israel, Jordan, Saudi Arabia, Lebanon, Syria, portions of Turkey and portions of Iran and this empire touched all of the major water ways in the region inclusive of the Mediterranean Sea, the Red Sea, the Persian Gulf, the Caspian Sea and the Black Sea.

The new Babylon arose out of the ashes of the Assyrian Empire, through the hands of a Chaldean king named Nabopolassar, who used war and diplomacy to create the new Babylonian Empire in 626 BCE (Mark 2018). It was however his son Nebuchadnezzar II,605/604-562 BCE, that took the new empire to its greatest heights conquering and ruling large portions of the known world and building some the most spectacular buildings and facilities ever built in Babylon or anywhere else in the world, some of which are still spoken about even today with much awe.

Some of these buildings included the following:

- The Hanging Gardens of Babylon – Considered one of the Seven Wonders of the ancient world (Mark 2018)
- Three beautiful palaces in Babylon – The Summer Palace, The Northern Palace and the Southern Palace.
- The Shrine to Marduk that stood 280 feet tall
- The Ishtar Gate to the city that was covered with bright blue glazed bricks
- The great ziggurat, 90 m x 90 m x 90 m high, Etemenanki (Lewis and Feldman 2015)
- The New Year Festival Temple.
- Three rings of security walls each 40 feet high around the city of Babylon.
- The expansion of the city to sit on both banks of the Euphrates River, covering 2200 acres.
- The golden statue of Marduk and many other beautiful statues. (Mark 2018)
- Elaborate temples of Esagila and Ezida and many other temples.
- The beautiful Processional Way (Mark 2018) that was 70 feet wide, half a mile long with walls over fifty feet high that was decorated with 120 lions, dragons, bulls and flowers in gold.
- The renovation and refurbishment of thirteen cities across the empire. (Mark 2018)

All of these works mentioned above gives an indication of the large volume of monumental construction works done by Nebuchadnezzar II in the new Babylon, while still maintaining the very strong agricultural heritage of the Kingdom long established by Sumer.

Assyrian Kingdoms.

The empires of Assyria arose from the city -state of Ashur in northern Mesopotamia, from where it grew in many stages until its eventual rise to power and its eventful fall from power. This empire rose twice in Mesopotamia, first time from 1120 -1100 BCE and the second time from 1020 -612 BCE and became the most prosperous and enduring era in the history of the middle east and in the world at that time.

The Assyrian Empire, while conquering a lot more lands and people and being more aggressive and violent than their predecessors, basically followed the same patterns as the other large Mesopotamian empires that had preceded them, with the importance of religion remaining paramount throughout all areas of life and agriculture and trading continuing as the foundation of the Empire's economy. It was, however, the looting of conquered nations which provided the funding for their many construction projects inclusive of many beautiful palaces, ziggurats, irrigation canals, for strengthening agriculture, and the walls for strengthening the defenses of their many cities around the empire. According to Belibtreu (1991) "The two principal tasks of an Assyrian king were to engage in military exploits and to erect public buildings" and these two tasks were regarded by them as religious duties, acts of obedience to please their major gods. The more aggressive nature of the Assyrians ensured that they made more enemies, fought many more wars, required a lot more money to continue financing their operations and this aggressive nature ensured that their second turn at empire lasted much longer than all of the earlier Mesopotamian empires combined. Finally, however, their many enemies, from both inside and outside of Mesopotamia, whom they had accumulated over their 400 years of dominance, got together and overthrew the Assyrian Empire.

The major civilizations of Mesopotamia, while different in terms of personnel of leadership, quality of leadership, the lands and peoples that they conquered, all ensured that they performed all of the functions that made the region important and prosperous, inclusive of ensuring:

- The continued growth and development of agriculture by building and maintaining irrigation systems to keep their most important industries alive,
- Keeping the Mesopotamian religious systems strong by empowering the priest, building new temples and doing regular repairs to the existing ones.
- The construction notable palaces, places, temples of worship and security walls.

All of these works had great negative impact upon the environment throughout the Mesopotamian and Middle Eastern regions ruled by the kings as they all left behind overworked and abused lands, damaged water ways and high levels of salt in the soils of the region, which all combined to forms deserts which still exist today.

11

Governmental Policies

Since the beginning of civilized human societies, many decisions have been made for the societies by those chosen to lead them, leaders with the direct intention of improving life or creating beautiful things to give pleasure to everyone, however, quite often the decisions taken by these leaders have resulted in the diminishing of the quality of life of humans and the environment. There are many examples of these problems both in ancient history and modern life inclusive of the Great Egyptian Civilizations, Sumer and other Mesopotamian Civilizations, the Indus Valley Civilization, the great Dust Bowl in Modern USA and desertification problems in modern China.

The ancient Egyptians have left great monuments of immense beauty and historical value which are still admired by most humans today, yet the creation of these beautiful things came at a very high costs that could not have been foreseen by the initiators of the Egyptian1200-year period of pyramid and monument construction. These initiators and the many that followed them could only see the great things of architectural beauty that would memorialize themselves for many generations to come and not the loss of their natural forests and the eventual onset and growth of desertification leading to Egypt becoming a part of a great desert for thousands of years.

The Sumerians were said to be the creators of the first irrigation systems in the ancient world and through this great innovation the Sumerians made Mesopotamia the bread basket of the region and allowed all the civilizations of Mesopotamia to grow rich and powerful as their agricultural surplus allowed them to acquire great wealth that was used to build great cities, build great armies and consequently to conquer the countries of the region many times over. Unfortunately, the design of the irrigation systems did not allow for the proper drainage of the fields and residual salts began to build up causing many fields to lose their capacity to produce and over time to become unusable and eventually these fields would dry up allowing for the onset of desertification, a process which eventually led to the creation of deserts in the region. Irrigation, the great technology that led to the intensification of agriculture, growing crops and animal husbandry, that built many empires also led to the downfall and eventual failure of the political and social power structure within the region.

The Indus Valley Civilization was the largest of the early civilization with a large population of approximately 5 million that occupied large expanses of land along the banks of the Indus River, lands which were utilized for the construction of over one thousand cities for housing the large population and for the practice of intense agriculture to feed this large population and for export to provide wealth to the few. The region that once housed this immense ancient civilization is now a part of the largest desert located in India and Pakistan.

The rise and fall of these three ancient civilizations were built upon the decisions, policies and programs of ancient rulers all of whom had the same desire to optimize the use of their local natural resources, to house and feed their people, build large cities, build large armies, build great building and monuments to demonstrate their achievements, to worship their gods and to honor their great leaders. The end result of all of these policies and programs was the destruction of ancient forests, in the case of Mesopotamia the destruction of great grass savannahs and reed lands, and the loss of many natural resources associated with forests, all of which led to the creation and growth of arid nonproductive lands which eventually dried out and became deserts causing a significant reduction in the amounts of lands available to feed and house their people. Unfortunately, the ideals of organized societies have not changed much over time as modern societies also have the need to feed and house large populations, to build great monuments and places of worship, and to build great armies, all of which places greater pressure on forests and land resources due to the much larger human populations. Today the policies that govern our societies are no longer made by tribal elders or priests, but by national systems of governance in most countries, called the government, which is made of groups of elected and selected people who make the policies and decisions on major national issues and sometime even on minor things. The government in all modern societies make policies on all major economic activities inclusive of agricultural, forestry and timber, energy, mining, industrial developments, commercial and residential developments, recreational developments, general land use, social policies and taxation required to finance all of their program. All such policies while created with good intentions usually create many unintended consequences many of which do significant harm to forest and the environment.

Agricultural Policies

Agricultural policies that negatively impact forests varies from government policies on politics, trade, taxation, expenditure, land use, water, air and subsidies provided on inputs such as fertilizers, Mlay et al (2002). Each of the policy for the named areas can incentivize the farming community to plant more crops which would automatically require more land and according to the World Bank (1996) "Policy failures outside the forest sector may even be more important" indicating that while these policies never directly referenced forests, they usually have significant impact upon them.

Politics. The political policies and systems of governance under which a society is managed significantly affect agricultural policies and practices and consequently how agriculture impacts forests and the environment all around the globe. The different political systems of governance include Liberal Democracies, Totalitarian Fascism,

Totalitarian Communism, Socialism, Military Dictatorships and various combination and mixtures of these.

The policies of Liberal Democracies are to create and support property rights laws, support the right of individuals and corporations to make a profit and allowing market forces to determine the selling price of agricultural products and in this system the farmer decides what crop to plant, depending on market conditions, how to utilize available water, fertilizer and pesticides to produce their best crop. The farmer also gets to decide how, where and when to sell his products, all depending on where and when they can get the best prices. The policies in Communist and Socialist totalitarian states eliminate the property rights of individuals and corporations and the state become the sole owner of all property and all decisions about what, where and when to plant are usually determined by the state with the farmers only role being to follow instructions irrespective of market forces. These states are also responsible for the distribution of the products reaped and also sets the price for all products in the official market place. The other political systems inclusive of fascism and military dictatorships, all follow a mixture of the state driven and market driven agricultural policies, unfortunately however, even with their much-publicized differences, Capitalism/Fascism v Communism/Socialism, no political system of governance has yet developed a set of agricultural policies that will eliminate or minimize the impact of agriculture upon forests and the environment in general.

An examination of the policies and practices of liberal democracies like the US and Brazil will highlight the great negative impact that their agricultural policies and practices have had upon the forests of both nations. In the US approximately 80 years, 1862 – 1939, of erroneous agricultural policies led to one of the worst environmental and ecological disasters that the nation ever faced, the Great Dust Bowl. According to Baumhardt (2003) and other sources the Dust Bowl was caused by three US government policies, the introduction of mechanized farming implements, over preparation of soil, overgrazing and the inevitable drought on the great plains. The policies were the Homestead Act of 1862 which provided white immigrants settlers with 160 acres of public land (read Native American lands), the Kinkaid Act of 1904, an act increasing the amount of land to 640 acre from 160 acres under the Act of 1862 and the Enlarged Homestead Act of 1909, all of which led to a great influx of immigrant non-farmers, desiring to become farmers across the great plains and thereby facilitating the passage of the disaster that would be called the "Dust Bowl" which ran from 1930-1940. These laws were passed by politicians who promulgated the folly called "Manifest Destiny" which was designed to give control of all native lands to the European immigrants by any means necessary, including using European religion to make the preposterous claim that it was the Europeans "sacred right" to take Native American lands.

In the case of Brazil, a political decision to grow it economy through export agriculture has led to the country having the highest rate of deforestation in the world as more land is always required to increase its agricultural output to meet the demands on the international market and according to Assuncao et al (2016) "Deforestation is intricately tied to decisions on land use for agricultural production". As indicated in the data shown in Chapter 7, Brazil is currently one of the largest producers and exporters of agricultural products in the world and with its drive to gain and keep agricultural market share, there is no immediate end in view for rainforest deforestation and the Brazilian government recently confirmed this by reporting that the current rates of deforestation were at their highest levels in 11 years in 2019 (Elassar 2019). Of course, Brazil is not the only country in the world that has ever used their lands and forests in this manner, as the USA, China and the many great civilizations of the past have done the same thing.

An examination of the policies and practices of two totalitarian states, China and Russia, will also highlight the damaging effects that their policies have had on the environment. China has made great strides in improving its economy and improving the living standards of a very large portion of their population through its rapid industrialization policies that it has practiced over the last 40-50 years and these policies have facilitated China's economic growth at rates as high as 10% per annum for many decades. The rapid rate and sustained pace of growth has grown their economy to become the second largest in the world, second only to that of the United States, with projections for overhauling the US economy in short order. These achievements, however, came at very high environmental costs and China is currently faced with many significant environmental challenges that will take great effort and time, similar to what it took to achieve the climb to its current position or greater, to overcome if they approach the problems with the same zeal as they pursued rapid industrialization. China's many environmental challenges include the fact that it is the largest source of carbon emissions in the world, it has poor air quality in most of its major cities, significant problems with the contamination of and scarcity of water, significant land contamination, desertification and drifting sand dunes that are threatening to cover many of its major cities, towns and villages. According to Albert and Xu (2016) "China's environmental crisis is one of the most pressing challenges to emerge from the country's rapid industrialization". Russia, the former great communist totalitarian state, had its own set of spectacular environmental and ecological failures based on their state driven agricultural policies, one of which was the spectacular failure of the Aral Sea, a lake which is today only a miniscule reminder of its former self. According to Conrad and Kobildjanova (2011) up to 1960 the Aral Sea was the fourth largest lake in the world and it was supported by two mighty rivers, the Amu Darya 2600 km long and the Syr Darya 2,212 km long and the lake had no outflow points. The status of the Aral Sea changed rapidly beginning in 1960 with the creation of an agricultural policy that required the Soviet Union to become a great producer of cotton on a global scale and this policy required the creation of large agricultural project for growing cotton for export and directed that the waters from the two rivers which fed the Aral Sea, were to be utilized for irrigating of cotton the crops. This use of the waters from the two rivers led to the elimination of inflows into the lake with the following long-term effects:

- The depletion of the waters of the lake.
- Increased salinization of the lake water which killed all salt sensitive fish that had their home in the lake.
- The receding of the lake waters many miles from their original shorelines and water levels falling up to 26 meters below 1960s levels.

- The drying out of the lake bed leading to dusts storms that now frequently carry the now exposed concentrated levels of salt and agricultural chemicals, that was formerly at the bottom of the lake, into people's homes and places of work causing significant health problems.
- The migration of the local population away from their homes and livelihoods around the lake. These people usually lived around the lake and made their living working on or around it, had to relocate to escape the dust storms, to find new employment and also to improve their health.
- The splitting of the lake into four bodies of water as with falling water levels the once mighty Aral Sea broke into two bodies of water in 1987 and by 2009 broke into four smaller bodies.
- The total volume of water in Aral Sea has declined by 92 % from its level in 1960.
- The total area of the Aral Sea has declined by 88 % since 1960.
- Many species of natural flora and fauna indigenous to the lake have disappeared and may now be extinct.
- The climate of the regions has been significantly changed going now from extreme cold in winters to extreme heat in summers quite unlike the conditions prior to 1960.

All of the four cases described above indicate that irrespective of the political or economic systems that may prevail in a society, many of the policies made by the leaders of these societies quite often lead to disastrous negative impacts upon the natural environment inclusive of forests, flora and fauna.

Trade Policies. By definition trade is an economic concept and activity that involves the buying, selling or exchanging of goods and services with compensation paid by the buyer and received by the seller or the exchange or swopping of goods or services between parties. In most economies trade takes place regularly between producers and consumers, thus the consuming public purchases the farmers products. The more desirable a product the higher the chance that it will be traded frequently and thus we have bread being sold every day of the week all around the world to meet the most basic human demand for survival. The frequency of this bread been sold will be dependent upon the number of people needing bread, money or goods available for the exchange and the amount of wheat, the main component of the bread, that is available to make the bread. If there is not enough wheat available to make the bread one of several things will happen, inclusive of the fact that price of the available bread will increase, some people will starve and in order to meet the demand for more wheat more fields of wheat must be planted thus requiring more forests to be destroyed until the demand for bread is met or satiated. This demand for bread has been used to build many great empires both in the ancient past and during modern times as nations and peoples with fertile soils and good supplies of water have learnt to grow more than they can eat and to trade their surplus with people, from near and far, whose soils are not so fertile or whose climate is not suitable for growing particular crops or who do not have sufficient water. The creation of this surplus for trading places significant pressures on the forests of the selling nations and can sometimes lead to these selling nations becoming buying nations, if they ever deplete their forests and their soils.

The great empires of Mesopotamia were all built on trading their surplus agricultural goods which was created using their fertile soils and their world leading irrigation technologies, however, after extended intensive use over thousands of years this technology created an unforeseen disaster due to a technical oversight on the part of the irrigation systems designers, who did not include a proper field drainage system in their engineered irrigation plans. This oversight led to thousands of hectares of formerly very productive lands becoming contaminated with high levels of salts and the high levels of salts significantly reduced the capacity of the fields to the point where they were no longer productive and had to be abandoned even after substituting crops that were more tolerant to salt. These abandoned fields dried out over time and consequently loss much of their soil to wind erosion leaving the once very productive lands to become barren deserts. This very real situation highlights the fact that intense agriculture for trading can and has depleted many forests in the past, is depleting many in the present and is still capable of doing so way into the future. In modern jargon the law of supply and demand can make vast tracks of primary and secondary forests disappear in a short period of time. This is a lesson that the people of Malaysia and Brazil are still learning as they destroy their natural forests in their desire to expand their economies by increasing their output of specific agricultural products.

The trade, import and export, policies of most nations will determine how much land is used for producing agricultural and other tradable goods and how much forests are affected.

Tax Policies. According to the encyclopedia Britannica -Taxation is the imposition of compulsory levies on individuals and entities by governments with the aim of raising revenues for governmental expenditures on things such as the country's infrastructure, the education of its people, providing healthcare for its people, taking care of the poor and indigent and the defense of the nation. The methods and means by which taxes are collected are usually defined by the tax policies of the nation and these policies, which are usually key policy instruments, have the capacity to negatively or positively impact the ability of a nation to attract and retains investments on a long-term basis (OECD 2013). This ability to negatively or positively impact investments in the economy also applies to investments in the field of agriculture and consequently has the same ability to negatively or positively impact forests and the natural environment. According to Miller (2015) any tax provision that encourages the expansion of agriculture is encouraging the many changes that must occur to facilitate agriculture, such as the destruction of species, flora and fauna, the use of chemicals, such as fertilizer and pesticides, that are harmful to humans and the environment. Thus, it can be seen that even when tax policies are intended to benefit farmers, the farming industry, food processors and consequently the buying public the unintended consequences of these "good" tax policies does further harm to forests and the environment. For example, a reduction of the tax or increase in the subsidies on fertilizers will aid farmers to acquire and use more fertilizers in their fields to facilitate greater production per acre planted, however, using more fertilizer in the production of a crop will facilitate the further flow of fertilizers from the fields into ground and surface water sources which will contaminate the water source, causing harm to aquatic flora and fauna and consequently reducing or eliminating essential human food and water resources. We often see the effects of excess fertilizer use in algal blooms in our streams, rivers, lakes and even the oceans and also other similar unintended consequences occur when taxes on lands, pesticides or even seeds for planting are adjusted to benefit the farmer, the industry and consequently the consumer.

Subsidy Policies. According the Scott (Investopedia 2020) a subsidy is a benefit given to an individual or an institution by the government with the intent of alleviating a particular public burden, promoting some social good or economic policy and this subsidy is normally in the form of a direct cash award or a tax reduction for a particular period of time. According to Amadeo (2020) agricultural subsidies are financial benefits paid by governments to agribusinesses to offset the risks associated with the vagaries of weather, disease, brokers and any unexpected disruptions in demands. In agriculture these gifts are intended to do several things, two of which are promoting the expansion in particular crops or curtailing production of particular crops such as may happen if there is an over production of dairy products which may cause the price of dairy products in general to fall to an unsustainable level. In a case like this the government could pay the farmers to dump their milk production or in more dramatic cases to slaughter their herd of dairy cattle. In the US only five crops are subsidized, corn, soyabean, wheat, cotton and rice and the subsidies provided have some positive and some negative effects which are as follows. There are several important positives outcomes associated with subsidies however the most important ones are shown below.

- Subsidies helps to stabilize the production and delivery of essential foods to the market place and provides stable jobs directly on farms, the agricultural processing industry, agricultural equipment manufacturers, suppliers and maintenance contractors, agricultural chemical manufacturers and distributors, haulage contractors, supermarkets and farmers markets, hotels and restaurants.

- Subsidies helps the agricultural industry to become competitive in the world market as most industrialized nations subsidize their farmers for the same reasons, stability of food production to feed their population, maintaining a reasonable cost on basic food items and employment opportunities.
- Subsidies also provide a significant level of protection against the possibility of price spikes created by commodity trading and the many other risks associated with farming.

Agriculture, while absolutely important to human existence, has many aspects that can quite negatively impact human lives and the subsidies provided by governments can greatly enhance these negative impacts. Some of the negative impacts of subsidies are as shown below.

- The benefits provided by subsidies while very helpful to the agricultural industry can have a very negative impact as the subsidy is locked into the five protected crops and can force farmers into a cycle of producing one of these protected crops which limits their ability to make changes even if the changes could create improvements such as the benefits created by rotation of crops that is very healthy for the land and the environment. This can turn subsidies into golden handcuffs.
- Farm subsidies are great for farmers in the industrialized world but they can do great harm to farmers and the economies of non-industrialized nations, especially those nations whose GDPs are overly dependent upon agriculture production, providing in some cases 50% or more of their GDP. The subsidized production of wheat(flour), corn (flour, oil), soyabean(oil) and rice has over many years displaced the production of many indigenous sources of carbohydrates and oil in many developing economies leading to much damaged to their economies and the health of their populations as their crops of potatoes, sweet

potatoes, yams, plantains and bananas have been shown to be much healthier than some of the imported grains.

- The most significant negative impact of subsidies is the environmental harm that it fosters in agricultural practices worldwide. Some of the practices include monoculture crops, the extensive use of fertilizers and pesticides, the stabilization of agribusinesses which gives them the ability to borrow money to expand their farming operations which inevitably leads to the destruction or harm to more forests and local ecologies.

Agricultural subsidies, as shown above, can become double-edged swords, as with the subsidies the farmer gains stability, the ability to expand and produce more while at the same time they also gain more power to harm the local environment and the economy and health of other nations. Faced with these realities it is imperative that subsidy polices and the programs that governments generate be more closely managed to prevent them from causing further harm to the local environment and the economies and health of smaller nations, while helping farmers in the developed economies to grow more needed crops.

Expenditure Policies.

Governments all around the world carry out long-term forecasting and budgeting in order to decide the amount of money to be spent to maintain the status quo or to facilitate change and growth in their economies. The exercise to determine the amount of money to be spent over a fixed period of time is quite often a function of the system of politics that is practiced within each country, with totalitarian communist nations using a multiple year planning cycle, the liberal democracies using a single year planning cycle and others using a mixture of these systems. Whether multiple or single year planning cycles the decision about and the announcement of the projected expenditures for a particular period quite often determines the actions that will be taken by farmers, the farming industries and food processors for that particular period. For example, the announcement by the government that it will be providing financial support to increase the volume of ethanol produced and used to replace fossil fuels in automobile fuels would cause farmers to increase their acreage in corn or sorghum or whatever crop that can be used to efficiently produce ethanol. As a consequence of this announcement of the proposed expenditure, forests in the locale where these crops are to be grown will be automatically placed under stress as new fields must be cleared and more fertilizers and pesticides must be used to ensure that the added expenditure by the farmers will yield a significant reward for their efforts and all of these actions combined will significantly impact local forests, the local hydrological systems and the local environmental and ecological systems.

Land Use Policies.

Each country has a limited amount of land available to it and each must consequently determine as a sovereign nation how to best use its available lands and from this formulate the necessary policies and laws to ensure the consistent use of the lands to meet their national needs. The bases of these policies and laws will be a function of the natural resources within the boundaries of the nation and how to best utilize these resources to best serve the people and the needs of the nation. This would therefore imply that the land use policies of an oil rich desert nation will be much different from that of a nation that has few minerals but rich agricultural lands and even much more different from a nation that is rich in minerals and prime agricultural lands. In ancient and modern times, the main concerns of the societies were how to use all of their rich natural resources found in their country to make themselves and their families wealthy without the due concern of how making themselves wealthy impacts all life on planet Earth, however, in the current "Climate Change Era" this approach is slowly but surely changing to recognize that the reaping of great wealth will be of no benefit to anyone if there is no place to enjoy it in.

According to the USEPA "Land Use" is the term used to describe human use of land and that the main uses of land usually fall under one of two categories of uses economic or cultural activities. Under the economic category there are activities such as agriculture, forestry, industrial and commercial activities, residential activities and mining, while under the cultural category there would be activities such as recreation, music and the arts, educational and spiritual pursuits.

Throughout early human history the use of land has been human centered, designated only to meet the needs of human societies and civilizations without any thoughts towards the many other forms of life that share the planet Earth, even the many other forms of life which are critical to continued human existence on planet Earth. The development of the need to designate land for particular purposes, Land Use Planning, began with some of the earliest civilizations with the dedication of arable lands close to fresh water for agricultural purposes, the dedication of less fertile areas for the development of urban centers inclusive of residences, palaces, government offices, temples and monuments. The many cities of the Indus Valley Civilization were all laid out on a grid and is a clear indication that significant land use planning took place during this era. The walled cities of Babylonia and the other Mesopotamian civilizations are also very clear indications that ancient planners were at work trying to make best use of the land available to them, unfortunately while these plans sustained these civilizations for millennia, these plans lacked many essential elements as the long-term results were the creation overused lands that succumbed to the forces of desertification which left large swaths of lands in these nations as barren hot deserts. The results obtained by ancient planners were not unique to them as even modern planners have quite often created problems similar to those that their ancient forebearers did, with some of their plans lacking the same essential elements inclusive of plans for continuity beyond the foreseeable futures for generations of human and animal existence that almost every planner thought was too far down the road for consideration.

The current era of existence now demands planning for future generations to ensure that they too will enjoy the many beauties and pleasures to be found in natural life on planet Earth and requires that all modern land use policy makers and land use planners create plans that will ensure Sustainable Land Management (SLM). According to the UNCCD Sustainable Land Management (SLM) is the adoption of land use systems that through appropriate management practices, enable land users to maximize the economic and social benefits of land, while maintaining or enhancing the ecological support functions of its resources, inclusive of soil, water, vegetation and animals. For sustainable land use practices to be established governments must create policies to support and enforce sustainable land management.

Water Policies.

Water is life, particularly fresh potable water, as the bodies of all living things, plants and animals, are made up of a very large percentage of water and this water must be replenished on a very regular basis or all species will die. In the humans, water makes up approximately 70-90 % of total body content (UNESCO) with the amount of water varying in each individual depending on age, health, other factors and according to UNESCO humans need 2.5 liters of water per day to sustain a healthy life. The amount of water contained in plants varies depending on species and similar to animal life, all plants need water to stay alive, grow, produce and reproduce. Ancient agriculture, the foundation of all civilizations and one of the main sources of vital nutrients for early humans, was built upon great supplies of water from some of the largest rivers in the world inclusive of the Mississippi, the Amazon, the Euphrates, the Tigris, the Indus, the Yellow, the Rhine, the Danube, the Nile, the Niger and the Zambezi. All of these rivers served large land masses and in many cases many nations such as occurs on:

- Continental Africa which has many large rivers inclusive of the Nile, Niger and Zambesi which serves up to 55 nations.
- Asia Minor has many rivers inclusive of the Euphrates and Tigris that serves six nations,
- India which has many rivers inclusive of the Indus and the Ganges that serves two nations
- China has many rivers inclusive of the Yangtze, Yellow, Mekong and one, the Mekong, that serves six nations.
- Continental Europe has many rivers inclusive of the Rhine and the Danube that serves many nations.

Separate and apart from the many national boundaries that these many rivers cross, they may also cross many different tribal boundaries with everyone demanding equal or superior access to this most important and precious commodity. Access to water while essential to life was not and is not always freely available to all people, as people with might usually dictated the terms on which less capable people got their water and these terms many times included subservience, monetary payments or complete subjugation by force of arms and while these situations still prevail in many places more modern times has seen the development of legally binding water sharing treaties and agreements between tribes and nations. Unfortunately, these nation-to-nation treaties and agreements do not always settle tribal differences about the sharing of water, which are usually settled at the tribal levels. The tribal agreements usually included animal watering for the tribes and people with large herds of grazing animals as historically, the absence of agreed terms and conditions did lead to skirmishes and conflicts among herdsmen of different tribes.

According to the US EPA the amount of water available on the planet Earth has not changed since the beginning of time, however, anthropogenic activities have significantly impacted the operation of the hydrological cycle over time and the impacts can be seen in the many areas where intense agriculture was practiced which resulted in the problems of forest fragmentation, forest degradation, deforestation, droughts, desertification and eventually the absence of water, plant and animal life.

The critical nature of water and the possibilities of the creation of significant health problems and conflicts, has forced the development of many policies and treaties governing the use of water in every nation and among nations. These policies included keeping water resources clean, maintaining watershed areas to encourage adequate rainfall, the distribution of water for human consumption, distribution of water for agriculture and industry, the equitable sharing of irrigation waters, the treatment of water for human consumption, the treatment of wastewater, the protection of surface and groundwater sources, the protection of aquatic flora and fauna, the sharing of water resources where rivers and lakes are shared by nations or states within a federation/federal system, or counties within a state or cities within a county, controlling the outflow of water from each source and controlling the purposes for which the water can be used.

The inequitable sharing of water by nations connected to great rivers remains a problem today as demonstrated by two very important long running cases that are still being discussed, the sharing of water in the middle east by Israel, Syria and Jordan and the use of the waters of the Nile River by Ethiopia, Sudan and Egypt. In each of these cases swords have been rattled and many threats made that could have resulted in conflict, however, policies, treaties and agreements have helped to prevent any real outbreak of physical conflicts thus far. In the case of the Nile which is very current, the Egyptian leader President Abdel Fatah al-Sisi is using very strong words to prevent Ethiopia from utilizing water which originates within Ethiopia's borders "Nobody will be permitted to take a single drop of Egypt's water, otherwise the region will fall into unimaginable instability" (AP). Mr. al-Sisi water policy could be considered to be tantamount to war mongering and it is very hard to understand as Egypt has built more than one dam on the Nile and Sudan has done the same yet he is enraged that the Ethiopians dares to desire to use waters that originates within its borders to the benefit of the Ethiopian peoples. The stance taken by all the nations involved highlights the need for new policies and treaties to immediately resolve this conflict as the conflicting water policies of each nation could become barriers to their peaceful coexistence.

In ancient times the main concern was the sharing of water resources for human consumption, animal watering and irrigation for agriculture, however, with the coming of the industrial age and the development of many destructive policies by industry and government, the need arose to develop more broad-based policies and to remove control of the many water resources from private hands. Among the greatest folly of the industrial age was the development and acceptance of policies that paved the way for industries to dump their waste, of every nature, into rivers, streams and lakes that were the main source of water for millions of people downstream of their operations, and these policies led to loss of human lives, the contamination of water resources, the contamination of the food chain and the destruction of much flora and fauna. Unfortunately, even with the development of policies and laws prohibiting certain behaviors, many destructive industrial practices are still being used today as some mining operations and their owners are still causing harm to many surface and groundwater sources with their mine tailings and chemicals used in processing even in the face of laws that prohibit such activities.

The dumping of industrial wastes into surface and ground water bodies are not the only the industrial policies which cause harm to water bodies and aquatic life, as the policies allowing the use of the kinetic and potential energy of moving water to create electrical energy, hydropower, technically a relatively clean form of renewable electrical energy production, have also caused and is causing significant harm to the environment, flora and fauna.

Forestry and Timber Policies

Every or almost every government in the world has a policy that dictates how, where and when the natural forestry that is endemic to its country may be utilized or destroyed to meet the economic and environmental needs of their nation, however, this does not mean that these policies are always enforced as intended as sometimes even institutions under the control of these governments infringe upon the established policies and associated regulations while making changes in other areas or when a new natural resource, metal or mineral, has been located. Historically the forestry and timber policies of governments, in nations where the concept of the free-market economy was paramount, were to allow almost every business or highly connected group to run wild reaping all the forests they could as quickly as they could, a policy that eventually led to the decimation of forest in Europe in the 18th century and 100 years later in the US. This policy was only changed in Europe when they realized that they were running out of wood to fire their newly established manufacturing plants. In the US the free market was allowed to destroy almost every forest from Maine to California and the reaping of forests only stopped when the reapers came upon the Pacific Ocean. Policy changes came in Europe after the near disaster of running out of wood and was as a result of private efforts to save industry which led to the beginning of the art and science of silviculture that eventually saved European forestry. In the US it also took the efforts of many private citizens to pressure their government to change its policies and call a halt to marauding US businessmen that were wantonly destroying forests for profit. The group of private citizens include men like John Muir, Ralph Waldo Emerson, David Henry Thoreau and James Audubon, all with different naturalist interests, but whose combined voices help to awake the conscience of the American society which forced the hands of American politicians.

In general, most forests today are operated and managed to produce timber and other forests products to meet the needs of the society in which they exist and for trading with external entities and these activities must be carried out while working under a national or local set of environmental policies and regulations, while at the same time abiding by the internal environmental policies of the organization associated with the forestry activity. The policies governing the operation of forestry businesses usually cover the following:

- The protection and preservation of existing forests and trees to ensure viability of all forests for future generations.
- The protection of the local environment
- The protection of the local ecology
- The protection of the ecological heritage, endemic flora and fauna
- Protection and preservation of the environmental services provided by forests and trees inclusive of clean potable water and clean air.
- Protection of surface and groundwater sources, inclusive of ponds, lakes, rivers, streams and aquifers.
- Protection of aquatic flora and fauna that have their habitat in lakes, rivers, stream and ponds.
- Protection of coastal regions and the aquatic flora and fauna in coastal regions
- Enhancement and protection of the economic and social benefits that may be earned from forest and trees, inclusive of timber and other forest products.

- Protection of avian and insect species.
- Protection of animals that reside in trees and other land animals which are endemic to local forests.

In addition to the many forestry and timber policies, the forestry and timber industries are also impacted by the same governmental policies as agriculture inclusive of political, trade, tax, subsidy, expenditure, land use and water and these policies will also significantly the forestry and timber business of the nation.

Energy Policy

Heating and lighting energies have always been and continue to be very essential to the existence of all life forms on planet Earth with the initial source of both heating and lighting energies being the Sun whose energy was all that was required to create and sustain life. However, the earliest climate changes brought about the need for additional sources of energy as many places became too cold for human habitation without additional sources of both heat and light. The material first chosen by humans to produce the required heat and light would have been material that humans had seen burn during lightening events, dried leaves, straw, dried dung and dried wood, and the use of these material would continue for millennia until the growing activities of humans would lead them to other material that could be burnt to generate as much heat and light, or greater, than fuelwood and the other materials did.

The dependence on fuelwood as the major source of energy became a part of most early civilizations and this dependence became even greater with the coming of the industrial age, starting in the 1700s, when the demand for fuelwood to provide heat and light beyond domestic requirements grew exponentially and the growth continued until other fuel materials such as coal were discovered to have similar or greater heat and light generation properties. According to Chan (2015) recent archeological finds at Xinjiang in China indicates that coal had been used as early as 3500 years ago for domestic heating purposes while its industrial use started later at a mine in Fusan around 1000 BCE.

This initial use of coal by the Chinese fostered the dawning of a new energy age that facilitated the end of the overwhelming dependence upon wood and slowed down the rate of destruction of natural forests, very small impact at first. The reports also indicated that the region of China where the archeological find was made did not have a lot of trees and coal, which was plentiful in the region, was used as a substitute. However, this new fuel was not utilized in Europe until 100-200 AD when the Romans used coal extensively for heating in England but its use did not grow much beyond this at that time as the rest of the country still had substantial supplies of wood.

The decimation of forests across Europe and later the US after the start of the industrial revolution forced these nations to seek and utilize alternative sources of energy and the most attractive solution was coal which occurred in copious amounts in both Europe and the US. This change of focus to coal, however, did not completely eliminate the use of wood within industry or on the domestic front, as many industrial processes such as the making of steel found that charcoal, a derivative of wood, made a much better steel and on the domestic front harsh economic circumstances made free wood gathered from forest the main fuel for the poor in the nations that allowed peasants to gather wood freely. In fact, the use of wood has continued into modern times even with the discovery, development and use of many new forms of fuels inclusive coal, oil, gas, nuclear, wind, solar, wave, geothermal and hydrogen fuel systems. Wood has remained a major source of energy for people all around the globe from the richest to the poorest nations and it is still used as a source of fuel in the US, the nation with the world's richest economy, and according to the US Energy Information Administration (2020) up to 2.5 million (2.1%) US households use wood as their primary heating fuel, while 9.0 million (7.7%) households use it as their secondary heating fuel and according to the FAO, in the rural areas of places like India, Pakistan, Cambodia, and the Philippines fuelwood use ranges from 59- 95% of the rural populations.

The physiological needs of all humans dictates that they all need heating and lighting energy for their daily existence and the recognition of this need has been addressed by the leaders and governments of most nations in the form of policies that are designed to ensure the delivery of required energy to most people within their respective nations. Unfortunately, the energy policies of many nations do not address the needs of the poorest people, the rural poor, as many people at this level still have to scrounge for wood wherever it is to be found, even to the environmental detriment of the country. The energy policies of most nations are usually focused on

- The delivery of electrical energy to meet the industrial, commercial, institutional, educational, urban and suburban residential needs of their nation. The provision of electrical energy in the rural areas of most countries is still not a fait accompli, but a work in progress.
- The primary sources of energy that produces this electrical energy usually includes the fossil fuels (coal, oil, gas) nuclear energy, hydropower, solar energy, wind energy and geothermal energy, with the fossil fuels producing the bulk of electrical energy all around the world. According to USEIA fossil fuel produces approximately 81% percent of electrical energy generated around the world during 2018.

The energy policies of most nations in the past, were focused on the delivery of the energy required to meet the national needs and were less focused on

- The environmental impact caused by the delivery of the fuel from the point of location of the primary energy source to the point at which it will be processed or utilized,
- The impact on the local environment in which the primary energy source is converted into electrical energy ready for delivery to customers.
- The environmental impact of the electrical energy and gas distribution systems upon the environment.

In the current climate change era, however, most nations are now attuned to the impact their use of fossil fuels are having on the environment and most are attempting to transition into using more environmentally friendly, sustainable and renewable energy sources and have revised their national policies to reflect the new future. Now as in the past, the decisions made by energy policy makers will continue to greatly impact the environment in which we all live, however, now the policy makers have a greater menu of energy sources to choose from, each of which will have its own impact on the environment. The policy makers job will now be to select the best combination of sources to meet their energy needs, to reduce their greenhouse gas emission, to reduce their impact on the environment and consequently play their role in keeping the global temperature rise below 1.5°C. The negative impact of the fuels from which they must make their energy choice are discussed below.

Fossil Fuels (coal, oil and gas). These fuels have the potential to negatively impact the environment at all points during handling and management inclusive of during extraction, transportation, processing, distribution, storage and ultimately consumption. During the extraction, transportation, processing, distribution and utilization of these fuels, very large volumes of fuel are consumed and very large volumes of carbon dioxide are emitted into the atmosphere, combined with the continuous risks of spilling at every stage of handling and utilization, marks these fuels as environmentally very risky to continue using. The goal of all current energy policies must be to minimize the use of fossil fuels based on their obvious negative impact on the environment, unless requisite technology can be created to prevent spilling and the emission carbon dioxide, particulate matter and all other criteria pollutants into the atmosphere.

During the last 20 years many energy policies have been modified to reduce or eliminate the use of all the fuels that are responsible for the increasing levels of the greenhouse gases, like carbon dioxide, in the atmosphere or there has been the introduction of policies requiring the use of technologies, such as decarbonization, that will capture and safely sequester the carbon dioxide emitted by the offending fuels. The target of these policies is the carbon rich fossil fuels, coal, oil and gas, with gas a cleaner burning fuel than coal and oil, being projected to be the transition fuel until the maturity of the cleaner renewable fuels and technologies. These new energy policies are the foundation upon which the fight against global warming and climate change are being waged on a global scale and has the support of the global bodies concerned with the negative impact that an increase of 2 °C globally could have on life and continuity of life globally.

In the modern and industrialized world, the main source of lighting and heating energy has become electricity which is derived from one of many fuel sources inclusive of coal, oil, gas, nuclear, wind, solar, hydro and geothermal energy along with several other sources that may soon become mainstream inclusive of utility-scale batteries, hydrogen fuel cells and other hydrogen technologies. In the current "climate change" era the policy of all governments and international bodies should be the reduction or elimination of the use of fossil fuels inclusive of coal, oil and eventually natural gas to reduce or eliminate the excess carbon dioxide in the atmosphere that is responsible for global warming and consequently the oncoming climate change. To achieve this goal all national energy policies must reflect a transition to sustainable, renewable non-carbon producing alternative sources of energy, inclusive of Solar Photovoltaic, Solar Thermal, Wind – onshore and offshore, Hydrogen Systems, Geothermal, Hydropower, Battery Power and nuclear power.

Unfortunately, all of these alternative systems, while not producing high levels of global warming carbon dioxide, have significant flaws that could still negatively impact the natural environment, humans, flora and fauna. Some of the flaws are shown below.

Solar Photovoltaics (PV). Large utility-scale solar photovoltaic power plants require extremely large volumes of land for installing the solar collection panels and facilities to house staff, batteries, transformers, switches and other solar power plant accessories needed to produce required volumes of electricity to serve industrial facilities and megacities. According to Ong et al (2013) of NREL, the total land required for photovoltaic systems ranges from a low of 7.6 – 9.1 acres/MWac for small PV plants and 7.5- 8.3 acres/MWac for large solar plants. Therefore, for a Solar PV plant generating 1000 MW the total land required would be 7500- 8300 acres which according to the Nuclear Energy Institute would be 10% more than the land required for an equivalent nuclear power plant. This large acreage of land would be exclusively used by the power plant as plants, trees, birds and land animal could impact the capacity of the plant which implies that the required lands must be cleared of all possible obstruction if the location is not already a bare desert or an abandoned or unused farm land. According to Gunerhan et al (2008) these large fields of solar panels could affect the local environment and ecology by disturbing sensitive ecosystem, delicate biodiversity, the thermal balance of the locale and the aesthetics of the surroundings. The absence of plants and trees will also ensure a loss of species with the loss of habitat and a significant disruption in the local hydrological systems as well.

Concentrated Solar Plants (CSP). The land requirements for these systems vary depending on the technology used and are as follows. Linear Fresnel 4.7 acres/MWac, Dish Sterling 10 acres/MWac, Tower 10 acres/MWac and Parabolic Trough 9.5 acres/MWac. CSP plants have greater land requirements and therefore multiplies the negative impacts of PV plants, while at the same time increasing the possible dangers to birds, bats and insects with their concentrated beams of solar energy.

Wind onshore and offshore. According to Denholm et al (2009) "There is no uniform definition of the total area of a wind power plant" however from the many projects examined, total required areas fall into general categories of direct impact of 1+/- 0.7 hectare/MW and a total area of 34+/- 22 hectare/MW depending on the type of land cover and topography. This great demand for land causes the wind power plants to affect the environment and ecology systems onshore with the main impact being the footprint of the towers, the permanent and temporary roads and temporary construction facilities. All of these activities require modification to the landscape involving the removal of trees, shrubs and other natural plant life and the harm becomes greater when natural forest lands are utilized in this way. These power plants also represent a problem operationally as the turbine blades have killed many species of birds and bats and according to the National Wind Coordinating Collaborative(NWCC) (2010) and Stewart et al (2004 & 2007) birds are generally impacted by the wind turbines in two ways, direct mortality from collision with turbines, meteorological towers and power distribution lines and indirectly from the avoidance of a location, habitat disruption, reduced nesting and breeding density and behavioral effects. For bats the dangers are direct collision and barotrauma, the harm the reduced pressure causes to the internal organs of the bats NWCC (2010) and Baerwald et al (2008). The Danish Energy Authorities, based on their experiences at two major offshore wind farms at Horns Rev and Nysted, have reported minimal negative impacts on aquatic flora and fauna with the exception of one species, harbor porpoises which left during construction of one of the major farms and have stayed away since.

Hydrogen Systems. Hydrogen system have been promoted by many scientists and engineers as the ideal fuel for the future as it is very clean and the only exhaust that it will ever emit is water or water vapor, however, there are a few issues that are also associated with hydrogen. Some of these issues are:

- Hydrogen is not freely available and it is only available as a part of many compounds such as water, H_2O, or the fossil fuels which are hydrocarbons which all contain different amounts of hydrogen. Hydrogen may be separated from these compounds by different methods such as the electrolysis of water, steam reformation of natural gas, partial oxidation of methane, coal gasification and biomass gasification, but these separation methods require high levels of energy to achieve and the energy utilized could be more than the energy that hydrogen will produce.

- Water, H_2O, is however, the only clean source of hydrogen as the other sources, the fossil fuel hydrocarbons, are all rich sources of GHGs that include Methane (CH_4), Ethane (C_2H_6), propane (C_3H_8) and butane (C_4H_{10}) which are all combinations of carbon and hydrogen for these highlighted gases and a combination of carbon, hydrogen, sulfur, oxygen and nitrogen for the other hydrocarbons depending on the locations from which they are sourced. All of these hydrocarbons will produce carbon dioxide the main greenhouse gas, when they are oxidized.

- In a hydrogen economy, with large volume of hydrogen being transported and used everywhere, there will be significant leaks and these leaks will significantly increase the amount of hydrogen in the atmosphere with the strong probability of directly impacting atmospheric chemistry and the dynamics of the other elements in the atmosphere. According to Derwent (2018) High levels of hydrogen in the atmosphere could affect "stratospheric ozone depletion through its moistening of the atmosphere and contribute to climate change through increasing the growth rates of methane and tropospheric ozone".

Geothermal Energy. Geothermal energy is on the surface an ideal source of free, relatively cheap renewable energy, but even this benign looking source of energy has some negative impacts upon the environment that must be given due consideration during the design and implementation stages of creating a geothermal power plant. Some of the environmental impacts includes

- Emission into the atmosphere of gases likes hydrogen sulfide, methane, ethane, propane and carbon dioxide,
- The use of high volumes of water and the impact of wastewater on surroundings,
- The impact of the power plant location and operation on wildlife and vegetation
- The impact of solid waste discharge into the environment,
- The land use requirement per MW of power produced and the impact of seismic activity and landslides caused by the development and construction of the site.

Hydropower Plants. Hydropower plants utilize the potential and kinetic energy of water to create relatively cheap and clean electrical energy for use in industrial and residential facilities, however, the creation of the facilities required to utilize the natural energies contained in water leave significant impact upon the environment, ecology, aquatic life, avian life, forests and trees. Some of the damage done to create hydropower plants includes

- The destruction of hundreds to thousands of square miles of natural habitats for many species of birds, insects and animals,
- The destruction of millions of trees and other natural forest cover,
- The disruption of the hydrological cycle,
- The disruption of the life cycle of many species of aquatic life forms that may have led to the extinction of many
- The destruction of many human habitats and historical sites.

Utility-Scale Battery Storage. Utility-scale battery storage is essential for all intermittent sources of power inclusive of solar energy and wind energy systems as they allow the collection and storage of excess electrical energy when solar and wind systems are performing at peak levels during the day and the release of this energy onto the grid after the hours of sunset, from these intermittent systems. In a comparison of the environmental impacts with gas utility power back up for intermittent systems, Balakrishnan et al (2019) found that as it relates to water eutrophication, "BESS (Battery Energy Storage Systems) showed a significant increase in impact compared to natural gas power due to raw material and production of the battery. The land use requirements for these battery storages will also be fairly high and will impact birds, bats, insects and other wildlife within the locale.

From the above it can be seen that policies will be required to determine the mix of energy sources that each government should utilize to meet their national energy needs while also meeting their international responsibility towards climate change. Therefore, a country with fossil fuel resources should have policies requiring the utilization of decarbonization technology to mitigate against large carbon emissions into the atmosphere and countries without fossil fuel resources should have policies that seek to optimize the use of renewable energy resources along with any necessary minimal fossil fuel, preferably natural gas, to maintain base loads. The energy policies of even fossil fuel rich nations must also must also give consideration to the use of other technologies inclusive of nuclear energy and future technologies such as fusion technologies and their possible impacts upon the nation and their environment.

In addition to the many policies governing the extraction and use of the many sources of energy the energy industries are also impacted by the same governmental policies as agriculture inclusive of political, trade, tax, subsidy, expenditure, land use and water and these policies will also significantly the forestry and timber business of the nation.

Mining Policies

The economic value of mining and mining related activities have morphed and grown significantly over the last three hundred years starting with the great growth in the use of iron and its related alloys in the fabrication and construction of items varying from the artistic to the everyday mundane. Iron and its many derivatives were not new material at the onset of the industrial revolution as they had existed and had been utilized for centuries, however, with the coming of the industrial revolution the utilization of iron and its related alloys, especially steel, exploded with the design and construction of a wide variety of items inclusive of ships, locomotives and rail systems, industrial and domestic heating and heat distribution systems, furniture, weaponry and even basic household items such as pot, pans, plates, cups, knives and forks. The great growth in the use of steel was later followed by a growth in the use of many other metals that have since become indispensable in all modern economies. The growth in the use iron and its derivative became even greater with the discovery of and the development of technologies to facilitate the utilization of fossil fuels to drive the wheels of the many new developments in the new industrial age.

Mining as an economic endeavor is many thousands of years old as many early civilizations had become enamored with the early group of "precious" metals inclusive gold, copper and silver and the "precious" stones inclusive of diamonds, rubies, pearls and garnets, all of which have maintained their places as precious items to be prized above all else inclusive of life-giving water, food and medicine throughout all ages and most civilizations. Only a few ancient civilizations did not highly prize these "precious" items and they only gave scant regards to them until they encountered the nations that sought them voraciously and would go out of their way to destroy peoples and nations to possess them. The transition into the industrial age and more urban societies gave greater value to these "precious" items and their relative scarcity when compared with pottery, China, farm products, timber, animals and the other metals gave them even greater economic and monetary value. These increased values made these precious metals and stones economically and socially very valuable to all nations that possessed them and made them want to possessed even more to bolster their "place" in the world.

This desire to possess more "precious" things became the driving force that saw many nations create policies to rob and steal, maim and murder, annihilate and destroy everyone that stood between them and these "precious" items as happened when the Spanish located the Americas and when England captured and colonized India, great parts of Africa, Australia, New Zealand and the Caribbean Islands. The location of these new worlds filled with these precious items was by itself not very satisfactory to the Spanish as the items that they sought were already owned by the native peoples of these lands and the Spanish had to devise new policies of how to transfer these precious items from the natives to their royal households in Spain and these new policies included of wholesale slaughter and genocide of the native peoples. These policies however required an adjustment of the very tenor of their religious systems of belief, as these belief systems clearly declared "thou shall not kill" and "thou shall not steal", which were the only tools available to them if the Spanish were to get the precious gold, silver and gemstones of the indigenous people of the Americas. One such policy that was devised to quiet their consciences stated that these natives were not really as human as Europeans were, therefore "God" made it ok for Europeans to kill, destroy and enslave them to get the gold, silver and gemstones. This policy even gave them the power to be inhumanely cruel, low, mean and willing to work their fellow human beings to death, without adequate food and water. In order to optimize their take of precious goods, policies were even devised to state the amounts of precious items to be shipped home each trip, the ships to be used, the route to travel to get home and the number people to be responsible for the transportation of the Queen's or King's precious items. Unfortunately for the Spanish, the English, Dutch and French were also devising their own set of mining policies to relieve the treasure ships on their way home. These mining policies were later modified after the signing of treaties between these nations and new policies had to be created on how to acquire gold, silver and precious stones without robbing their fellow Europeans.

In North America, the Spanish had only found very small portions of the available gold and mineral wealth and the policy of the new British government on how to acquire the wealth of the natives, after the expulsion of the Spanish empire, was go kill the natives and find all the mineral wealth of the continent, a policy that was quite successful as they decimated the Native Americans and filled Fort Knox with gold, built the largest oil companies in the world and built some of the largest mining, processing and metal trading companies in the world. In today's modern economic environment most of these old-style mining policies are no longer viable, as most of the natives all around the world are dead and passed into history and most of the mineral rich lands are in the hands of the invaders. From available evidence, however, the new policies of most mining companies, aided and abetted by most governments, appear to remain in the same grab, rob and go vein, in other words just get the gold, silver, diamond, pearls, iron, copper, bauxite, uranium, coal, gas, oil and all of the very valuable items out of the ground and move on to the next mineral rich location. All of which must be done with minimal concerns about the people that inhabit the location, soil conditions, forests, wildlife, rainfall, surface and subsurface water systems. The evidence of this mind set is highlighted by the number of mine tailing piles and mud lake locations around the world, the number of recorded and unrecorded fish kills and the decimation of other aquatic species associated with the use of mercury, cyanide, arsenic and sodium hydroxide spills associated with gold and bauxite mining activities. The acknowledged harm done by mining activities must also include the amount of droughts suffered in mined out lands all around the world, the loss of potable water due to contamination from mining operations, the loss of livelihood, displacement of native people and the loss of species caused by associated mining operations.

According to Crawford (2015) there can be no question of the importance of mining activities to the economic growth and development of nations as it generates jobs, creates revenues for governments to provide healthcare, education and infrastructures for their nations. It also facilitates the development of a more skilled workforce and it provides profits for the private companies that most governments that own mineral resources utilize to extract, process and sell the final products of mining. However, mining as an endeavor cannot stand by itself and it must be managed to ensure that it can be integrated in a seamless sustainable economy, where it leaves all mined out locations as green, verdant oases of life that all local species can once again thrive in as they did prior to the advent of mining activities, a condition that is now the policy of all mining institutions around the globe. If these policies advocated by mining institutions are to be of value, they must be matched by the national policies of all nations with mineral wealth and mining operations, as private companies will attempt to satisfy the needs of their policies and regulations by doing only the minimum required or less if allowed to, as is happening currently in many areas of the world. In addition to the many policies and regulations governing mining, the mining industry is also impacted by many other government policies inclusive of political, trading, taxation, subsidies, expenditure, water and air and land use.

Climate Change Policies

The global nature of the climate change phenomena dictates that the problems associated with it cannot be resolved by the policies and regulations of any one nation, no matter how wealthy, as the problem is global in nature affecting all 197 sovereign member states of the United Nation (UN) and requires the participation of all to make their contribution to the resolution of the problem by managing the related problems within their own boundaries, by creating or adopting policies and programs, similar to those recommended at the highest levels of international governance, to manage or eliminate source of greenhouse gases (GHGs) and all other factors that has precipitated the problems of global warming and consequently climate change. Historical evidence indicates that global cooperation of this nature is quite feasible as was demonstrated with the problems related to ozone depleting substances (ODS) and its resolution utilizing the policies created under the Montreal Protocol, which was created and approved by all members states of the UN. The Paris Agreement is very similar in nature to the Montreal Protocol and with all member states working together the problems associated with human influenced climate change will be successfully managed and eliminated over time.

CHAPTER

12

Forests Restoration Projects

Forest and trees have over time come to be seen by most humans as commodities to be monetized through their conversion into one of several forms inclusive of timber, fuel wood and pulp for paper or the monetization of the crops which they produce inclusive of fruits and nuts. The trees, however, that are not good for conversion to pulp or timber or which produce no edible crops are usually viewed as lacking value and therefore not worth growing or keeping. The commoditization of forests and trees can have both positive and negative long-term impacts upon the environment as the positive impacts will ensure that so long as there is a human population there will be a need for forests and their products and all effort will be made by producers to ensure that these needs are met. On the negative side, however, the trees that do not meet these existing criteria and for which humans have not yet discovered their true "economic" value stands a very good chance that they will be eliminated or their presence minimized in the environment and this action will negatively impact flora and fauna which are dependent on such trees. We have seen in the recent past and in current times the implementation of such practices with many forests being replanted with only one species of trees, a specie that has high commercial value, to optimize the value for the owner of the forests, however, this folly has been recognized for the damage that it can do and many nations and institutions have tried to apply the brakes to this practice.

While the heavy commodity bias towards forests and trees still exists, there has been significant movement in the last 300 years or more to use trees in a more economically prudent manner to ensure that there will be sufficient trees available to continue meeting the economic needs of modern society and filling their roles of providing protection and food to humans, animals and the environment. This transition started with the recognition by humans that the natural forests were disappearing due to overuse and that there may not be enough timber for future generations. This recognition forced the industrialists of that era, among the highest users of timber at that point in time, to acknowledged that humans were using timber much faster than it was being produced in forests (von Carlowitz 1713) in each country and that recognition led to the need for a more scientific approach towards the use of existing forests and also forced a change in attitude towards forests and trees. These early thinkers realized that to be able to meet the timber demands for their current and future operations they had to get a handle on how much timber was required for their operations annually, how much timber was available and how much would need to be planted to meet their present and future demands. One of the first step required to establish the actual number of trees available for use by industry and others, was to do a physical count of trees and according to LaBau et al (2007) "The first record of a statewide, in the US, forest inventory was in 1830 in Massachusetts" as reported by Cameron (1928). This first forest inventory in the US was an effort to inventory the forest supply of trees and based on the then existing usage patterns that were developing, make some projections about the future availability of timber. This survey and many others like it done earlier in Europe, sowed the seeds for the development of the practice and science of what would be later called forestry, which was said to be an art born of necessity and not of pleasure. Fernow (1911) stated it like this "... the development of the forestry idea belongs essentially to the 19th century and more specifically to the second half, when the rapid development of railroads had narrowed the world and the remarkable development of industries and material civilization called for increased draft on forest resources". Thus, the art of forestry was developed not to preserve forests or the environment but only to fill the gap that had been created by the great draft of new industries, so industry took, and in an effort to continue replicating itself, industry gave back. This narrow focus on the needs of industry only saw the development of monoculture forests that were planned and planted only to meet the specific needs of industry, without due consideration about the best interest of the environment.

In more recent times the focus of the forestry industry and related government agencies has been broadened significantly to include much greater use of the art and science of forestry to include such things as:

- Using trees to clean up and recondition the air and water in urban centers.
- Using trees to prevent both water and wind soil erosion and countering the effects of desertification.
- Using trees to clean up chemically polluted sites.
- Using trees to control and clean up storm water flows.

This shift in focus has also included the development of policies for the sustainable growing and reaping of forests and the elimination of monoculture forests as a sustainable solution to forestry and environmental problems.

Urban Trees

The creation stories of many early civilizations indicate that the first humans came to life in a garden, an early forest, where trees and plants provided the required oxygen for humans to take their first breaths and where they continued life in the natural shelter provided by forests along with the first sources of nutrition inclusive of edible plants, fruits, nuts and animals that sustained human life for many thousands of years. This relationship between humans and the forest, with the forest as the provider and home or a place of solace, continued for many millennia even after humans had moved away from living directly under the forest canopies and started living together in villages or communities that were in close proximity to the forests. This move away only impacted the relationship in a small way as the forest still acted as a rich larder that humans continuously returned to for food in the form of fruits, nuts, protein (in the form of fowl, deer, hog, fish), vegetables and starchy tubers before the development of agriculture. Unfortunately, the development of agriculture required the destruction of vast amounts of forests further separating humans from their natural homes, while providing them with a more consistent source of nutrition. The consistent and greater availability of foods and forest products in a modern society has, however, never dulled the need in humans to return to their ancestral homes for regular topping up that only a forest environment can provide through activities like fishing in that quiet stream, not so much for the fishes, but for the peace that it gives us or hunting game in the wooded hills and valley as our forefathers did many thousands of years in the ancient past, not because that same meat cannot be obtained in a supermarket, but because it is the "manly" thing to do in the modern world, or to walk in the isolated places to be where only the sights and sounds of nature can be observed. Fishing, hunting, and living in isolation are, however, only a few of the many ways that humans have sought to reconnect with the forests as many other adopt hobbies like bird watching, tree hugging, hiking and cycling forest trails, visiting nature parks, skiing, climbing mountains, climbing rocks and trees, catching and releasing fishes and many other outdoor activities to reconnect with humanity's true home, the forests.

For many, these hobby activities are insufficient and they must move out of the great urban centers to live in the suburbs to get fresh air, a patch of grass, some trees, birds singing and a small area where a garden could be planted, however, moving to the suburbs created other problems that made living away from urbans centers very difficult. These problems included the distance to proper health care if the need ever arose, distance to schools for children, the distance that many had to travel to get to and from work, to and from the ball park, and to and from places like old churches, old theatres, pharmacies, families and friends. The difficulties associated with suburban living, however, did not kill the desire to be closer to nature while staying close to all of the needed amenities of modern life and this desire led to a return to a model that was attempted a couple centuries earlier in some cities like early Philadelphia, bringing the trees into the urban centers. William Penn's instruction to his designer was quite clear, he wanted a "green country town" that included much open space, five centrally located major parks and gardens with tree lined boulevards and according to Stevens et al (1999) Penn wanted a "greene Country Towne which will never be burnt and always be wholesome". This concept of a town with a lot of green is currently the new direction that is being adopted by many cities, towns and municipalities based on the recognition of the knowledge that forests provide many great benefits for the human population and as Nowak and Greenfield (2015) puts it, "it is common sense that trees are good for us", but it is more than common sense, it is written in the human deoxyribonucleic acid (dna), it is in human genes.

The recognition of this and the fact that fifty percent (50%) or more of the US's (82%) and the world's populations are now located in urban centers makes the transfer of trees into urban centers even more important. Since the planting of the first trees in urban centers, in the modern era, many tangible benefits have been observed and studied with some surprising results inclusive of:

- Trees make communities healthier by removing air pollution, thereby lowering the level respiratory systems related illnesses, making communities more sociable and safer and consequently lowering the levels of domestic violence.
- Trees make businesses more profitable by putting shoppers in a better mood so that they extend their shopping trips, shop more frequently and be willing to pay as much as twelve percent (12%) more for goods and services.
- Trees save home owners money on their energy bills as the trees significantly affect the micro climates around the homes.
- Trees improve the value of a residence by 1% for each large tree in front of the house.

These are benefits in addition to the traditional benefits associated with forest:

- Inspiring people with their beauty and facilitating a transformation in human moods and attitudes
- Reducing human exposure to UV rays and helping to prevent skin health problems.
- Absorbing carbon dioxide and storing carbon to maintain balance in the biosphere.
- Providing fresh oxygen every day, for the human and animal population.
- Removing pollution from the atmosphere, soil and water.
- Reducing storm water runoff, polluting surface water bodies with silt and increasing water absorbed into aquifers after a precipitation event.
- Reducing negative wind impacts, especially during cold weather.

Studies conducted by Nowak and Greenfield (2015) concluded that urban trees save 850 lives and prevents 670,000 incidences of acute respiratory symptoms per year and they also concluded that "Although pollution removal by trees equated to an average air quality improvement of less than 1 percent, these effects illustrate that planting urban trees does not just beautify the city but provides beneficial ecosystem services, making cities healthier for human inhabitants". Research conducted indicates that tree coverage in urban and metropolitan centers across the US varies between 27 and 33 percent respectively on average (Dwyer and Nowak 2000) and with local projections tree coverage in urban centers are supposed to increase significantly in the next 20 years.

From the data available from the USDA Forest Services and the many described benefits of urban trees one could quite easily come to the conclusion that tree coverage in all urban area across the US would have been improving over the last two decades, however, this is not the case as a recent report, Declining Urban and Community Tree Cover in the United States, written by Nowak and Greenfield (2018) indicates that between 2009 –2014, cities and communities across the US have been losing 36 million trees per year. The loss of all 36 million trees cannot be prevented, as some losses are due to factors beyond human control, inclusive of hurricanes, tornadoes, flooding, natural fires, old age, pest and disease. The loss of so many trees in cities and communities across the US each year, however, raises the issue of how seriously municipalities across the US take the issues related to the presence or absence of urban trees and their many advertised benefits.

Utilization of Trees to Prevent Desertification and Soil Erosion

The only answer to deforestation, desertification, degradation of the forest and soil erosion is trees (FAO), and the benefits of trees can only be achieved through replanting of old forests, reforestation, or planting new forest in areas where none existed before, afforestation. Reforestation and afforestation programs must take into consideration the best trees for the selected location and the trees must be utilized in a manner that is best suited to bring the desired result in each location and not applied in a one size fit all manner. Several large-scale reforestation and afforestation programs have been and are being implemented in many countries to halt the effects of desertification, to reduce or eliminate soil erosion, to block desert sand drift, to improve the general aesthetic of a region and also to expand and improve agricultural production. Some of the programs attempted in the past and current programs include the following:

- Stalin's Great Plan for the Transformation of Nature
- Roosevelt's Great Plains Forestry Projects (Shelterbelts)
- China's Three-Norths Shelterbelt Forest Project (Great Green Wall of China)
- The African Unions Great Green Wall of the Sahara
- The state of Israel Making the Desert Bloom

These programs represent only a few of the programs that different countries, institutions and people have tried to eliminate the problems related to loss of vital trees stocks and the examination of each of these shall highlight the success or failure of each approach.

Stalin's Plan for the Transformation of Nature

Joseph Stalin in 1948, under immense pressure from the drought of 1946 and famine in 1947 that killed anywhere from 0.5- 1 million persons in the Soviet Union (Josephson 2016), along with his technocrats and scientists devised and promulgated expansive plans to transform agriculture and nature in the Soviet Union with a view to eliminating the possibility of future droughts and starvation. The proposed works were massive in scope and had a very ambitious project completion date of 1965. The plan included the following elements:

- The planting of a massive shelterbelt of trees on 5.7 million hectares of land that would eliminate soil erosion and alter the microclimates in the various regions to aid agricultural production output.
- The construction of several regional irrigation systems inclusive of dams, reservoirs, ponds and irrigation canals across European USSR to provide water for all agricultural projects and electrical power to improve industrialization.
- The introduction of grassland crop rotation and other scientific methods to ensure high crop yields.
- Land Planning and Management to maximize land use and improve overall output from the Soviet Union.

Unfortunately for Stalin and his team, he died in 1953 and the work on this grand plan ceased in the Soviet Union, as he and his ideas immediately fell out of favor with the new leadership team in the country. Putting it succinctly Brain (2010) said "Indeed afforestation on a massive scale was the environmental panacea of choice for dictators in the twentieth century" and it still may be, however, the ideas proposed by Stalin and his team of scientists such as the shelterbelt, irrigations systems, hydropower systems, crop rotation and land use management, while not original, were good ideas as they were all tools that were used in the US and elsewhere previously and are still used today to resolve some of the problems associated with desertification and the depletion of forests and would probably have produced some success if the programs had been properly planned. Unfortunately, the portion of the plans that were completed proved to be quite disastrous and some significant natural resources were depleted and destroyed and included the once mighty Aral Sea.

Roosevelt's Great Plains Forestry Projects

The "Dust Bowl" of the 1930s inspired President Franklin Delano Roosevelt and his team of technical advisers to conceive of and implement forestry projects in the great plains of the US to eliminate the problems caused by bad US government policies and poor farming practices, over an eighty years period on the Great Plains region of the country. The solutions as initially proposed, however, were not seen or accepted as being suitable for the problems facing the farmers and the country in general and were rejected by the Congress of the US the first time that it was presented in 1934 and was only approved on a second attempt in 1935. According to Sparrow (2018) President Roosevelt attacked the Dust Bowl problem on several fronts inclusive of:

- The Farm Security Administration provided emergency relief, promoted soil conservation, resettled farmers on more productive lands and aided migrant farm workers who had been forced off their land.
- The Soil Conservation Service helped farmers enrich their soil and stem erosion
- The Taylor Grazing Act regulated grazing on overused public lands
- The Roosevelt Shelterbelt Project, created by an Executive Order, fought wind erosion by organizing farmers, Civilian Conservation Corps and Work Progress Administration workers in a program to plant over 200 million trees from Bismarck, North Dakota to Amarillo, Texas to form a belt to block and regulate the destructive winds of the Dust Bowl era.

Some individuals consider Roosevelt's Shelterbelt Project to be one of the greatest environmental success stories of our time as the program appeared to have eliminated the dust storms, however, the shelterbelt project alone did not resolve the problems, and it took changes in agricultural policies and practices to eliminate the root causes of the problem.

China's Three-Norths Shelter Forest Project (Great Green Wall of China)

The Gobi Desert is growing and causing significant environmental and health problems in some of the major cities of China including the capital city Beijing and nearby communities. The Gobi Desert has already covered up several villages and small cities and continues to threaten other areas while causing up to $50 billion dollars-worth of economic losses each year and forcing tens of millions of people to leave their homes to relocate to safer environments. The Three-North Shelter Forest (Great Green Wall of China) program was designed to place 100 billion trees between the Gobi Desert and the major population and commercial centers in China thus creating a barrier to the movement of sand and other forms of pollution. Since the commencement of the project in 1978, 60 billion trees have already been planted with the balance to be planted by 2050 (Levin 2005). However, the completion date is twenty-eight away and according to many international agencies the problems are still not been addressed and Luoma (2012) indicates that many scientists and conservation groups are expressing concerns about the long-term viability of China's reforestation push. Some people consider that the planting of 60 billion trees since 1978 by the Chinese population to be a sign of success and that this program sets the standard for other nations that may want to tackle the problems of deforestation on a large scale in the future and the completion of the project in 2050 should be applauded by the whole world even if the planting of these trees does not achieve all of the set goals. This project will be the laboratory to prove what works, what needs to be done differently and if reforestation of deserts or deserted areas can be achieved successfully over a 72 years period.

The Great Green Wall of The Sahara.

The Sahara Desert is one of the oldest and largest hot deserts on the planet, Schuster et al., (2006) "After the mid-Holocene (approximately 6000 years ago) arid conditions developed throughout North Africa culminating in the formation of the Sahara Desert, which is the largest warm climate desert on earth". The Sahara Desert is approximately 3.6 million square miles large and runs from the Atlantic Ocean on the west coast to the Red Sea on the east coast of Africa, covering many North African Nations inclusive of Algeria, Morocco, Tunisia, Mauritania, Mali, Niger, Chad, Libya, Egypt and Sudan. To the south of the Sahara Desert is a region referred to as the Sahel, which is a semi-arid belt of tropical savannahs around the Niger River Valley and the Sudan Region of Sub-Saharan Africa and the countries that make up this region includes Burkina Faso, Cameroon, Central African Republic, Eritrea, Ethiopia, Nigeria, Senegal and South Sudan.

The problem associated with the Sahara, as with all deserts, is that given the right conditions it will grow to engulf fertile lands and with the Sahel being a vast savannah region which supports agriculture and animal grazing, the chances of this region becoming a part of the Sahara is great due to its overuse from growing crops, over grazing by herds of cattle, goats and sheep and due to the current semi- arid climate of the region. The encroachment of the desert and other climate changes occurring in Africa, encouraged the African Union to devised a plan in collaboration with international financial institutions, such as the World Bank, the International Monetary Fund and the African Development Bank, to plant a belt of trees right across the Sahara Desert and the Sahel region. This belt of trees would run from Senegal on the Atlantic Coast to Djibouti on the Red Sea Coast a total distance of approximately 4,835 miles and covering an area of 11,662,500 hectares of land. The Great Green Wall Initiative (GGWI), as the program is called, was the brainchild of leaders of the African Unions in the 1970s who saw the great expanse of fertile lands in the Sahel disappearing before their eyes and wanted to do something to create a positive change.

The original initiative was conceived by the leaders of 11 countries in the Sahel in 2005 and was officially launched in 2007 under the leadership and guidance of the African Union and since that time the number of countries participating has grown to 21. The initial plan was for the program to plant trees in the focus area as shown on the map, but the program has now been modified to include Sustainable Land Management (SLM) projects and sustainable management of water and arable lands projects. According to the Global Environmental Facility and the World Bank Group (2019) "today the GGWI is focused on integrated management of natural resources as a means to transform livelihoods and landscapes by improving crop and livestock productivity, restoring degraded lands and promoting resilient landscapes for food security". The original goals of the GGWI were as follows:

- The eradication of famine in the Sahara and the Sahel
- Reversing of land degradation trends in the Sahara and Sahel by 2025
- The transformation of the vast arid lands of Sahara and the Sahel in rural production and development hubs by 2050.

All of the above are worthy and ambitious goals and according the United Nations Convention to Combat Desertification (UNCCD) brochure (2016) they have to date observed some good results in several nations inclusive of Ethiopia, Burkina Faso, Niger, Mali, Nigeria, Senegal and Sudan. Some the reported successes include:

- Ethiopia – 15 million hectares of degraded lands restored.
- Burkina Faso, Mali and Niger – 2 million seeds and seedlings plant from 50 native species and 2500 hectares of land restored.
- Nigeria – 5 million hectares of land restored, 200 miles of windbreak were established, 260 miles of shelterbelt were established, 135 hectares of community woodlots were established, 235 hectares of community orchards were established and 138 hectares of community vegetable gardens were also established.
- Senegal – 11.4 million trees were planted, 24,600 hectares of degrade lands were restored, 6250 miles of firewalls were

established and 10,000 hectares of land established using natural regeneration processes.

- Sudan – 2000 hectares of land were restored.

None of the above could have been achieved without the establishment of great employment opportunities, great training programs and great community inputs in all the countries named.

Making the Desert Bloom Again (Israel)

The slogan "Making the Desert Bloom Again" made the state of Israel famous for its many achievements in the field of agriculture inclusive of the development of drip irrigation systems, citrus groves in the deserts, greenhouses for growing flowers and vegetables for export, in an effort to produce their own food and make themselves self-sufficient and food secure in a hostile environment. However, what is not as well-known is the fact that one of the earliest challenges that they issued to themselves, starting as early as 1908, long before Israel was a state, was to plant as many trees as was possible in both arid and semi-arid environments in an effort to stabilize and restore as many degraded locations as possible. The country rose to the challenge and succeeded in planting over 240 million trees from 1908 – 2008 and earned a place as the only country in the world, over the last one hundred years, to have a net gain of trees. According to Schiller (2008) the main goals of all the afforestation efforts since 1908 has been the improvement of landscape and soil conditions, prevention of soil erosion, the creation of work for the poor immigrant population and the creation of places where people could relax after a bruising week in the harsh climate of the land. Schiller also indicated that the production and utilization of timber was never the primary consideration and this allowed the existing natural forests to survive even as they built up afforested areas, which only added to the current forestry status of 100,000 hectares of afforested lands and 85,000 hectares of natural scrub vegetation.

The country's afforestation successes were facilitated by some very important factors inclusive of:

- A great desire to survive in a harsh natural and political location.
- The willingness of Jews everywhere to give to finance the forestry projects as the cost to ensure success of any afforestation program anywhere in the world is very high.
- The development of the necessary science, education and training programs to ensure success of the programs.
- The willingness to keep on trying even after significant failures such as establishing monoculture forests in the early stages of the project and the destruction of wetlands.
- The historical and cultural attachments to tree planting within the national Jewish culture.

The one hundred plus years of afforestation in Israel has by all measures to date, produced the results as set out in the planned objectives of improving the landscape, preventing soil erosion, creating employment and creating recreational facilities for the people, as thus far the 240 million trees that were planted have greatly improved the national natural landscape, created 150 forests and 400 parks and provided employment for a significant portion of the nation's population. These activities have also facilitated the restoration of degraded soils, in arid and semi-arid regions which has helped to strengthen agricultural production and provided employment for many persons. However, according to Ginsberg (2000) there were many other add on benefits as "not only has the physical appearance of Israel been transformed by the long-term afforestation effort, but the social fabric of Israel has been influenced as well".

The afforestation activities have also created in Israel a large body of knowledge on the science and technology of forestry, afforestation, forest fragmentation, forests degradation and desertification, which they have been sharing with the world as consultants on two of the largest afforestation projects ever attempted, the China Great Green Wall and the Great Green Wall of the Sahara, and many other smaller projects around the world.

Phytoremediation Projects

Phytoremediation is the process of using plants and trees to resolve environmental issues caused by the spill or dumping of chemicals such as hydrocarbons, solvents and other pollutants in locations where they pose long-term health and environmental threats to humans and the environment. The solutions to these problems are usually designed to use specific trees or plants to absorb, store or convert the pollutant using a permanent stand of tree, shrubs or grass which will all add to the stock of trees, shrubs and grass in the particular location. Phytoremediation methods have been used to resolve environmental pollution problems in many Superfund sites across the United States and at contaminated sites across Europe and has been used to resolve contamination caused by Petroleum Hydrocarbons, PCE, TCE, Chlorinated Solvents, Aromatics, Ketones, Alcohols and Asbestos. Some of these projects already in progress or completed includes:

- Groundwater Phytoremediation for removal of solvents at Solvents Recovery Service of New England (SRSNE) Superfund Site in Southington, Connecticut, USA. (Ferro et al 2005)
- Phytoremediation to remove TCE at a Superfund Site at LaSalle, Illinois, USA. (LaSalle Electric Utility) (Lindner 2004)
- Phytoremediation to remove TCE at a Superfund Site at Aiken, S.C., USA. (Savanah River Ecology Labs, SRS) (Lindner 2004)
- Phytoremediation to remove petroleum hydrocarbons at an abandoned gasoline station in Axelveld, Denmark. (Epps 2006)
- Phytoremediation to remove petroleum hydrocarbons at the Amsterdam Terminal in Netherlands. (Van Epps 2006)

The method used at each site was a function of the chemical pollutant, the location, the contaminated medium, water and or soil, the size of the contaminated site, the type of plant selected and the jurisdiction in which the polluted site exists. According to Switzguebel et al (2002) "recent developments in Europe and the USA show that the approach is somewhat different on both sides of the Atlantic." It is said that in Europe the approach is driven by research results, which are then applied to problems, while in the USA the approach is more application and experience driven. Phytoremediation is a proven scientific method of using trees or plants to remove many different environmental pollutants on both sides of the Atlantic and in many cases the phytoremediation methods have been proven to be more effective than other methods in removing the pollutants and is also more cost effective.

13

Review

There are many things that have contributed to the demise of forestry all over the world and some of these things includes ancient civilizations, agriculture, timber production, mining, energy, the industrial revolution, natural disasters, diseases and government policies and programs. Relevant effort will be made to examine each sector.

An examination of the historical timeline will show that the existence of plants and trees preceded the existence of animals and humans by an estimated 400 million years, during which time plants and trees worked assiduously with sunlight to convert many of the harmful chemical by-products, left after the large energy burst that brought the planet Earth into existence, into substances that were more favorable and conducive to the existence of animal life on the planet. In the process plants, trees, and other autotrophs:

- Were the only life forms in the primeval soup that could survive in the conditions that existed 400 million or more years ago when they first appeared.
- Developed respiratory systems that utilized carbon dioxide to produce oxygen, a relatively new gas. that was more conducive to the development of animal life on the planet.

- Transformed an atmosphere filled with 98% carbon dioxide and 1.9% nitrogen and minute percentages of oxygen and other gases into an atmosphere rich in Nitrogen 79% (an inert gas) and Oxygen 20% (a gas that fosters animal life), Carbon Dioxide 0.035% and minute quantities of other gases and water vapor (Yu 2001).
- Built up a very deep layer of oxygen that was converted to ozone by a process of photodissociation using ultra violet radiation (UVR). This protective layer reflects a high percentage of the solar incident radiation back into space and produced conditions at the earth's surface that would better support animal lifeforms.
- Blocked 95 % of the UV radiation that penetrated the ozone layer thereby creating under their canopies, nurseries for the creation of new life.
- Populated the whole earth and kept the soils of the earth together to foster the development of other life forms and to keep other life forms safe from the extreme actions of water and wind and also fostered the development of the hydrologic cycle.
- Continued evolving until the appearance of new species of trees and plants that flowered and bore fruits, some of which became food for both animals and humans.
- Provided food for animal and human sustenance and shelter from the elements which created a long-term relationship, with animals and humans being totally dependent upon plants and trees for their sustenance and later livelihood. In the hunter-gatherer phase of their development humans enjoyed the fruits of the land without making any input into how the plants existed and according to Czartoryski (2011) "Before the agricultural revolution humans spent more time on the planet as hunter-gatherers, relying on nature's resources and their own survival instincts to sustain themselves". In this phase humans reaped the fruits of the trees, used their shade, burnt their branches and moved on to the next location where the fruits and animals were more available without any considerations to the trees and the plants in the old location. This moving on process could be beneficial to plants and trees if the roving population of humans

did not stay in one place too long, which they quite often did, obliterating nearly every valuable plant and tree before seeking new locations rich with all their favorite foods.

- Many species of plants and trees were faced with destruction when humans became farmers as these farmers were only interested in domesticating and reproducing particular species of plants, trees and animals. The selective domestication, breeding and reproduction of particular plants ensured the longevity of these plants and the decline of those not so selected and the habitat provided by those not selected was necessarily destroyed to create room for the selected species to thrive and thus many forests along with many unknown species of plants were destroyed, made extinct, to ensure the development of species such as wheat, barley, rye, oats, apples, oranges, bananas, potatoes and the many other species of plants that are reproduced cyclically to feed humans until today. Agriculture which was responsible for the extinction of many species of plants and animals also started the process of fragmenting and degrading forests which eventually led to desertification and the creation of hot deserts. The reality was that the Earth, the non-domesticated animals and plants paid a very high price when humans developed agriculture, because even as humans were now caring for particular plants and animals, their caring activities were limited to the selected plants and animals and consequently their actions led to the destruction of other plants and animals. The farmer was at times doing much more harm to the environment when compared to the hunter-gatherer who only took what he needed and moved on, allowing the flora and fauna left behind to regrow.

- Forests rich in natural biodiversity were continually and significantly reduced to meet the nutritional, heating and shelter needs of the continuously growing human population and this inadvertently led to modifications in the patterns of local climates that had been developed by trees over the earlier 400 million years and these changes amplified as human populations grew, became more stable, expanded the areas cleared of trees and the flora and fauna that had developed under the canopies of the trees.

Agriculture

By definition, agriculture is the science or practice of cultivating crops and animal husbandry that allows humans to produce their food and other necessary products to meet their nutritional and shelter needs and is therefore an essential activity for sustaining human life. The practice of agriculture, however, requires open land space for the proper propagation, growth and development of crops, as most plants require direct sunlight for the best crop yields. Thus, we have the practice of agriculture extending human life and increasing the population with a better food supply which then leads to the ever- growing need for the clearing of more forest lands. This ever-growing demand to clear more lands to feed a growing population raises the question of how much land will be required, now and in the future to meet the world's growing population's nutritional needs and the answer to this question is vitally important as the amount of arable, arid, semi-arid or even desert lands on the planet is limited and the amount of forest that can be cleared is even more limited. In the quest to provide sufficient food to meet the world's nutritional needs, one of the issues that must be examined in depth is the amount of land that was and will be required to continually feed the earth's population while preserving forests and the natural environment. The questions related to this issue have been answered many times over the millennia as humans have continually found ways to improve their production of food to feed the ever-growing population and according to Thrall et al., (2010) some of the ways selected over millennia have included:

- The development of irrigation systems to provide adequate water to increase agricultural production.
- The selection and domestication of plant species and the creation of hybrids that produced more, were more resistant to disease, more resistant to salt intrusion, more drought resistant and in general more resistant to environmental conditions.
- The selection and domestication of animal species and the creation of hybrids that produced more, were more resistant to

disease, had a greater tolerance to drought and other negative environmental conditions.

- The development of land use practices such as crop rotation that enhance the production of crops.
- The development of various methods of pest control.
- Growth in knowledge about crop and animal sciences.
- Growth in knowledge about soils and soils conditions and the development of fertilizers
- The advancement of the agricultural sciences with the aid of technological advances.
- The growth and development of high-tech solutions through research.

Impact of Agriculture

The development of agriculture ensured a more consistent supply of nutritious foods for human consumption, which made them healthier, taller and stronger, extended their lives and gave them stability, all of which exacerbated the problems faced by all other forms of life on the planet. Basically "agriculture was also responsible for helping humans create and develop stable societies" (Thrall et al., 2010) and this stability in turn fostered the growth and development of human civilization and consequently population growth and a demand for more land. With agriculture firmly established, stable humans then had more time on their hands and began developing philosophies, religions, music, art and culture, all of which also placed great demands upon the natural forests around them as each activity demanded space to perform and material for the construction of facilities and instruments. Some communities developed special places for religions, the most important aspect of life in most early civilizations, special places for food storage and built bigger houses to accommodate their other activities, while others developed less stringent demands on the forest and lands around them by seeing the forest, its plants and animals, as works of art in themselves and the forests as clean beautiful places that were good enough to worship in and for some people to worship, as forests provided special non-temporal (spiritual) inspiration to many people and later religious leaders over the centuries.

In general, the majority of humans developed a laissez faire approach to natural forests while working assiduously, through the arts and science of agriculture, to multiply continuously the animals and plants that they had domesticated as they understood implicitly that without the care and attention provided by humans that these domesticated plants and animals could disappear and leave the human population hungry again. Humans also knew implicitly that they needed to provide food and water for their cattle, goats, sheep, pigs, donkeys, horses, mules, camels, dogs and even cats if they wanted them to provide milk, meat, wool, skin, bear burden and provide companionship. They also knew that they had to provide water and nutrients for the crops that they planted, yet they did not develop the same concept for forests that had been providing animals and humans with all the goods and services that they needed for 2- 7 million years. This awareness that the life-giving forests required care only came to them during the many natural crises that they faced every thousand years or so and a very long time after they had domesticated animals and some plants.

Fortunately, not all early humans abused the forests as many ancient peoples revered and worshipped forests and trees and through this reverence preserved many religious groves and many species of flora and fauna that would have been lost otherwise all around the world. These preservers of forests may, however, have been in the minority since the development of organized religion and may have been restricted by the majority who had adopted different religious and or philosophical beliefs and therefore may not have shared the views of the "tree huggers". This majority may have seen the forest disappear before their eyes but did not give it a second thought as in their minds there would always be other forests across cross the river or on the other side of the border, somewhere nearby where timber and forest products would be available in great abundance for sale or taking. This way of thinking appeared to have become the modus operandi of many ancient and even modern societies such as the ancient Egyptians who bought timber from Lebanon to help in the construction of their pyramids after they had depleted their own forests and the Europeans, thousands of years later, who pillaged, murdered, captured and colonized other people to get their forests and trees free.

The Future of Agriculture

The agricultural production of the six nations, Australia, Brazil, China, Germany, Nigeria and USA, examined earlier, clearly indicates that agriculture plays a very important role in providing nutritional sustenance for the growing populations of these countries and can give an idea of what appears to be justifiable reasons for clearing forests in their respective locations in different sections of the planet. The amount of forest cleared, however, was usually a function of agricultural methods used in the past and the level of efficiency achieved while using these methods. Over the last 100 years there have been significant improvements in crop yields in the developed nations of the world inclusive of US, Canada, China, Europe, Africa, Australia, New Zealand and elsewhere based on a number of factors.

These improvements came about as result of the application of new technologies highlighted by Miller (Smith 2016) and included:

- Genetically modifying plants to resists natural pest.
- Genetically modifying plants to allow higher plant densities per acre
- The use of Integrated Pest Management Programs.
- Utilizing precision planting technology
- Utilizing global positioning system in agriculture
- Improved soil testing technology to provide faster test results
- Formulating fertilizers to meet exact needs of particular soils
- Mapping plant genomes to allow more rapid breeding of new varieties.

These technologies created the following improvements:

- The creation of new varieties of crops
- Increasing plant density from 4-5000 per acre to 30,000 per acre for a particular crop.
- Reducing the use of nutrients while improving yield
- Quadrupling of corn yields, improving nutrient quality, improving drought resistance and improving nitrogen use efficiency.

- Increasing wheat yields by more than ten folds by the creation of a dwarf variety and development of plant resistance to known pests inclusive of the Hessian fly, the cereal mite and the greenbug.
- Increasing sorghum yield by 25%
- The creation of new and more effective herbicides and pest management control programs.

These changes, which occurred between 1911 – 2011, brought great improvements inclusive of reduction in the number of farmers required to feed the population, a significant reduction in acreages of farmland required for the same, improved yields and a major increase in the amounts of crops reaped each season. Along with the increased food production these improvements have allowed for many acres of land to be returned to forest in both Europe and the US and has thereby helped to foster the reforestation of once cleared lands. These achievements in the field of agriculture, from 1911- 2011, however, were and are not an endpoint in themselves as the world's population keeps growing and there will need to be even greater improvements in the next one hundred years with the growth in population expected to reach 9.7 billion by 2050 and 11.2 billion by 2100 (UN Department of Economic and Social Affairs {DESA}).

All of the many improvements in agricultural production have been fostered by technologies that have improved agricultural productivity and efficiency and these improvements have seen one acre of land producing much more than previous years and thereby reducing the amount of land required to produce the amount of food needed to feed a large and growing population and these improvements have also reduced the need to continually deplete forest lands. However, the Earth's population is now reaching new highs every year and the need to continuously improve agricultural productivity and efficiency must be an ongoing process of change and improvements if forests are to be saved and nutritional needs of the human population adequately met simultaneously.

Timber

Timber by definition is wood that is suitable for construction or for carpentry and this wood is a product of trees taken from forests located all around the world and unfortunately, this use of trees to produce timber is now responsible for significant environmental problems inclusive of drought, forest fragmentation, forest degradation, desertification, dust storms, soil erosion, water shortage, starvation, great flooding, poor water quality, loss of habitat for animals, generating 12% of world's greenhouse gases (World Bank) and in general causing significant harm for humans and the natural ecosystems alike. The production of timber causes all of the aforementioned problems for forests and according to Dudley et al., (1995) "Research carried out by the World Wildlife Fund (WWF) suggests that the international timber trade is now the primary cause of forest degradation and loss in those forests that contain the highest levels of biodiversity." If taken to its logical conclusion, the global effort to reduce or eliminate the effects of climate change, must include actions to reduce or eliminate logging from biodiversity rich forest and forests in general, however, reducing or eliminating logging would have significant economic consequences for both rich and poor nations as the production and sales of timber and forest products generates up to US$600-850 Billion annually, approximately 1% of the world's GDP and employs millions of people around the globe (World Bank). Therefore, based on the economic activities generated and the money earned, any effort to reduce or eliminate logging could increase the rate of poverty around the world and these realities must be given due consideration in the discussions to find ways to continue using forest output without doing further harm to the environment and this must lead to the concept of sustainable forestry.

Sustainable Forestry Management

"A narrow focus on …the role of forest as carbon sinks at the expense of the other forest values would be unsustainable" (Collaborative Partnership on Forest 2008). To avoid "unsustainable" practices while striving to create balance in environmental and ecological systems, the focus of all human engagements with the forests and the general environment must therefore be directed in such a manner that human utilization of the forests and forests products do as little harm to the forest and the inhabitants of the forest as possible, while at the same time ensuring the continued existence, ad infinitum, of forests. The existence of places like the Sahara Desert, the Gobi Desert, the Mohave Desert, the Thar and the many other hot deserts around the world and the current problems associated with forest degradation, deforestation and desertification, clearly indicates that humans have failed and continues to fail greatly to ensure the existence ad infinitum of sustainable levels of forests.

The FAO, however, indicates that sustainable forest operations and management will ensure the following:

- The survival of forest and forest ecosystems.
- The enhancement of the environmental, sociocultural and economic functions of forest.
- The optimization of climate change mitigation.
- Provision of optimum support to help the forest and the people dependent upon forests and forest products, to adapt to the new conditions created by climate change.

The benefits to be obtained from sustainable operations and management of forest resources shall include greater food security for all, improved economic conditions for the people at the lowest level, general overall economic improvements, sustainable land use practices and elimination of, forest fragmentation, forest degradation, deforestation and improved environmental conditions. The implementation of sustainable operations and management of the world's forests usually requires the establishment of strategic frameworks, policies and programs, created at the highest levels of governments, without whose support the establishment and long-term survival of these new forestry practices would not be possible. The integrated approach recommended by the FAO includes five major elements, Policy and Governance, Management Planning and Practices, Forest Product and Services,

Intersectoral Cooperation and Coordination and Monitoring and Assessment which all inter relate to produce optimum outcomes.

The recommended tactical tools to be used to achieve the long-term goals includes Carbon Sequestration, Forest Carbon Stock Conservation, Strengthening Adaptive Capacity of Trees and Forest, Strengthening Adaptive Capacity of Forests Dependent Communities and Mitigation Adaption (FAO, Collaborative Partnership on Forest, 2008).

Carbon Sequestration

Increase natural carbon sequestration by increasing the forest stock, tree count and tree coverage in every region of a country inclusive of urban areas, farming communities, arid areas and by replenishing degraded forests and shrub areas. This can be achieved by utilizing afforestation, reforestation and forest restoration techniques, practices and best management systems suitable to the different locations and the capacity of the project management teams.

Forest Carbon Stock Conservation

This deals with forest carbon stock conservation through the reduction in the many pressures on forest from deforestation and forest degradation practices associated with our many survival and economic activities. This reduction can be achieved by utilizing sustainable forest management systems and practices, integrated fire management systems, fervent management of the health and vitality of forests, strong oversight and management of forest biodiversity to ensure the growth and maintenance of existing species and continuous monitoring and management of existing protected areas, increasing the size of protected areas and monitoring and protecting existing wildlife.

Strengthening Adaptive Capacity of Tree

In order to ensure continuity and longevity of our existing forest all effort must be made to strengthen the adaptive capacity of existing forests and trees in our fragile forest ecosystems. This strengthening can be achieved by monitoring and management of forest biodiversity, managing forest health and vitality to reduce or eliminate all vulnerabilities, intensifying fire management systems and creating and using adaptive management system that will continuously monitor and make necessary changes as may be required based on any and all perceived changes.

Strengthening Adaptive Capacity of Communities

All communities that live in close proximity to forests and who are dependent upon the forest to sustain life and liberty are quite vulnerable to any significant change that may occur in the forest environments and ecosystems and therefore all effort must be made to make the community more aware of the fragility of the forests and what they can do to help to prevent any pending or likely environmental events that could negatively impact them. Some of the things that could be done may include:

- Efforts to educate the community to improve their ability to cope with environmental changes such as the effects of climate change and also to help them to use the forest and forest products in way that will do less harm to the environment.
- Help them to see the many possible opportunities that they can take advantage of to make things better for themselves even with any difficult environmental problem that may arise.
- Create employment opportunities that will allow the community to participate in making forests more resilient to events that will negatively impact them.
- Help the community to adopt proper land use planning and best management practices to ensure that their activities will not continue to negatively impact the forests.

Mitigation Adoption

In this framework there is built in flexibility to modify, adopt or change direction as required to achieve the desired output through the Mitigation- Adaptation feedback mechanism.

Mining

Mining, historically, was never on the same plane as providing for the most basic human needs, as it never satisfied any of the basic physiological needs for food, clothing, shelter and probably only developed as humans became sedentary and had more time to sit, contemplate and become creative and according to the US National Mining Association (NMA) evidence suggest that gold was first used about 4000 BC to make decorative objects in Eastern Europe and it appears that most of the early finds of copper and later gold were only used for aesthetic purposes such as the adornment of the leader of the community, the religious leader and probably the place of religious gathering and worship, according to Hur (2020) "Gold played an important role in ancient Egyptian mythology and was prized by pharaohs and priests". Over time the need for these gold adornments created a demand that could only be met by actively going out and seeking for copper and gold in the locations where the first pieces were found, in the rivers and lakes, or in the forest and as the populations grew the demands and the search for precious metals and gem stones for adornment grew and as economic value was placed on these adornments and the finding and processing of them, mining became another way to obtain the things required to meet the basic needs. The mining of precious metals, gems stones and later minerals developed to become a major human economic activity that created another route by which humans could gain the basic items needed to survive and this trade in metals, gem stones and minerals would later be greatly expanded to become some of the most highly valued traded goods.

Mining as an economic endeavor was later greatly impacted by discovery of another metal, which while not as aesthetically pleasing as gold or copper, was much better for making tools and implements of war such as swords, knives, arrow heads, lance points, shields and armor for protection and this new metal was iron and it revolutionized the world and elevated the status of the other metals as it began replacing copper in the making of tool, weapons and later household items. Mining expanded over time as other new metals were found and new uses were developed for them until the modern era where the same process continues and mining has grown to become one of the largest industries across the globe generating hundreds of billions of dollars in revenues. Today mining is a major economic driving force in the global economy and the products provides many essential goods and services that affect every sector of the world's economy, inclusive of the provision of items for domestic household use, medicine, agriculture, construction, manufacturing and processing industries, transportation, power generation and transmission, armaments of war, food preparation, food processing, water and wastewater treatment, lighting, heating, ventilation, air conditioning & refrigeration, telecommunication systems, computing & electronic controls systems and entertainment, just some of the many areas that the mining industries provide essential and critical material.

The economic value of mining is unquestionable as many nations derive a significant portion of their GDP from mining activities that take place within the economic boundaries of their nations under license or by direct actions of sovereign governments. The money earned from licensing fees and taxes on the earnings of mining activities plays a very vital role in providing the basic services required by humans in all nations especially those that are more dependent upon nationally provided services. Mining, like agriculture, has made itself indispensable as it produces many items which make modern life possible and therefore it is not possible to eliminate mining because it has become a most important and necessary human activity. What must therefore be examined and managed are the follow:

- The efficiency of mining operations and mining methods
- The efficiency of land use designs for mining operations in an effort to reduce the footprint of every mining operation,
- Improving the efficiency of mining transportation,

- Improving energy efficiency in mining operations,
- Minimizing the impact of mining on forests, local ecological systems and the local hydrological systems,
- Minimizing the time period required to complete the extraction of the ores and to complete the land restoration of the mined-out areas, as required, to reduce the many losses suffered at all mined out locations with the loss of their natural forests, flora and fauna and even rainfall levels.

Sustainable Mining

Mining in general deals with the location and extraction of deposits of desired metals, gem stones and minerals that are of high economic value and the supply of these desired elements cannot be replenished in any reasonable period of time, this description fits the classical definition of "unsustainable". When viewed from this angle and against the definition of sustainability created by the Bruntland Commission (1987) "sustainability, as the ability of the current generation to meet their own needs without compromising the ability of the future generations to meet their own needs", makes mining unsustainable as the elements once removed cannot be regrown by any process to benefit the future generations. The United Nations, national governments and the multinational mining companies, in recognition of the value of both forests and the mining industries in world economies have developed policies and programs which are directed at promoting 'Sustainable Mining', an oxymoron, which requires all mining companies to restore natural conditions on all mined-out lands, as mining not only permanently eliminate known deposits of metals and minerals but it also permanently scars, disfigures or destroys the original landscape and the environment in which the mine is located, making the location no longer suitable for many activities and in some cases making the location unsuitable for all activities. To make the concept of sustainable mining palatable the definition for sustainability in mining must therefore be modified to take into consideration several factors as proposed by Strongman (2002), which includes the following:

- The mining activity must be economically and financially viable
- The mining operation must be designed, built and operated on an environmentally sound footing.
- All mining activities must be carried out in a socially responsible manner.
- All mining activities must be implemented using Best Management Practices (BMPs) under the guidance of internationally agreed upon policies, standards and management systems.
- Mining must provide sound long-term benefits for all stakeholders inclusive of the local communities and people.

In addition to Strongman's points above, there must be a requirement for the timely reforestation of all mined out lands, where mining activities have led to the demise of forests and associated ecosystems. Currently, in bauxite mining nations, such as Jamaica, the mined-out lands are converted into pastures and lands suitable only for subsistence farming and animal husbandry, which cannot provide the environmental service typically provided by forests. Since the beginning of bauxite mining in Jamaica in 1952, rainfall levels have fallen and the country currently suffers significant drought each year. The same problem occurs all around the world where mining activities have caused the demise of forests and therefore it become imperative that the restoration of forests become a primary legal requirement in all mining operations around the globe.

Impact of Industrial Revolution

The industrial revolution was a major turning point in the life of humans and forests as there was an explosion in the demands for energy, with wood as the first energy source that fed this revolution, at a scale which had never existed before and this demand for energy has been growing ever since. This demand for energy has kept growing based on the expansion of industries all around the globe, the electrification of commercial, institutional and residential facilities with the invention of new business and household appliances and the spread of these new electrical appliances and tools all around the globe. This spread has ensured that every office building, commercial spaces, institutional and residential facilities in developed, in upper income and low-income developing societies have become totally dependent on electrical energy as these facilities had electrical lighting, heating and cooling systems, electrical stoves, fridges, clothe irons, washing and drying machines, mixers and blender, electrical kettles, televisions, computers and musical sound systems. The overall impact of the industrial revolution on forests was cataclysmic and was probably similar in effect to a new ice age when compared to the damage that it did to forest in general, however, while doing great harm to forests all over the world it also opened the minds of humans to the great damage that was taking place in the environment as a result of human activities, as prior to the advent of the industrial revolution in the 1700s, there is no evidence that humans had never shown much inclination towards taking care of forests or silviculture, the growing and cultivation of trees, and this lack of interest was given a reality check in the 1700s when there was a near collapse of forests in Europe and many other places, as the demand for wood became greater than the rate at the existing stressed forests could produce them.

This great demand for timber was driven by the many new machines of the industrial revolution that utilized wood as their primary or only source of energy and this reality check, the fact that Europe was running out of timber, forced many to review their approach as they realized that at the rate at which they were going through the natural forests of Europe, they would not have any wood to run their factories in a fairly short period of time. The focus then was not on the depletion of the natural forest and the extinction of many species but on the loss of their only source of energy and thus their ability to smelt iron, their manufacturing and other industrial activities. In fact, this same approach is still being taken by the industrial world today as even with the knowledge developed about forests and trees in the last three hundred years, the best approach that humans have developed today, speaks only about to how to "best use trees" or "sustainably use forests and trees" which could imply that trees are only important as they meet the economic needs of humans and based on the economic needs of humans, we must ensure that there will always be sufficient trees around. While this position may be economically and logically sound, it is not a nature balanced position that seeks to ensure the continued existence of every species of plants and trees irrespective of human needs. The best or sustainable use position could also imply that if humans ever developed an economic substitute for the use of forest products and trees, it may become convenient to get rid of trees or stop paying attention to the environmental and ecological need to ensure the continued survival of all species of trees.

Energy

Since humans first learned to make fire, they have reaped timber from forest for use as a fuel for cooking and heating to meet their most basic survival needs and this trend continued until the 1800s when a timber crisis in Europe forced humans to find new sources of energy to replace wood and one of the first such new source was coal, which was naturally located beneath the surface of the earth, underground. The use of coal was followed later by oil, gas and many new technologies, based on electricity, developed around the world, but these new fuels have not completely displaced wood as a primary source of fuel for humans, especially those that live close to locations that produce wood in forest and non-forest locations. These people can be found in both developed and developing countries all over the globe and according to the USEIA, in the USA, in 2018 wood energy accounted for approximately 2% of residential energy consumption, while in 2015 it accounted for 11%.

According to the Food and Agricultural Organization (FAO) Wood "is still the most important single source of renewable energy providing about 6% of the global total primary energy supply" and the FAO also states that greater than 2 billion people continue to use wood for cooking and heating around the globe, which they source directly or indirectly from forest or non-forest source of trees and this population of 2 billion is approximately 25% of a population of 7.8 billion and can cause great damage to forests all over the world as can be seen from the history of the United States with a population significantly much less than 2 billion, probably less than100 million from 1650-1850, did great damage to forests in the US. According to Blakemore (2018) by the 1500s Britain was running out of firewood and the poor population was bearing the brunt of the shortage as they could not afford the price being charged for wood at that time and to escape the harsh conditions these poor people formed the bulk of those that would take to the seas to find a new life in the colonies in the US, 100 years later. Yet in 200 years 1650 -1850 these same people would decimate half of the forest and all of the non-forest trees in the Northeastern section of the US, creating a firewood crisis similar to the ones that they ran away from in Britain.

The damaged caused by the gathering of firewood on the major continents, Africa, Asia, Europe, North and South America, indicates that if not properly managed even the richest forest in the world can be quickly destroyed and history will always repeat itself with respect to our forests and other natural resources as people can always find a good "economic" reason to destroy forests irrespective of the damage that may be done to the environment, the ecology and life in general on the earth, as greed and sometimes need always trumps environmental concerns. Unfortunately, this is a global concern as people everywhere behave irresponsibly when resources appear to be free as described by William Forster Lloyd in 1833 in his 'Tragedy of the Commons" theory (Hardin 1968) which state that "individuals use up resources shared by many to benefit themselves,". These are individuals acting selfishly to benefit themselves at the expense of the majority with everyone ending up suffering.

Wood's place as the primary source of energy was eclipsed with the development of electricity, the development of coal as a source of energy and the development of the means to convert coal into the much in demand electrical energy. The transition into coal was later followed by the development of the other fossil fuels, oil and gas, as sources of energy that could be converted to produce electricity. The development of "power plants" to convert the fossil fuels into electrical energy started a process, the development of locations just to create electrical energy, that has continued until today even with the development of the newer renewable energy sources, with the renewable energy sources demands for land creating a significant negative impact upon forest and trees as these systems required the use of great swaths of lands, lands that were usually covered in trees or shrubs in many locations. This can be clearly seen in hydroelectric power plants that required the inundation of very large areas of lands to form large dams and reservoirs to produce the potential energy needed to produce electricity. The inundation of the land usually led to the destruction of millions of trees and other plants even though these trees were not burned to produce energy, they were just destroyed in the quest to create "renewable" hydropower. The same applies to the development of solar energy that requires large swaths of land on which to layout thousands of panels to collect the energy from the sun, again while solar energy does not require the use of wood, its uses of land usually occupied by trees automatically displaces trees within the environment, as trees would negatively affect the ability of the solar panels to collect solar energy. The only exception to this is when solar panels are installed in treeless barren desert.

Ancient Civilizations

Many ancient civilizations through their practices of intensive agriculture, monument building, timber production and sale, mining and smelting of metals have left many deserts and or arid regions in their wake as shown in the cases of the Indus Valley Civilizations in India and Pakistan, the major Mesopotamian Civilizations in Iraq, Syria and Turkey, the Egyptian and Sudanese Civilizations on the African continent. The existence of deserts in the locations of many early civilizations such as the Indus Valley and Iraq is an established fact, however, some archeologists and environmentalists would argue about the exact cause of desertification and the destruction of the environment. Many have developed the concept called ecocide, which is the extensive destruction of ecosystems by humans, Gauger et al (2013), as there may be an alternative element, sometimes brought to location by humans, that may be responsible for the damage to the environment and ecology. The definition of ecocide, however, is broad enough to cover direct or indirect cause and intentional and unintentional causes as another definition presented by Gauger et al (2013) indicates "it was recognized by others, however, that ecocide often occurs simply as a consequence of business rather than being a result of predetermined, intended direct attack on the environment". In the case of the environmental and ecological failures on Rapa Nui, Hunt and Lipo (2009) acknowledges that environmental and ecological catastrophes occurred after the arrival of the Polynesians and that the population of the native palms fell rapidly, they however, indicated that the reduction in human population that followed was only as a direct result of making contact with Europeans, who carried diseases that the Polynesians had no resistance to and the enslavement and physical abuse of the people of Rapa Nui. However, while acknowledging that the harm caused to native populations by the arrival of the Europeans is historically correct, it is also true that whenever there are environmental and ecological catastrophes the human population of the affected areas are always negatively impacted as happens when an event such as an extended drought occurs. Extended droughts produce environmental and ecological catastrophes which are related to deforestation and when they occur, agricultural production is always negatively impacted and crop productions fail creating a shortage of food which consequently leads to starvation and death, as has been the experience around the world on multiple occasions. This natural sequence of events is not unique to any location on the planet and would have occurred on Rapa Nui, if it had been affected by environmental and ecological catastrophes as described and secondly the two sets of events are not mutually exclusive as the population could have been reduced by starvation prior to the arrival of Europeans and by contact with the Europeans.

The second point raised by Hunt and Lipo (2013) was that it was the rats and not the humans that caused the destruction of the palm trees and that this should again remove the responsibility from the human populations, however, according Norrington (2018) "much of the damage done to forestry appears to have been done before evidence of fires on the island" and this could suggest that rats were on the island prior to the arrival of the arrival of the Polynesians that settled the island. If this was the case it could establish the case that it was the arrival of humans and their activities that hastened the loss of trees on the island, however, if the rats were brought to the island by humans, the anthropogenic activities are still totally responsible for the rapid destruction of the tree population of the island, because if humans had not ventured to the island there would be no rats and without rats all the trees on Rapa Nui would still be present.

The same logical thought process also applies to salt intrusion caused by the lack of proper field drainage in the agricultural fields of Mesopotamia and Egypt which eventually led to the reduction in the productive capacity of the soils and consequently desertification in regions that had some of the largest water supply and irrigation systems in the world. Of course, lower Mesopotamia had no trees to destroy only reeds, grass and shrubs and the loss of these accentuated the problems caused by necessary human activities, as agriculture was the source of nutrition and the mainstay of the economies of both Egypt and Mesopotamia. Desertification in the locations of ancient civilizations in Mesopotamia, Egypt, Sudan, India, Pakistan and many other locations around the globe, clearly bear the marks of anthropogenic activities and the consequent climatic changes which occurred due to the loss of forests and grass coverage. There are many who would seek to promulgate the idea that deforestation and desertification are products only of the last 300 or so years, however, there are also some views that clearly state that ancient civilizations had a much bigger impact on the earth's environment and ecology than was previously thought (Klivert 2019). The environmental changes created by ancient civilizations, however, cannot be viewed in the same light as the changes that are occurring today, as today's changes are happening in the face of the accumulation of a great body of knowledge about the long and short-term effects of forest fragmentation, forest degradation and deforestation and the many things that can lead to desertification.

Unknown Ancient Civilizations

Current archeological thought indicates that the Sahara Desert used to be a green lush verdant area that was occupied by humans a very long time ago in the ancient past and other evidence, inclusive of large groundwater sources under the Sahara Desert, also clearly point to the fact that the necessary hydrological conditions required for the infiltration of water into the underground aquifers also existed. The conditions to facilitate infiltration of precipitation include surface coverage to prevent rapid runoff, temperatures that prevented the immediate evaporation of precipitation and tree coverage that encourages the penetration of the soil. According to D'Atanasio et al (2018) the 'Green Sahara' landscape was characterized by the presence of savannahs, forests and an extensive system of rivers, streams and lakes and today when the Sahara Desert is only a desert it still has two major rivers, Nile and Niger, twenty or more lakes, with Lake Chad having the only potable water. Stirn (2020) provides the following information that supports the concept of a 'Green Sahara':

- The archeological sites at Sabu-Jaddi, and many other locations in eastern Sudan, contains more than 1500 rock drawings spanning 10,000 years of human history in the region.
- These rock drawings depict animals from early times, cattle from the later Kerma period (2600- 1450BC), boats of Egypt's New Kingdom (1570-1069 BC), Christian period motifs and more.
- The climate of the Sahara region was once drastically different than it is today, during a time that has become known as the 'African Humid Period', approximately 13,000-3000 BC, when seasonal monsoons from Central Africa would move northwards delivering large volumes of rainfall to the northern parts of the African continent.
- The wide savannahs of the regions were covered with elephants, giraffes and gazelles and the ponds and rivers filled with hippopotamus, crocodiles and fish.
- The area was also covered with a large variety of plants and animals that provided a rich larder for the human occupants of the region.

Other historical data also indicates that Lake Chad used to be the largest freshwater lake on earth, up to twenty times larger than Lake Ontario (Mann and Stager 2017) and this lake was reduced in size due to the activities of humans and their domesticated grazing animals that caused the degradation of the forests, the onset of desertification and full desertification. This historical view dismisses the theory that the desertification of the Sarah was caused by the tilting of the earth's axis as had been postulated by many (Boissoneault and Wright 2017).

The size of the Sahara Desert is approximately 3.5 million square miles, which makes it the largest hot desert in the world and it is much larger than the deserts created by the Indus Valley, Mesopotamian, Egyptian and Sudanese civilizations combined. The relative size of these deserts compared to the Sahara and the duration of each civilization, Mesopotamian Civilizations 5000- 612 BC, Egyptian Civilization 3000-1070 BC, Indus Valley Civilization 2500-1750 BC, may be an indication that the much older and larger Sahara may have contained, at different points in time, many much older and probably much larger civilizations that are yet to be discovered and recognized. If the Sahara has been a desert for 10,000 years as indicated by NASA, then the anthropogenic activities to create the unknown civilizations and consequently produce the desert must have taken place during the previous 10-30,000 years or earlier, based on the duration of the later civilizations and the size of the deserts created by them. When the size of the deserts created by the known early civilization are compared to that of the Sahara Desert it could safely be said that the Sahara Desert must have been created by many different more ancient civilizations over different periods of time.

Diseases

Plant diseases and invasive insect pests destroy millions of plants every year and according to FAO estimates, the loss to the agricultural sector is in the region of $220 billion due to plant diseases and $70 Billion due to invasive insect pests annually worldwide and these costs do not include the damage done to non-agricultural trees and plants. According to Fei, the volume of trees killed each year by the 15 most invasive diseases and insects is approximately six million US tons and this level of loss is relatively small as it represents only 0.04 percent of "the total live biomass in the contiguous US" Wallheimer (2019). This 0.04 percent is, however, indicative of the current level of forest penetration, less than 35 percent, achieved to date by the many invasive tree pest, approximately 450, that are in the US and the damage done could increase significantly with greater forest penetration. Researchers have also established that approximately 40 percent of American forested lands face a direct threat from these invasive tree pests.

Policies and Programs

The development of policies and programs that will see us formulating "best practices" with regards to forests and trees and every other elements of our natural environment, would be more sustainable if humans work to recreate the balance that existed with trees, plants, animals and the rest of nature prior to the industrial revolution when we did not see everything, including our fellow human beings, as resources or assets to be used only as required, because trees and plants represent much more than resources or assets to be consumed at the pleasure of humans. Trees and plants are an essential and unique part of the universe and they play as vital a role as the sun, land, rivers, lakes and seas in sustaining all animal life on planet Earth and until all humans develop this approach there will always be rampant destruction of forests, even under the guidelines of sustainability, to meet human needs. Sustainability is only setting a high bar, relative to the immediate past, which may be lower than the ones set by the many different religious groups in earlier times and those religious tenets gave way under the pressure of growing populations. This is quite evident in places like Ireland, UK, India and Nigeria where different religious grouping such as the Druids, Animists, Buddhist and Hindus and others, venerated and worshipped trees for many centuries yet this veneration and worship did not prevent the problems associated with the degradation of forest, deforestation and desertification. The statistics in the varying places are as follows:

- In Ireland, a land that initially had 80 % forest coverage, currently has only 11% forest coverage, the lowest forest coverage in Europe (Hickey 2016) up from less than 1% 100 years ago.

- The UK has only 13 % forest coverage with England 10%, Wales 15%, Scotland 19% and Northern Ireland 8 % (UK Forest Research).
- Nigeria has a forest coverage of only 9 %, down from forest coverage of approximately 66 % just over one hundred years ago.
- India has a forest coverage of 21.4 % (Forest Cover Current Affairs 2020), higher than Ireland, UK and Nigeria but rather low for a country with the population and size of India.

The tree venerating and worshipping cultures also had great problems with the loss of forest and trees, however, these relationships developed along religious lines allowed for the preservation of many small patches of old growth forests in many areas of the world which consequently ensured the continued existence of many species of flora and fauna that would have otherwise have been lost to humanity forever. The action of these cultures that ensured the continued existence of many species should be examined further to help in the selection of the positive elements that can be utilized to further benefit forests around the world and to provide guidance on prioritizing the true value of trees. The advent of climate change and the role that trees could play in mitigating the probable damage arising from it could see the world is entering into a new culture of tree "veneration", without the obvious religious connotations under the many new policies and programs that are being devised to use trees in the environment to curb and minimize the effects of climate change.

In any attempt to create a new perspective about the importance of trees, the old perspective must be examined to establish why trees are negatively impacted by human societies and find ways to minimize these impacts. Historically trees were deliberately destroyed or removed for reasons closely associated with the very survival of the human species inclusive of clearing land for agriculture (deforestation), timber production for the construction of human shelters (deforestation and forest degradation), wood for fuel (forest degradation) and non-timber forest products (forest degradation). Deforestation is a function of direct human activities that converts forests to non-forest land (IPCC 2008) and this conversion, in the ancient past, was mostly for agricultural purposes, shelter and monuments, however, later practices expanded to include such things as large residential developments, industrial and manufacturing developments, large mining and other economic activities. According to the IPCC (2008) Forest degradation is defined as 'direct human- induced long-term loss (persisting for x years or more) of at least Y per cent of forest carbon stock (and forest values) since time (T) and not qualifying as deforestation. Some forest degrading activities in the tropics includes (GOFC-Gold 2008):

- Selective logging
- Large-scale and open forest fires.
- Collection of fuel wood and non-timber forest products
- Production of charcoal, grazing, sub-canopy fires and shifting cultivation.

Many institutions, local, national and international, have developed and implemented policies and programs that are directly aimed at fostering the growth, regrowth and sustainable use of forest and forest products and all of these policies and programs have achieved a certain level of success. However, in the face of the threat from global warming, soil erosion, desertification, environmental pollution and the continued loss of forest due to forest fragmentation, forest degradation and deforestation, it appears that these policies and programs have not, to date, achieved the many goals set by the different organizations. The end result is forests loss, associated hydrological problems, global warming, desertification and consequently climate change which could have many disastrous consequences for life on earth.

Deserts and Desertification

Deserts and desert ecologies represent an important part of the natural biosphere even though the absence of trees, water and a large body of animals gives an appearance of emptiness, the absence of life, a great void and an unproductive waste land. However, what some deserts really represent, even with their arid beauty, could be the endpoint of anthropogenic activities that have permanently changed once fertile green lands into dried out unproductive barren waste and they could also show what could happen to the rest of the planet if action is not taken to reverse the damage done over many millennia. The creation of deserts, desertification, by whatever means can never be called a success story as it reduces the amount of lands that is and would be available to support life on the planet, as desertification means that more fertile lands will be converted to dried out arid unproductive lands that can only support a very small amount of life at a time when more land will be required to support the growing human populations of the world and the required flora and fauna that makes human life possible. In the long dark past there were many that saw deserts and desertification as the problems of others, especially those other that lived on the African and Asian continents where the oldest and biggest deserts are located, however, current data will clearly indicate that more deserts are being created, desertification, due to anthropogenic activities all around the world especially on the larger land masses. The most vulnerable areas have been shown to be the Western United States, the Sahel Region of Africa, Asia Minor, Central Asia and the Australian continent. The areas that are currently vulnerable to becoming deserts, separate and apart from the many existing deserts, can be found on any map highlighting desertification across the globe. This frightening picture of growing deserts caused by anthropogenic activities demanded urgent responses and many governments and international bodies have reacted with many policies and programs to first decelerate the pace of growth, and finally reverse the process of desertification. These policies and programs included, afforestation and reforestation programs in the worst affected areas in the world and the sustainable use of the lands and forests across the globe for agriculture, timber production, power generation, residential, commercial and industrial facilities and extraction of metals, gemstones and minerals. In countries like the USA these policies and program were initiated and implemented at all levels of governance, inclusive of the federal, state and local levels, thus giving people at all levels, especially at the community level an opportunity to understand and appreciate the value of forests and to actively participate in programs to plant and grow more trees locally.

Some of the laws, policies and programs that were developed and legislated at the Federal level and mirrored at the State levels includes:

- Sustainable Forest Management – USDA
- Sustainable Agriculture Management –USDA
- Sustainable Mining Practices – BLM
- Federal Land Policy and Management Act of 1976 - Created for the distinct purpose of managing publicly owned lands for the benefit of the people of the US. - BLM
- Forest Reserve Act of 1891- Policies and programs establishing Forest Reserves, forests to be preserved in perpetuity, to exclude logging and the mining of metals and minerals.
- Creative Act 1891 – That required that national forests must be managed for the people of the US.
- Weeks Law of 1911 Programs for the restoration of forest on former private lands.
- Organic Administration Act 1897 – Establish national working forests by the setting aside of public lands.
- National Forest Policy of 1922 – Lead the expansion of national forest in the Eastern US and the protection and restoration of millions of acres of land.
- The General Land Exchange Act of 1922- Empowered the Secretary of the Interior to obtain title to private lands that are located within National Forest Boundaries.

The policies, programs and legislation highlighted in the US are only examples, as the developed world inclusive of the Australia, European Union, Japan, Russia and Canada, have policies, programs and legislations that are as well developed and as well implemented as those in the US and are producing similar results to those in the US. In the developing nations the policies, programs and legislations are in place, in most instances, but may not be as well established and implemented, however, many with the help of the United Nation's Food and Agriculture Organization (FAO), they are working to improve their policies, programs and legislations to greatly improve their capacities.

At the international levels the FAO creates policies and programs that are aimed at facilitating efforts, in the less developed countries of the world, to utilize and preserve their existing forests in a sustainable manner, to use their agricultural lands in an efficient and sustainable manner and to develop afforestation and reforestation programs to grow and regrow forests to prevent or eliminate desertification. Two of the best-known afforestation projects are being done in collaboration with the FAO, are the Great Green Wall of the Sahara and Sahel which was design to stop the expansion of the Sahara Desert into the Sahel Region of Africa and eventually to encourage the afforestation and reforestation of lands in the countries closely connected to the Sahara Desert and China's Three- Norths Shelterbelt Program (Great Green Wall of China), designed and implemented by the government of China, with the support of the UN(Xin 2019) that was designed to stop the spread of the Gobi Desert which is currently encroaching on many village, towns and cities, inclusive of the capital city Beijing which is currently affected quite regularly by sand storms.

Impact of NGOs

There are also several Non-Governmental Organizations (NGOs) which are making significant contributions in an effort to support some important ideas such as the concept of sustainable forest management and some of them have come together to form an international body called the Forestry Stewardship Council (FSC) whose aim is to directly influence the sustainable operations and management of forests worldwide, through the creation and establishment of policies, programs and standards, which all participants in the forestry industry worldwide voluntarily agree to abide by. The FSC is an international non-profit organization and it was formed by a group of timber users, timber traders, environmental and human rights organizations, which had their first meeting in 1990 and was officially established by 1994(FSC). The ranks of this organization have grown to include a wider group of supporters, inclusive timber users, timber traders, environmental and human rights organizations, forestry professionals, indigenous people organizations, community forest groups and forestry product certification groups. The work of the

FSC is guided by their Global Forest Strategy which is designed to" halt and reverse the loss and degradation of forests and all kinds of woodlands (particularly old growth forest by 2000) and the Principles of Ethical Forestry and Plantation Principles (Rainforest Alliance).

The Principles of Ethical Forestry is based on the need for:

- A Forestry Management Plan
- Forestry Security
- The creation of social and economic benefits for all
- The rights of local people to benefit from the forests
- The assessment and mitigation of environmental impacts
- Maintaining sustained yields of forest products
- Maximizing the economic potentials of the forests
- Ensure that consumers pay the true cost to produce forest products
- Ensure the appropriate consumption of forest products
- Creating forest plantations to ensure the growth of replacement trees and affected ecosystems.

The Plantation Principle requires the following:

- A set of specific management objective
- A designed plantation layout.
- The planation of multi-crop trees to ensure diversity in consumption
- The selection of species for planting based on their overall suitability to existing conditions. Native trees are usually best suited for each location.
- Ensuring the proper proportion of overall forestry management areas
- Continuous monitoring and measuring of soil conditions to maintain and improve soil structure as required.
- Minimizing pest outbreaks using environmentally sound principles and practices
- Continuous monitoring of the plantation operations to assess the potential for negative on-site and off-site ecological and social impacts.

In the last 100 years many nations have begun to show that they understand the importance of forests and trees, not only as natural resources to be reaped, used or sold as humans see fit, but as a major ally of life on the planet. This realization has produced, for good and bad reasons:

- Policies, programs and legislations prepared and enacted by national governments, which are all designed to ensure that forests and forest products will exist in perpetuity for the use and enjoyment of all generations to come.
- The creation of strong vibrant international bodies dedicated to the long-term management, development, protection and long-term use of forests globally.
- A great swelling in the number of NGOs, such as WorldWide Fund for Nature, Environmental Defense Fund, The Nature Conservancy, The Audubon Society, the American Bird Conservancy, Forestry Stewardship Council, who are purpose driven to protect forest and the natural environment and who have played a significant role in pushing for greater levels of care for the environment and the fight back against the forces that view forest and the environment as only resources to be used.
- A great growth in the number of educational institutions, programs and degrees in nations across the globe that are focused on forestry education, which started with Hans Carl von Carlowitz in the early 18th century in Germany.
- The development of millions of astute forest experts at all levels around the globe.
- The accumulation of great bodies of knowledge that has filled up many libraries with forestry data and information and the need for sustainable growth, development and use of the earth's forest and other natural resources.
- The creation and development of plans to find, minimize or eliminate the causes of the immense loss of forests which have occurred since the start of the industrial revolution on into the modern era.
- The creation of programs to replant old forest lands and plant new forests on lands that were not forest previously, everywhere possible.

The acknowledgement by most nations of the problems relating to destruction of forests, the creation of the great bodies of knowledge, the creation of experts, the formulation and the implementation of plans to plant new forests or replant old forest lands, certification programs to ensure that forest are being sustainably operated and managed, the push to recycle and reuse old wood, has to date only produced fair results, results which are not commensurate with the efforts already put in place by almost everyone concerned. According to the Rainforest Alliance (2016), a founding member of the FSC, the loss of forest is still significant as "Each year we lose 32 million acres (13 million hectares), 26 times the size of the Grand Canyon or 60 acres per minute." This level of losses is not sustainable and this indicates that even with the current active afforestation and reforestation policies and programs, that many countries around the world are pursuing, a lot more must be done to reduce the pressure on one of the earths vital organs or true sustainability will never be achieved and the earth will continue to lose valuable flora and fauna, and the ability to care for its growing human population.

The pressures placed on forest by 'modern living' is a direct function of growing human needs, developed tastes and patterns of consumption, which will never abate until ways are found or learned to differentiate what is truly needed and what are just a function of tastes and patterns dictated by what many have called modern existence. An example of the problems created by 'modern living' is the use of well-designed, aesthetically pleasing packaging that every food product must now be presented in, according to the food marketing specialists around the world, and packaging material is usually made from the processing of logs which had been reaped from forests and which over time has been responsible for the loss of large volumes of trees all over the globe. The general paper industry consists of many other sectors and plays a significant role in the economies of many countries around the world as it employs millions of people, generate revenues, profits and pay taxes. The industry, in order to maintain its relevance, also works very hard to continually improve the level of efficiency related to their production processes, the quality and quantity of their products, while also seeking to gain market share. Unfortunately, even with significant improvements in the efficiency of the packaging industry the pressure on forest remains the same or is even greater as according to Burg and Lingquist (2019) "Packaging is growing all over the world, along with tissue papers and pulp hygiene products". The growth in these two areas are however, only a part of the whole picture as indicated by Burg and Lingquist (2019) "And a broad search for new applications and uses for wood and its components is taking place in numerous labs and development centers", which indicates that even in the face of the coming changes predicated by global climate change the industrial economic complexes built upon the use of forests have no plans to ease the pressure on trees.

Howard and Liang (2018) clearly indicate, in their 2015- 2019 Annual Market Review and Prospects, the strong relationship between economic growth in the US and the use of timber and forest products, with the rate of growth of the economy paralleling the rate of growth in the use of timber and forest products. The review shows continuing strong demands, with small annual fluctuations, for all forms of timber and forest products inclusive of sawn softwood, sawn hardwood, softwood log trade, hardwood log trade, pulpwood, structural panels, hardwood plywood, particle board and medium density fiber board, hardboard, insulation board, fuel wood, wood energy and biomass energy. The current approach, as indicted by Burg and Lingquist (2019) in the packaging industry, and reported by Howard and Liang (2018) clearly points to the reasons for the low level of success being achieved by the many well-intentioned policies, programs and laws initiated by international bodies, governments and people all around the world.

The timber, forest products, paper and packaging industry economic complex are responsible for many things affecting forestry including the following:

- The great demands placed on forest by competing entities.
- Minimizing the effects of the many other factors which are maintaining great pressure on forest, inclusive of meeting the demanding and competing basic needs of a growing human population.

- The level of effort and finances required to ensure the success of many well intended forest programs.
- The genuine absence of empathy for the needs of the peoples of the world by those who are only focused on using the natural resources of the world to create wealth for the financial benefit of a few only.

Carbon Capture and Storage

Carbon capture and storage is proven technology that has the capacity to help reduce the amount carbon dioxide in the atmosphere and therefore represents an option in the fight against global warming due to greenhouse gases and to mitigate against the effects of climate change. Unfortunately, this tool has become entangled in a fight between those environmentalists that think that the only solution to the problems associated with climate change is the complete elimination of the fossil fuel industry and those, in the fossil fuel industry, that think that carbon capture and storage will ensure (CCS) that there is no need to stop using fossil fuels, as long as the tool, CCS, can reduce carbon dioxide in the atmosphere to the required level to decelerate rising global temperature before the earth reaches the critical tipping point of an increase in temperature of 2^0C above the pre Industrial Age level, that will bring on the full blown effects of climate change.

If the aim of all involved is to truly eliminate or prevent a disaster directly caused by human activities only, then this fight is unfortunate and quite wasteful and all effort must be made at all levels to quash it immediately because the fight is not about personal positions on critical issues or about undermining any particular industry, it is about averting possible cataclysmic environmental events that could completely alter life on planet Earth. CCS is a tool with a capacity to make a difference that has been acknowledged at the highest level by the IPCC and must be utilized in the best way possible to benefit all inhabitants of the world.

Forest Restoration, Afforestation and Reforestation Efforts

The three major projects examined clearly indicates that it is possible to tackle large desert and desertification problems with programs and projects design to use the tools of forest restoration, afforestation and reforestation. These projects also indicate that all such projects will require great effort, perseverance, significant financial support and an extended period of time to complete. The results achieved in Israel took one hundred years, while the Chinese Green Wall was designed to be completed in seventy-two years and the revised version of the Green Wall of the Sahara indicates that full completion of the project will also take a relatively long period of time to complete. The Green Wall of the Sahara is already achieving significant short-term results.

The results in the arid Sahel regions of Africa also indicate that starting the fight against the problem in the early stage before a full-blown desert has been created can bring significant results in a relatively short period of time and this result can significantly impact the lives of all who live in the environments as it will create new opportunities to produce many goods and services that would not have been possible prior to the implementation of the project. These programs are however not without their critics in the environmental community as many doubt that either the Chinese or African projects can achieve the lofty goals stated at the beginning of the projects, which is significant, however, while achieving all the goals of a project is very important for all project managers this cannot be used as the benchmark for success in any of these programs. The success must be measured by the planting of the one hundred billion trees by 2050 in China and the effect that planting these trees have had over the 72 years life of the project to date and the projected impact for the next 72 years upon the environment in China. The success in the Sahel region must be measured by the increase in food production in the region and the elimination of food shortages that have negatively impacted the lives of the people in the region for many decades. Secondly the results achieved by both of these projects cannot be seen as an end point in themselves but as new starting points to continue the fight against deserts and desertification.

Conclusion

The existing condition of forests, which are the lungs and the immune system of the planet earth requires a change in paradigms, a 180 degree shift away from our present sustainability course, which is far better than every other previous approach, but which still cannot reduce effectively the rate at which humans are destroying forests, to a course that will lift the discussion about the very existence of humans on the planet if we continue to abuse and destroy the very elements that make the earth livable. The facts are simple, without trees and plants there would be no oxygen to breathe, no ozone to block out dangerous UV Rays, no shade to further protect relatively delicate plants and animals which are essential to life on earth, no fruits, nuts, vegetable, grains or roots to consume and consequently no human beings or animals.

The discussions about the importance of trees and plants have been ongoing from the beginning of human existence according to the Jewish and Christian creation stories, and confirmed by other early creation myths from other cultures around the world inclusive of the Epic of Gilgamesh, Native American creation story and Native Australian Aborigines creation story among others, which points to the following:

- The first man and woman came to life in a forest, rich with plants and animals, as it was trees and plants of the forest which created the oxygen to give humans and the other animals the breath of life.
- The forest provided everything that the first pair of humans needed to live.
- The pair were "given instructions" that they should not utilize every tree in the forests.
- The subsequent utilization of all of the trees in that particular forest, over thousands of years, lead to the first major climate change that made food scarce and forced humans to adjust their lifestyle, which initially only involved finding and reaping the output of trees and plants in the forest (hunter-gatherers), to

becoming tillers of soil (farmers) to produce their food by the efforts of their own hands.

- The ideal existence found by humans was created by trees and plants over a 400 million years period and was significantly damaged by human activity over a period of 2-7 million years and this set a pattern followed much later in time in Africa, Asia, the Americas, Europe and Oceana.

- That first climate change was not the last, as climate changes became a permanent feature of life on planet earth, with cyclical increases and decreases in forest coverage causing significant changes in climate conditions as humans change their patterns of consumption due to natural phenomena such as volcanic activities, earthquakes, natural fires, impacts by meteorites, the ice age or the mass destruction of human life and curtailment of activities caused by war and disease, as was experienced in the Little Ice Age (Mann 2002) in the Northern Hemisphere inclusive of both the North America and Europe. In North America the arrivals of other humans with new ways of life, new animals and new diseases caused the destruction of 90 % of the Native American population and the curtailment of 90% of their activities, while in Europe and the destruction human lives due to the black plague and other diseases created the same impact.

The discussions, then as now, have always been earnest and sincere followed by some actions to regrow forests or use of alternative sources of energy as occurred in Europe during the 16th, 17th and 18th centuries, only to return to a period of complete relapse and the continuation of policies that saw the decimation of forest in places like Ireland, England, Scotland and Wales. Forestry coverage in Ireland fell to 1% or less in the 19th century and is now at 11%, while forest coverage in the UK (England, Scotland, Wales) is currently on average at 13%. The discussions in the early 18th century, reached a high point when people like von Carlowitz realized that their mining or other operations would be halted because Europe was running out of forest timber which provided their main source of energy and his realization of the destruction that was occurring and the negative impact that it would be having on his immediate business activities at the present time and in the near future, led him to start the first school for silviculture that lead to a significant growth in the body of knowledge about forest and created a significant change in the German and later wider European approach to forest growth and utilization of forest products. Unfortunately, this conversion in Germany and the wider Europe, may have come too late for the forests of the Americas, as the many Europeans that migrated to the new world brought with them the earlier culture of wanton destruction of forests that lasted well into the 20th century, causing problems such as desertification and dust storms, which were a function of their agricultural practices, their lack of appreciation for the aesthetic value of forests, flora and fauna, their fear of the unknown, thought to be contained and hidden in the new forest of the Americas, and their inherent desires to make the new lands look like the old lands from which they came.

The discussions today while couched in much broader social, economic and environmental terms are still focused mostly on the long-term economic value of forests to humans, with all other concerns being secondary, which provides the basis for the approach that parlays policies, programs and legislations about sustainability and the need to protect and regrow forest, while economic growth, through many industries, destroys the forests faster than we can grow them. If real long-term changes are to occur, greater social, spiritual, environmental and economic value must be placed upon forest and trees, with forests becoming the standards by which a nation's wealth is determined instead Gross Domestic Product, gold, precious metals, gemstones or US dollars as none of them by themselves can provide for basic human needs. The point could also be made that placing greater economic value on gold has brought the forests of the world to a point that makes them unable to supply their former bounty to humans.

14

Solutions and Alternative Pathways

The body of knowledge about trees and forests accumulated since the early 18th century or earlier contains more than enough information to permanently resolve the issues related to forest fragmentation, forest degradation, deforestation and desertification and this body of knowledge has been integrated to create policies, legislations, regulations and practices at the local, national and international levels as embodied in agreements like the Paris Accord and other international agreements, that if conscientiously applied would ensure the life of forests and trees well beyond sustainable levels and take forests to a point of flourishing within defined and expanded forest boundaries and within urban centers. Unfortunately, with all the good intentions of governments, local, national, and international bodies such as the UN, the body of knowledge, legislations and practice, to date, have not yet produced the desired results except in a few places and millions of trees are still being lost on an annual basis due to anthropogenic activities and the losses, net losses, are happening in the presence of the many great afforestation, reforestation, soil conservation and other agricultural programs and practices that have been initiated within the last seventy years. The body of knowledge contains solutions that are tried and proven and includes the following:

- Increasing the efficiency of land use to increase agricultural production to ensure that nutritional needs of the world's population are met.
- The development of hybrid crops and utilizing crops that require less land and less water.
- The utilization of new science and technological methods inclusive of genetic modifications to increase productivity and resistance to disease, insect pest and drought.
- The utilization of GPS and precision planting technology to optimize land use.
- The replanting of forests on the lands taken out of agricultural production with the increased efficiency in productivity and yields.
- The utilization of other crop growing technologies inclusive of hydroponics, indoor vertical farming, automation and robotics, livestock technology, modern greenhouse technologies, precision agriculture, artificial intelligence, blockchain and other developing technologies to increase efficient food production.
- The modification of land use regulations to ensure increased forests coverage on a permanent basis.
- Establishing of regulation to ensure that mining companies reestablish permanent forests in the areas that they have mined out.
- The establishment of legislation and regulations to limit mining in critical forests around the globe.
- The reestablishment of high fiber fast growing plants, as a source for pulp to meet the growing demands for paper and paper products, inclusive of kenaf, hemp, bamboo, sugar cane, rice-stalks, wheat and barley stalks and other suitable waste from agricultural production.
- The genetic modification of several species of trees to make them drought resistant and more durable for use in afforestation and reforestation projects.
- The planting of forests to utilize excess carbon dioxide within the atmosphere and the utilization of Carbon Capture and Storage Systems to the provide necessary additional carbon sequestration capacity.

These solutions contained in the existing body of knowledge and established practices has to date produced significant results in the increase of efficiency in food production and if these older solutions are coupled with newer proposed measures they could together produce even greater results and lessening of the burden on existing forests and help to foster the restoration of more old forest and some of these proposed new measure are as follows:

- The modification of food packaging and distribution standards to ensure the reduction in the amount of paper-based packaging material required and therefore the amount of damage done to forest to meet the needs of this industry.
- The modification of logistics related to the transportation of food and essential products to reduce or eliminate the use of wood fixtures and the complete replacement of all wood pallets with pallets made from recycled plastics only, to reduce the pressure placed on forests and also to prevent waste plastics from entering the natural environment.
- The establishment of international regulations requiring specific increases in forest coverage to meet a permanent national minimum coverage in all nations around the globe, through the dedication of a percentage of the lands that are currently exclusively used for grazing. The national minimum coverage must be a function of the level of industrialization of each country's economy. The US and most major agricultural economies dedicate much more lands for grazing animals than they do to forests, to meet the demands for beef, lamb, mutton, goatmeat and deer meat in their respective populations. The implementation of these changes would force dietary changes on the part of people in the developed world that consume large volumes of beef, lamb and mutton and these dietary changes can produce many significant health and environmental benefits as red meat is known to negatively affect the health of humans and cows are known to produce large volumes of methane, a known greenhouse gas.

- The lands taken from grazing should be dedicated to forests reserves or transfer the equivalent amount of existing working forest to forest reserves, that is lands that are off limits for any form of business or production activity ad infinitum.
- The modification of designs and material requirements of residential facilities, all across the globe to reduce the amount of timber required, to reduce the pressure on forests.
- The modification of national, state and local legislation to limit the spread of urban sprawl to allow more space for forests and natural vegetations. The use of more high rise dwelling could greatly help to minimize or eliminate urban sprawl.
- The creation and implementation of regulations to make all urban centers more livable by ensuring that a specific percentage of lands for development, 40-50% are dedicated to parks, forests, trees and natural plant coverage and that these requirements become an integral legal requirement for planning approval. These regulations must also include requirements for green roofs and the use of renewable energy in all urban centers to reduce and eliminate where possible the heat island effect that now negatively impacts all urban centers and to reduce the amount of "dirty" energy taken off the grid.
- The utilization of waste plastics in ecological and environmentally safe ways. Plastic waste is currently a major scourge to the environment all around the globe and it is a problem which will not be resolved until several profitable and environmentally sustainable ways can be found to utilize it. One possible solution may be to the utilize the waste plastics in the fight against desertification by the creation and utilization of artificial trees made from this waste plastic to perform some of the functions of natural trees inclusive of providing habitat for birds, insects and other tree dwelling animals, blocking the direct rays of the sun and thereby shading the soil to reduce the drying out effect of solar radiation, forming a barrier to reduce or eliminate soil erosion by wind and water and absorbing a portion of precipitation. The artificial trees could be provided with water absorbing material for leaves and bark. While artificial trees will

never perform all of the important functions of natural trees it is very possible that the functions that they will perform will be sufficient to:

- Attract birds, insects, tree loving animals,
- Use their structure to block and trap some of the seeds that are transported by the wind which will then be deposit under their canopy where they may germinate and create new life around the lifeless trees.
- The birds and insects that are attracted may also deposit seeds but to encourage the growth of new plants in a barren region the space under the canopy of the artificial trees could be seeded, provided with small patches of good soil with the needed bacteria and soils animals and watered in the early stages to get the process going.
- The shade provide by these artificial trees will also reduce the vaporizing effect of solar radiation and this will allow a greater portion of any precipitation to infiltrate into the soils.
- Artificial trees could be used in many different conditions and for many different purposes inclusive of recreating conditions to facilitate the replanting of desert areas, enhancing of the beauty of residential communities while eliminating problems associated with plant diseases and maintenance, providing temporary shade until newly planted trees are grown and providing good shade for seeds transported by wind and birds in arid areas.

- The establishment of laws and regulations to limit the size of agricultural fields and ensure that shelterbelts remain a permanent fixture in all agricultural fields globally. In recent years many farmers have started removing the shelterbelts to improve the efficiency of using their mechanized equipment and there is new evidence to suggest that it is possible for the conditions needed for Dust Bowl, are again being created and it could return in a relatively short period of time.

Carbon Capture and Storage.

As established earlier, while trees and plants are the perfect tools for the removal of carbon dioxide from the atmosphere, in the current climate change era trees and plants alone are no longer be sufficient to remove the excess carbon dioxide at a sufficient pace to mitigate against the expected impact of the oncoming climate change and another method of direct removal, carbon capture and storage must be utilized. Carbon capture and storage, the process of withdrawing carbon dioxide directly from the atmosphere or directly from fossil fuel burning, carbon dioxide producing equipment and storing it securely, is of greatest importance if the problems associated with climate change are to be mitigated and minimized, since climate change is being driven by the amount of excess carbon dioxide in the atmosphere. Historically the preferred methods for the removal and storage of the excess carbon dioxide were terrestrial sequestration methods using forests, improved soil conservation methods and the reestablishment of wetlands and grasslands, however, it has been established that these methods are currently insufficient and that new methods are required to improve the capacity to remove carbon dioxide from the atmosphere.

While carbon sequestration in all forms present a very good options for removing excess carbon dioxide, the best option would be the production and emission of less carbon dioxide into the atmosphere which would require new carbon free green methods of producing electrical energy, green transportation systems, green methods of production in manufacturing, industry and agriculture. In the best interest of life on earth and the natural environment, the best option for carbon sequestration would be a combination of the following:

- Reducing the production and emission of carbon dioxide in the atmosphere by reducing or eliminating the use of fossil fuels.
- Optimizing the use of terrestrial sequestration by mandating the increase of forest coverage to agreed levels globally, improving agricultural methods and restoring wetlands and grasslands.
- Utilizing CCS methods at every location where fossil fuel is still used to create electrical energy or to do other work in industry.

The installation of CCS equipment, the facility to transport and stored the carbon dioxide must be a basic requirement for the purchase and utilization of all fossil fuels.

- Utilize CCS methods to directly pull carbon dioxide from the atmosphere as required.
- The creation of more large reforestation and afforestation projects similar to the green Wall of China and Green Wall Initiative of Africa in other desert regions of the world.
- Continuation of both the Green Wall of China and Green Wall of the Sahara until the ultimate outcome is achieved, the transformation of these massive deserts.

Economic Pathways

All of the solutions presented above are directly related to forests, trees, agriculture, new technologies, legislations and regulations at the local, national and international levels that could facilitate a reduction of the many pressures on forests, however, none of these solutions will have the desired long-term results and success without also creating and fostering an alternative approach to current economic outlooks and practices. This alternative approach would involve the modification of the existing economic system of valuation as created and maintained by the world's economic and monetary free market systems, where the "market" determines the value of everything. These free-market systems have been shown to be great for regulating the cost of commodities, based on supply and demand, however, these systems have not to date provided an answer to the diminishing stock of forests and species as in any drive to make the markets work better new products must always be created and marketed and this need for new and better products allows the free market to maintain consistent pressure on natural forest resources. This proposed modification of the systems of economic valuation if reasonable and allowed could reduce the pressure on forest resources, however, if the proposed changes are to have any value they must necessarily place greater importance on the things that are more essential to life relative to things like precious metals, mineral and gems as in the current free market a few ounces of gold or a few karats of diamond or a few barrels of oil are seen as much more valuable than trees in a forest that has the potential to directly feed, heal and shelter humans and animals, which none of the former things can do directly.

Historically the most basic function of gold, silver, platinum, diamonds, gems and pearls are as ornaments or decoration for the human body yet for many centuries they have been given much higher economic values than food, medicine, shelter and water, based upon the existing systems of economic valuations which are heavily slanted towards these items and thereby providing the economic basis for justifying the destruction of forests to find, process and sell these "precious items". It is therefore probable that readjusting upwards the economic value placed on forests relative to that placed on metals, minerals, concrete and steel, could significantly reduce the economic pressures on forests all around the globe. However, any proposed change to the system of international economic valuation, an issue that would have far reaching global impacts, would have to be agreed upon by all nations to eliminate any and all repercussions that would arise from making any such monumental change.

The complete set of mechanisms required to make the necessary changes are way beyond the capacity of this writer and the scope of this book, however, limiting the supply of wood and forest products on the international markets for set intervals and then allowing the laws of supply and demand to force the necessary changes could go a long way towards increasing the value of timber and forest products and with the help of strict controls help to ease the pressure on forest. It should also be noted that any increase in value achieved by the adjustment of economic value of forests relative to precious metals could serve to increase interests in the creation and ownership of forested lands and could consequently lead to an increase in the acreage covered in privately owned forests and could also create an opportunity to increase the monetization and trading of more live forest stocks that would create more wealth for the forest owners. This monetization of live forest could also allow the public to participate, through the acquisition of forest stocks and shares, directly in saving forest and the environment, which is of common interest to all humanity. Any increase in relative economic value of forests would also redound to the benefit of the many nations with rich forest resources that provide a source of income derived from the international trade in timber and forest products, a trade which is currently valued in the hundreds of billions of dollars annually. Naturally, the countries with the greatest forest resources should be the greatest benefactors of any upward valuation of forests, however, this may not the case as in reality many nations with smaller forests are bigger participants in the international trade in timber and forest products than many larger nations with larger forest resources based on current international trade and other practices. This is typically the case with continental Europe versus continental South America and continental Africa, as several countries in Europe, such as Sweden, Finland and Germany produce and trade much more timber and forest products than much larger countries such as Brazil and all of the South American nations that share the Amazon Rainforests. These South American nations face great international pressures to reduce or eliminate their timber, forest products and agricultural businesses due to the environmentally sensitive nature of the of the location of their forests, Amazonia.

The economic and social pressures being placed on these nations to save the Amazon Rainforests due to its ecological and environmental importance to the global community, appear to be inequitable, as the Amazon Rainforests benefits the whole human population and therefore the pressures should be the borne by all humanity and not only by these nations, as these nations of South America have the same economic needs to provide food, healthcare and shelter for their growing populations in the same way that the European nations do. It should therefore mean that if the Amazon Rainforests are to be saved in the interest of all humanity, which they should be, then all nations need to play a role and this could be achieved if all nations that are linked to the Amazon are provided an income equivalent to the possible earning from the Amazon lands, to curtail logging and expansive growth in agriculture that demands the clearing of more lands in the pristine tropical rainforests. These same economic and social pressure are also being applied to African nations which also own rich tropical rainforests and are trying to utilize them as assets to improve the status of their nations.

Spiritual and Educational Pathways

The proposed changes in economic valuation, economic programs to prevent the destruction of the Amazon and African Rainforests, the reforestation of former forest lands, afforestation of new lands, programs to reduce and eliminate deserts, the planting of urban trees, the utilization of artificial trees, the refinement of agricultural and mining practices to minimize the loss of forests and all programs designed to increase forest coverage may not be sufficient to save existing forests and create the necessary new forests if the relegation of forests and trees to levels of commodities only is not changed. This attitude and outlook, commoditization of forests, is responsible for how most modern humans view forests and the reason why so many forests have disappeared and continues to disappear all around the globe and for real lasting changes to be achieved this outlook must be modified to reflect a little of the veneration accorded forests and trees by so many ancient cultures around the globe who have, through their many different approaches, managed to preserve little pockets of life that would have been lost forever without their outlook. Properly understood these ancient approaches, which on the surface clashes with some of the major religious philosophies, can be enhanced to explain the true place of trees in the universe and the care required of humans to ensure their continued and eternal performance of their roles to support life on the planet.

Unfortunately, the required change in philosophical outlook cannot be achieved overnight but only through long-term improvement in forest education within all modern societies and the transfer of these ideas to modify human behavior towards forests can only start through a modification of the educational approaches provided to our children at the earliest levels, starting at home. This new outlook must then be carried into the classrooms from kindergarten through high school and on through to the tertiary levels of education where all environmental programs at the associate, bachelor and master levels must be required to have forestry as an area of concentration.

References

Introduction

Christenhusz, M.J.M and Byng, J. W. (2016) The number of known plant species in the world and its annual increase. Phytotaxa https://www.researchgate.net/publication/303371386_The_number_of_known_plant_species_in_the_world_and_its_annual_increase/link/573ed32808ae

World Most (2011) Top ten oldest trees in the world. World Most. Retrieved from: http://worldmost.org/oldest-tree

Chapter

Kinver, M. (2017) World is Home to "60,000 Tree Species"

Mark, J., Newton, A. C., Oldfield, S. and Rivers, M. () The International Timber Trade: A working List of Commercial Timber Tree Species, Faculty of Science & Technology, Bournemouth University, Botanical Gardens Conservation International

Lloyd, E. (October 2018) Secrets of The Lost Ancient Sahara Civilization, Ancient Pages.

Action Against Desertification, Ethiopia. Food and Agricultural Organization, United Nations. Retrieved from: www.fao.org/in- action/action-against-desertification/countries/africa/ethiopia/en/

Gul, S., Siddiqui, Z.S., Noman, A. and Rasheed, F. (August 2017) Tree Anatomy and Physiology. Retrieved from: https://www.researchgate. net/publication/319306758_Tree_Anatomy_and_Physiology

Bales, C. (2012) Basic Tree Anatomy. Texas Forest Service. Retrieved from: https://www.treefolks.org/wp-content/uploads/2012/09/Clay-Bales-Tree-Anatomy-part-1.pdf

Pettersen, R.C. (1984) The Chemical Composition of Wood. US Department of Agriculture, Forest Service, Forest Products Laboratory, Madison, WI 53705. Retrieved from https://www.fpl.fs.fed.us/documnts/pdf1984/pette84a.pdf

How to Calculate the Amount of CO 2 Sequestered in a Tree per Year Retrieved from: www.unm.edu/~jbrink/365/Documents/Calculating_tree_carbon.pdf

Johnson, S.E. and Abrams, M. D. (2009) Age class, longevity and growth rate relationship: protracted growth increases in old trees in the eastern United States. Oxford Academic. Retrieved from: https://academic.oup.com/treephys/article/29/11/1317/164901

Rost, T. L. () The organization of the plant body. Department of Plant Biology, University of California, Davis. Retrieved from: http://www-plb.ucdavis.edu/courses/bis/1c/text/Chapter4nf.pdf

Chapter 2

King, H. M (2015?) Pangaea Supercontinent. Geology.com. Retrieved from: https://geology.com/articles/supercontinent.shtml

Thomas, P. (January 2000) Trees: Their Natural History. Cambridge University Press. Keele University Retrieved from: https://www.researchgate.net/publication/259357794_Trees_Their_Natural_History/link/0a85e53958b701a4eb000000/download

Janick, J. (2005) The origins of fruit, fruit growing and fruit breeding. Plant Breeding Rev 25:255–320. Retrieved from: https://hort.purdue.edu/newcrop/origins%20of%20fruits.pdf

Nix, S. (2020) "Evolution of Forests and Trees." ThoughtCo, Feb. 11, 2020, thoughtco.com/evolution-of-forests-and-trees-1342664. Retrieved from: https://www.thoughtco.com/evolution-of-forests-and-trees-1342664

Harari, Y.N (2014) Sapiens A brief history of humankind. Signals McCLelland and Stewart. Retrieved from: www2.southeastern.edu/Academics/Faculty/mrossano/grad_cog/ancestral%20landscapes/sapiens%20book.pdf

Chapter 24 – Gymnosperms. Retrieved from: www-plb.ucdavis.edu/courses/bis/1c/text/Chapter24nf.pdf

Angiosperm: Flowering Plants Retrieved from: :courses.washington.edu/bot113/summer/WebReadings/PdfReadings/ANGIOSPERMS.pdf

Chapter 25 – Angiosperms. Retrieved from: http://www-plb.ucdavis.edu/courses/bis/1c/text/Chapter25nf.pdf

Brown, C. S. (2014) MesoAmerica: Civilization. Retrieved from: https://school.bighistoryproject.com/media/khan/articles/U7_Mesoamerica_2014_800L.pdf

Anitei, S. (2008) Inca Human Sacrifices: Children for the gods. Softpedia news Retrieved from: https://news.softpedia.com/news/Inca-Human-Sacrifices-79148.shtml

Stevenson, Mark. (2005) Brutality of Aztecs and Mayas corroborated. Los Angeles Times. Retrieved from:https://www.latimes.com/archives/la-xpm-2005-jan-23-adfg-sacrifice23-story.html

Ingber, S. (2017) Photos: Trees that tell stories about the world we live in. NPR, WAMU 88.5 American University Radio. Retrieved from:

https://www.npr.org/sections/goatsandsoda/2017/10/15/557121926/photos-trees-that-tell-stories-about-the-world-we-live-in

What is Your Tree Sign According to Celtic Tree Astrology Retrieved from: https://blog.fantasticgardeners.co.uk/whats-your-tree-sign-according-to-celtic-tree-astrology/

Tree Lore. Retrieved from: https://druidry.org/druid-way/teaching-and-practice/druid-tree-lore

Barnett, R. (2007) Sacred Groves: Sacrifice and the order of nature in ancient Greek landscapes. Landscape Journal26:2, University of Wisconsin Press, 252-269. Retrieved from: www.nonlinearlandscapes.com/sacred-groves

Tacitus (2013) The Germany and Agricola of Tacitus. The Oxford Translation Revised with Notes. Retrieved from: https://www.gutenberg.org/files/7524/7524-h/7524-h.htm

Khan, M.L., Khumbongmayum, A.D. and Tripathi, R.S. (2008) The sacred groves and their significance in conserving biodiversity. An Overview. International Journal of Ecology and Environment 34(3) 277-291, 2008, National Institute of Ecology, New Delhi. Retrieved from: https://www.activeremedy.org/wp-content/uploads/2014/10/ml-khan-et-al-2008-the-sacred-groves-and-their-significance-in-conserving-biodiversity.pdf

Corvillo Arroyo, S. (2015) Sacred Groves Retrieved from: https://foresttaenglish.wordpress.com/2015/06/01/sacred-grove/

Polidor, A. (2004) Sacred Groves of India. Sacred Land Film Project. Retrieved from: https://sacredland.org/sacred-groves-of-india-india/

Goodin, D.K., Wassie, A. and Lowman, M. (2019) The Ethiopian Orthodox Tewahedo Church Forest and Economic Development: The Case of Traditional Ecological Management. Journal of Religion & Society, Volume 21(2019) ISSN 1522-5668 The Kripke Center.

Retrieved from: https://dspace2.creighton.edu/xmlui/bitstream/handle/10504/121318/2019-3.pdf

Shrivastava, J.L.(Dr.), Masih, S.K.(Dr.) and Homkar, U. (Dr.) (2009) Assessment of Status and Role of Sacred Groves in Conservation of Biodiversity at Different Levels in Madhya Pradesh – District Chhindwara. MP State Biodiversity Board, Bhopal (MP) and State Forest Research Institute, Polipather, Jabalpur (MP). Retrieved from: www.mpsbb.nic.in/completedProject/SG.pdf

Corbin, A. (2008) Sacred Groves of Ghana. Sacred Land Film Project. Retrieved from: https://sacredland.org/sacred-groves-of-ghana-ghana/

Chapter 3

Rahula, W. (1974) What the Buddha taught (revised edition). Grove Press, New York. Retrieved from: https://web.ics.purdue.edu/~buddhism/docs/Bhante_Walpola_Rahula-What_the_Buddha_Taught.pdf

St. Matthew (AD 100) The Gospel According to Matthew. New Testament of the Christian Bible, King James Version. Retrieved from: https://www.kingjamesbibleonline.org/Matthew-Chapter-4/

Schneider, R.J. (2019) Thoreau's Life. The Thoreau Society. Retrieved from: https://www.thoreausociety.org/life-legacy

Bassett, C.G. (2015) The environmental benefit of trees on an urban university campus. University of Pennsylvania. Retrieved from: https://repository.upenn.edu/mes_capstones/66/

Coder, R. D. (Dr.) (1996) Identified Benefits of Community Trees and Forests. University of Georgia. Retrieved from: https://nfs.unl.edu/documents/communityforestry/coderbenefitsofcommtrees.pdf

Nowak, D.J., Crane, D. E and Stevens, J.C. (2006) Air Pollution Removal by Urban Trees and Shrubs in the United States. USDA Forest Service Northeastern Research Station 5 Moon Library, SUNY-ESF

Syracuse, NY 13210. Retrieved from: https://www.researchgate.net/publication/222411712_Air_Pollution_Removal_by_Urban_Trees_and_Shrubs_in_the_United_States/link/5bab75ee299bf13e604cda8e/download

Brahimi-Horn, M.C. and Pouyssegur, J. (2007) Oxygen a source of life and stress. Elsevier, FEBS Letters, Volume 581, Issue 19, 31 July 2007, Page 3582 -359. Retrieved from: https://www.sciencedirect.com/science/article/pii/S0014579307006667

Johnson, M.P. (2016) Photosynthesis. Portland Press. Retrieved from: https://www.researchgate.net/publication/309466837_Photosynthesis

Nowak, D.J. (2002) The Effect of Urban Trees on Air Quality. USDA Forest Service Syracuse, New York. Retrieved from: https://www.nrs.fs.fed.us/units/urban/local-resources/downloads/Tree_Air_Qual.pdf

Sterling, T.M. (2004) Transpiration - Water Movements through Plants. Department of Entomology, Plant Pathology and Weed Science, New Mexico State University. Retrieved from: https://www.sciencemag.org/site/feature/misc/webfeat/vis2005/show/transpiration.pdf

Ansari, A. S. (2003) Influence of Forests on Environment. XII World Forestry Congress 2003, Quebec Canada. Retrieved from: www.fao.org/3/XII/1018-B2.HTM

USDA, NRCS (2000) Soil Erosion NRCS, USDA. Retrieved from: https://www.nrcs.usda.gov/Internet/FSE_DOCUMENTS/nrcs142p2_010152.pdf

Tatarko, J. () Wind Erosion: Problem, Processes and Controls. USDA-Agricultural Research Services, Engineering and Wind Erosion Research Unit. Retrieved from:
https://www.nrcs.usda.gov/Internet/FSE_DOCUMENTS/nrcs142p2_019407.pdf

Khan, M.A. and Ghouri, A.M. (2011) Environmental Pollution: Its Effects on Life and Its Remedies. International Researchers Journal, Vol.- II, Issue – 2 April 2011. Retrieved from: www.retawprojects.com/uploads/Paper_23.pdf

Rodrigues-Eugenio, N., McLaughlin, M. and Pennock, D (2018) Soil Pollution: a hidden reality. Rome, FAO, 142 pp. Retrieved from: www.fao.org/3/i9183en/i9183en.pdf

Ali, M., Bhat, A.K., Dolkar, T. and Malik, M.A. (2018) Phytoremediation: A plant-based technology. International Journal of Current Microbiology and Applied Sciences. ISSN:2319-7706 Volume 03 (2018). Retrieved from: https://www.ijcmas.com/7-3-2018/MansoorAli,etal.pdf

USEPA (2000) Introduction to Phytoremediation. EPA/600/R-99/107. Retrieved from: https://clu-in.org/download/remed/introphyto.pd

IFAD(UN) () Desertification. Rome, Italy. Retrieved from: https://www.unisdr.org/files/1794_VL102205.pdf

Camhi, A.L (2009) Reforestation Challenges and Opportunities. Mongabay. Retrieved from: https://news.mongabay.com/2009/11/reforestation-challenges-and-opportunities/

Haupt, F. and Von Lupke, H. (2007) Obstacles and opportunities for afforestation and reforestation projects under the Clean Development Mechanism of the Kyoto Protocol. FAO,

Advisory Committee on Paper and Wood Products, UNFCCC. Retrieved from: http://www.fao.org/forestry/12713-0f8177c8e7d25bea8226c3e1c3240805a.pdf

Chapter 4

Nasa, Climate Science Investigations (CSI). Retrieved from: http://www.ces.fau.edu/nasa/module-2/how-greenhouse-effect-works.php

Stute, M. (2007) The climate system, EESC 2100 Spring 2007. Retrieved from: https://eesc.columbia.edu/courses/ees/climate/lectures/greenhouse.html

Leys, A.J. (2012) How is carbon stored in trees and wood products? Forest Learning, Forest and Wood Products of Australia. Retrieved from: https://forestlearning.edu.au/images/resources/Howcarbonisstoredintreesandwoodproducts.pdf

Seinfeld, J.H. and Pandis S. N. (2006) Atmospheric chemistry and physics: from air pollution to climate change- chapter 1 atmosphere: history and evolution of the earth's atmosphere. Retrieved from: https://catalogimages.wriley.com/images//pdf/0471720186.01.pdf

Yu, J-Y. Composition and structure of the atmosphere. Retrieved from: https://www.ess.uci.edu/~yu/class/ess5/Chapter.1.composition.all.pdf

Sundquist, E., Burrus, R., Faulkner, S., Gleason, R., Harden, J., Kharaka, Y., Tieszen, L., and Waldrop, M. (2008) Carbon sequestration to mitigate climate. US Geological Survey. Retrieved from: changehttps://pubs.usgs.gov/fs/2008/3097/pdf/CarbonFS.pdf

PG&E Gas R&D and Innovation (2018) Carbon capture and sequestration/alternative carbon markets. Retrieved from: https://www.pge.com/pge_global/common/pdfs/for-our-business-partners/interconnection-renewables/interconnections-renewables/Whitepaper_AlternativeCarbonMarkets.pdf

Herzog, H. (2009) Carbon dioxide capture and storage. Massachusetts Institute of Technology, Energy Initiative. Retrieved from: https://sequestration.mit.edu/pdf/2009_CO2_Capture_and_Storage_Ch13_book.pdf

Vincent, W.F. (2009) Cyanobacteria. Encyclopedia of Inland Water, 2009 pg 226-232. Retrieved from: https://www.sciencedirect.com/science/article/pii/B9780123706263001277

Chapter 5

Bronaugh, W. (2012) North American Forest in the Age of Man. American Forest. Retrieved from: https://www.americanforests.org/magazine/article/north-american-forests-in-the-age-of-man/

Lesson 3: Economic Importance -Timber and Forest Products. Retrieved from: hub.rockyview.ab.ca/mod/book/view.php?id=794&chapter id=1143

Hamblin, J. (2014) The dark side of almond use. The Atlantic, Health. Retrieved from: https://www.theatlantic.com/health/archive/2014/08/almonds-demon-nuts/379244/

Barthel, M., Jennings, S., Schreiber, W., Sheane, R., Royston, S., Fry, J., Khor, Y.L. and McGill, J. (2018) Study on the environmental impact of palm oil consumption and on existing sustainability standards. Luxembourg, European Union. Retrieved from: https://ec.europa.eu/environment/forests/pdf/palm_oil_study_kh0218208enn_new.pdf

Ladrach, W. (2009) The effects of fire in agriculture and forest ecosystems. International Society of Tropical Forest. Retrieved from: www.istf-bethesda.org/specialreports/fuego_fire/fire_ecology-eng.pdf

San-Miguel-Ayanz, J., (2019) Climate change, forest fires and greenhouse gas emissions. European Commission Joint Research Center Space, Security and Migration Directorate Disaster Risk Management Unit, Ispra, Italy Retrieved from: https://europeanlandowners.org/images/Climate_Change/190320_CC_FF_GHG_by_JRC_San-Miguel-Ayanz.pdf

Alexander, K. (2018) 12 Northern California wildfires sparked by PG&E power lines, Investigator says. SFGate. Retrieved from: https://www.sfgate.com/bayarea/article/12-Northern-California-fires-caused-by-PG-E-power-12979955.php

Iles, J. and Gleason, M. (2008) Understanding the effects of flooding on trees. Sustainable Urban Landscapes, Iowa State University, University Extension. Retrieved from: https://store.extension.iastate.edu/Product/sul1-pdf

Arthur, M., Saffer, D. and Belmont, P. (2010?) The Nile River and Aswan Dam. Water: Science and Society, The Pennsylvania State University. Retrieved from: https://www.e-education.psu.edu/earth111/node/887

Gleick, P.H. (2013) Three Gorges Dam Project, Yangtze River, China. Water Briefs 3. Retrieved from: http://worldwater.org/wp-content/uploads/2013/07/WB03.pdf

Li, K., Zhu, C., Wu, L. and Huang, L. (2013) Problems caused by the Three Gorges Dam construction in the Yangtze River Basin: a review. NRC Research Press. Retrieved from: https://www.usi.edu/science/geology/jdurbin/PDFs/GEOL481-critiques/Rachel-Three-Gorges-Dam.pdf

Platform for Sustainable Alentejo (2005)The Alqueva Dam: How the EIB helped to finance the environmental destruction in Portugal Retrieved from: https://bankwatch.org/documents/alqueva_dam_02_05.pdf

Sumner, D. A. (2013) The Economic Impact of California's Almond Industry: A Report Prepared for the Almond Board of California. Retrieved from: https://aic.ucdavis.edu/almonds/EconomicImpactsofCaliforniaAlmondIndustry_FullReport_FinalPDF_v2.pdf

Philpott, T. and Lurie, J. (2015) Here's the problem with almonds. Environment. Retrieved from: https://www.motherjones.com/environment/2015/04/real-problem-almonds/

Nigeria Land use - Geography (indexmundi.com) 11/27/2020. Retrieved from: https://www.indexmundi.com/nigeria/land_use.html

Chapter 6

Merrill, D. and Leatherby, L. (2018) Here is how America uses its land. Bloomberg, July 31,2018 Article. Retrieved from: https://www. bloomberg.com/graphics/2018-us-land-use/

Bradshaw, C.J.A. (2012) Little left to lose: deforestation and forest degradation in Australia since European colonization. Journal of Plant Ecology, Volume 5, Issue 1, March 2012, page 109-120. Retrieved from: https://academic.oup.com/jpe/article/5/1/109/1294916

Barson, M., Randall, L. and Bordas, V. (2000) Land cover change in Australia. Bureau of Rural Sciences, Department of Agriculture, Fisheries and Forestry- Australia. Retrieved from: data.daff.gov.au/brs/data/warehouse/brsShop/data/report.pdf

Mfon, P., Mfon, G., Akintoye, O. A., Olorundami, T., Ukata, S. U. and AdesolaAkintoye, T. (2014) Challenges of deforestation in Nigeria and the millennium development goals. Modern Scientific Press company, Florida, USA. Retrieved from; https://www.researchgate.net/publication/303047811_Challenges_of_Deforestation_in_Nigeria_and_the_Millennium_Development_Goals

Bogoni, J.A., Pires, J.S.R., Graipel, M.E., Peroni, N. and Peres, C.H. (2018) Wish you were here: how defaunated is the Atlantic Forest biome of its medium-to large-bodied mammals? PLOS ONE, 2018; 13(9): e0204515 DOI:10.1371/Journal.pone.0204515

Williams, A. (2018) Europe's lost forest – study shows coverage halved over 6 millennia. University of Plymouth. Retrieved from: https://www.plymouth.ac.uk/news/europes-lost-forests-study-shows-coverage-has-halved-over-six-millennia

Elwell, F. () The industrial revolution. Rogers State University. Retrieved from: faculty.rsu.edu/users/f/felwell/www/Ecology/PDFs/IndRevolution.pdf

Chapter 7

Pollini, J. (2014) Slash-and burn agriculture. Responsive Forest Governance Initiative, University of Illinois at Urbana Champaign https://www.researchgate.net/publication/268150234_Slash-and-Burn_Agriculture/link/54626a780cf2837efdaff9ab/download

Stief, C. (2019) Slash and burn agriculture explained. ThoughtCo. Retrieved from: https://www.thoughtco.com/slash-and-burn-agriculture-p2-1435798

USGS (2007) Investigating the environmental effects of agriculture practices on natural resources: scientific contributions of the US Geological Survey to enhance the management of agricultural landscapes. USGS. Retrieved from: https://pubs.usgs.gov/fs/2007/3001/pdf/508FS2007_3001.pdf

Gilbert, J. (2016) Land grabbing investors and indigenous peoples: new legal strategies for an old practice? Oxford Academic, Community Development Journal, Volume 51, Issues 3, July 2016, Pages 350-366. Retrieved from: https://academic.oup.com/cdj/article/51/3/350/2566503

Laltaika, E. I. and Askew, K.M. (2018) Modes of dispossession of indigenous lands and territories in Africa. Retrieved from: https://www.un.org/development/desa/indigenouspeoples/wp-content/uploads/sites/19/2018/01/Laltaika-and-Askew_UN-paper_rev3.pdf

Fois, F. and Machado, S.M.M (201How indigenous peoples' lives are being destroyed by global agribusiness in Brazil. Innerself. Retrieved from: https://climateimpactnews.com/politics/3242-how-indigenous-peoples-lives-are-being-destroyed-by-global-agribusiness-in-brazil

Australian Bureau of Agriculture and Resources Economics and Sciences (ABARES) (2019) Australian Crop Report No 192 December 2019. Department of Agriculture, Australian Government. Retrieved from: https://www.agriculture.gov.au/sites/default/files/documents/austcroprrt20191203_v1.0.0.pdf

Fast Facts (2019) Australia' beef industry. Meat and Livestock Australia. Retrieved from: https://www.mla.com.au/globalassets/mla-corporate/prices--markets/documents/trends--analysis/fast-facts--maps/mla-beef-fast-facts-2019.pdf

Fast Facts (2019) Australia's sheep meat industry. Meat and Livestock Australia. Retrieved from: https://www.mla.com.au/globalassets/mla-corporate/prices--markets/documents/trends--analysis/fast-facts--maps/mla-sheep-fast-facts-2019-1.pdf

Global Summary (2018) Goatmeat. Meat and Livestock Australia. Retrieved from: https://www.mla.com.au/globalassets/mla-corporate/prices--markets/documents/os-markets/red-meat-market-snapshots/2018-mla-ms_global-goatmeat.pdf

Workman, D. (2020) Barley Exports by Country. World Top Exports. Retrieved from: http://www.worldstopexports.com/barley-exports-by-country/

Workman, D. (2020) Brazil's top ten exports. World's Top Exports. Retrieved from: http://www.worldstopexports.com/brazils-top-10-exports/

Nag, O.S. (2017) The top wheat exporting and importing countries in the world. Economics, World Atlas. Retrieved from: https://www.worldatlas.com/articles/the-top-wheat-exporting-and-importing-countries-in-the-world.html

World Soybean Production 2020/21 Retrieved from: http://www.worldagriculturalproduction.com/crops/soybean.aspx

Compassion in World Farming (2019 Statistics: broiler chickens. Compassion in World Farming. Retrieved from: https://www.ciwf.org.uk/media/5235303/Statistics-Broiler-chickens.pdf

Meyer, A. (2010) Brazil Agriculture. Retrieved from: https://www.brazil.org.za/agriculture.html

China in Brief, Agriculture. Retrieved from: http://www.china.org.cn/e-china/agriculture/crop.htm

Smith, R. (2016) Eight major factors that have changed agriculture in the last 50 years. Retrieved from: https://www.farmprogress.com/equipment/eight-major-factors-have-changed-agriculture-last-50-years

https://www.mdpi.com/1999-4907/10/10/933/pdf

http://publications.dyson.cornell.edu/outreach/extensionpdf/1996/Cornell_AEM_eb9603.pdf

The World's Top Ten Tea Producing Nations. World Atlas. Retrieved from: https://www.worldatlas.com/article/the-worlds-top-ten-tea-producing-nations.html

Chapter 8

Fernow, B.E. (1911) A brief history in forestry: In Europe, the United States and other countries. University Press Toronto and Forestry Quarterly, Cambridge Mass. Retrieved from: https://archive.org/details/briefhistoryoffo00fern/page/n6/mode/2up

LaBau, V.J., Bones, J.T., Kingsley, N.P., Lund, H.G. and Smith, W.B. (2007) A history of Forest Survey in the United States: 1830- 2004. USDA, Forest Services, FS 877, June 2007. Retrieved from: https://www.researchgate.net/publication/259812871_A_History_of_the_Forest_Survey_in_the_United_States_1830-2004

Stevens, S.K., Magda, M.S. and Trussel, J. B. B. () Philadelphia. Encyclopedia Britannica. Retrieved from: https://www.britannica.com/place/Philadelphia/The-people

Nowak, D. J. and Greenfield, E. (2015) Trees improve human health and wellbeing in many ways. Forest Service, USDA, US Forest Service Northern Research Station, Research Review No. 26, April 2015. Retrieved from: https://www.fs.fed.us/nrs/news/review/review-vol26.pdf

Nowak, D. J. and Greenfield, E.(2018) Declining urban and community tree cover in the United States. Urban Forestry and Urban Greening 32 (2018) 32-55, Elsevier. Retrieved from: https://www.fs.fed.us/nrs/pubs/jrnl/2018/nrs_2018_nowak_005.pdf

Levin, E. (2005) Growing Chin's great green wall. ECOS 13, Oct-Nov 2005. Retrieved from: www.ecosmagazine.com/?act=view_file&file_id=EC127p13.pdf

Luoma, J. (2012) China's Reforestation Programs: big success or just illusions? Yale Environmental 360, Yale School of Forestry and Environmental Studies. Retrieved from: https://e360.yale.edu/features/chinas_reforestation_programs_big_success_or_just_an_illusio

Schuster, M., Duringer, P., Ghienne, J-F. and Vignaud, P. (2006) Age of the Sahara Desert. ResearchGate. Retrieved from: https://www.researchgate.net/publication/51372753_The_Age_of_the_Sahara_Desert

Global Environmental Facility and World Bank Group (2019) The Great Green Wall Initiative: Supporting Resilient Livelihoods and Landscapes in the Sahel. Global Environmental Facility and World Bank Group. Retrieved from: https://www.thegef.org/sites/default/files/publications/gef_great_green_wall_initiative_august_2019_EN_0.pdf

UNCCD (2016) The Great Green Wall: Hope for the Sahara and Sahel. UNCCD and The Global Mechanism. Retrieved from: https://www.unccd.int/siteels/default/files/documents/26042016_GGW_ENG.pdf

Schiller, G. (2008) Afforestation of Palestine and later Israel. Department of Natural Resources, Institute of Plant Sciences, Agricultural Research Organization, The Volcani Center, Bet Dagan, Israel. Retrieved from: http://www.forestandwater.uni-goettingen.de/IsraelPDFdocs/ Schiller%20afforestation_in_Palestine_Israel.pdf

Schwitzguebel, J-F., van der Lelie, D., Barker, A., Glass, D.J. and Vangronsveld, J. (2002) Phytoremediation: Europe and American trends, successes, obstacle and needs. Journal of Solis and Sediment 2,91–99(2002). Retrieved from: https://link.springer.com/article/10.1007/BF02987877

Ferro, A. M., Kennedy, J., Zollinger, N. and Thompson, B. (2005) Groundwater Phytoremediation System-Performance at the SRSNE Superfund Site. de maximis inc. Retrieved from: https://clu-in.org/phytoconf/proceedings/2005/2B_Ferro.pdf

Lindner, A.S. (2004) Phytoremediation of TCE at Two Superfund Sites. Environmental Engineering Sciences, University of Florida. Retrieved from: https://www.niehs.nih.gov/news/assets/docs_f_o/lindner_508.pdf

Van Epps, A. (2006) Phytoremediation of Petroleum Hydrocarbons. US Environmental Protection Agency, Office of Solid Waste and Emergency Response, Office of Superfund Remediation and Technology Innovation, Washington DC. Retrieved from: https://clu-in.org/download/studentpapers/A_Van_Epps-Final.pdf

Nowak, D.J. and Greenfield, E.J. (2009) Urban and Community Forest of the Southern Atlantic Region. Northern Research Station, Forest Service, USDA. Retrieved from: https://www.nrs.fs.fed.us/pubs/gtr/gtr_nrs50.pdf

Doubravka, O. (ed) (2016) In the name of the great works: Stalin's plan for the transformation of nature and it's impact on Eastern Europe. Retrieved from: www.environmentandsociety.org/mml/name-great-work...

Chapter 9

Siqueira-Gay, J., Sonter, L.J. and Sanchez, L.E. (2020) Exploring potential impact of mining on forest loss and fragmentation within a biodiverse region of Brazil northeastern Amazon. Elsevier, Science Direct. Retrieved from: https://www.sciencedirect.com/science/article/abs/pii/S0301420719307470

Frelich, L.E. (2014) Forest and Terrestrial Ecosystems Impact of Mining https://www.savetheboundarywaters.org/sites/default/files/attachments/frelich_2014_-_report_september_22_2014.pdf

Priyadarshi, N. (2009) Effects of Mining on environment in the state of Jharkhand, India: mining has caused severe damage to the land resources of the area. Retrieved from: http://www.ismenvis.nic.in/WriteReadData/CMS/156EFFECTSOFMINING.pdf

Williams, C.E. (2005) Iron and steel Environmental impact. In K. Hillstrom and LC Hillstrom (ed.), The Industrial Revolution in America, Volume 1: Iron and Steel. ABC-CLIO, New York, pp 157-182 Retrieved from: https://www.academia.edu/1862606/Iron_and_steel_environmental_impact

The making of iron and steel. Retrieved from: http://www.seaisi.org/file/TheMakingofIron&Steel.pdf

Macintyre, S. (2009) A concise history of Australia (3rd edition). Cambridge University Press, New York, USA. Retrieved from: http://seas3.elte.hu/coursematerial/GallCecilia/S_Macintyre_A_Concise_History_of_Australia.Ch1.pdf

Johansson, T. (2003) Jamaica deforestation and bauxite mining –applying the Coase theorem (Masters Thesis). Lulea University of Technology. Minerals & Energy – Raw Materials Report, Journal. Retrieved from: www.diva-portal.org/smash/get/diva2:1029248/FULLTEXT01.pdf

World Aluminum (2018) Sustainable bauxite mining guidelines, 1st edition, Australian Aluminum Council Ltd and Associacoa Brasiliera de Alumnio. Retrieved from: www.world-aluminium.org/media/filer_public/2018/05/18/170518_sbmg_final.pdf

Rahm, M., Julian, B., Lauger, A., de Carvalho, R., Vale, L., Totaram, J., Cort, K.A., Djojodikromo, M., Hardjoprajitno, M., Neri, S., Vieira, R., Watanabe, E., do Carmo Brito, M., Miranda, P., Paloeng, C., Moe Soe Let, V., Crabbe, S. and Calmel, M. (2015) Monitoring the impact of gold mining on the forest cover and freshwater in the Guiana Shield. Reference year 2014. REDD+ for the Guiana Shied Project and WWF Guiana. pp 60. Retrieved from: http://d2ouvy59p0dg6k.cloudfront.net/downloads/gold_mining_final_report_1.pdf

Da Silva, O., (2019) Top copper production by country. Copper Investing News, Retrieved from: https://investingnews.com/daily/resource-investing/base-metals-investing/copper-investing/copper-production-country/

Stanley, J., Wilkinson, S.T., Moreno Ramirez, D., Maier, R.M. & Chief, K. (2015) Tribal educational module: copper mining and processing (PDF Document) Retrieved from: https://www.superfund.pharmacy.arizona.edu/learning-module/tribal-modules

International Copper Study Group (2019) World Copper Factbook 2019) Retrieved from: https://www.icsg.org/index.php/component/jdownloads/finish/170/2965

Arcia, J. (2018) Copper mines destroying forest in Panama's Mesoamerican biological corridor. Mongabay Series: Forest Trackers Global Forest Reporting Network. Retrieved from: https://news.mongabay.com/2018/12/copper-mine-destroying-forests-in-panamas-mesoamerican-biological-corridor/

Holmes, F. (2019) Top 10 gold producing countries. US Global Investor, Advisor Perspectives. Retrieved from: https://www.advisorperspectives.com/commentaries/

Renier, T. and Howell, J. (2020) Red Dirt – chapter 1: mining the land: the past and future of bauxite -alumina industry in Jamaica. Jamaica Environmental Trust(JET).

Chapter 10

McCafferty, G., G. (1996) Reinterpreting the great pyramid of Cholula Mexico. Ancient Mesoamerica. Cambridge University Press, USA. Retrieved from: https://www.academia.edu/210173/1996_Reinterpreting_the_Great_Pyramid_of_Cholula_Mexico

Schmitz, E., R. (2012) The great pyramid of Giza: decoding the measure of a monument. Roland Publishing, Nepean, ON, K2G 5Y3. Retrieved from: thegreatpyramidofgiza.ca/book/TheGreatPyramidofGIZA.pdf

Wenke, R., Nolan, J. and Amran, A. (1995) Dating the pyramids. David H. Koch Pyramid Radiocarbon Project, Archaeology "Dating the Pyramids" Volume 52, Number 5, September/October 1999. Retrieved from: www.ancient-wisdom.com/egyptghiza.htm

Gadalla, M., (2016) Egyptian pyramids revisited. Tehuti Research Foundation, Greensboro, NC. Retrieved from: https://egypt-tehuti.org/wp-content/uploads/2018/02/The-Egyptian-Pyramids-Revisited-Expanded-Third-Edition-sample.pdf

Ross, L. (2013) Nubia and Egypt 10,000 BC – 400 AD: From Prehistory to the Meroitic Period. The Elwin Mellen Press, NewYork. Retrieved from: https://www.researchgate.net/publication/283504727_Nubia_and_Egypt_10000_BC_to_400_AD_-_From_Prehistory_to_the_Meroitic_Period

Draper, R. (2008) The Black Pharaohs. National Geographic Magazine. Retrieved from: https://whbailey.weebly.com/uploads/1/5/7/3/15738528/national_geo_-_black_pharaohs.pdf

Sofaer, A. () The primary architecture of the Chacoan Culture: a cosmological expression. Retrieved from: https://solsticeproject.org/images/pdfs/24-Lekson_Chapter_9%2520%25282007%2529.pdf

Lekson, S.H., (2006) The archaeology of Chaco Canyon: Chaco Matters. School of American Research. Retrieved from: www.sarpress.sarweb.org

Holloway, A. (2014) Unravelling the mystery of the Chaco Canyon culture collapse. Ancient Origins. Retrieved from: https://www.ancient-origins.net/news-evolution-human-origins/unravelling-mystery-chaco-canyon-culture-collapse-001916

Posey. J. (2015) Why did the Anasazi Collapse? Jeff Posey Author Notes. Retrieved from: http://www.jeffposey.net/2015/09/08/why-did-the-anasazi-collapse/

Mann, D., Edwards, J., Chase, J., Beck, W., Reanier, R., Mass, M., Finney, B. and Loret, J. (2007) Drought, vegetation change and human history on Rapa Nui. Quaternary Research, Elsevier. Retrieved from: www.bio-nica.info/biblioteca/Mann2008EasterIsland.pdf

Mian, M. () Indus valley civilization. Retrieved from: www.chem.rutgers.edu/~kyc/Teaching/Files/264/1115maria.pdf

Dani, A. H. and Thapar, B. K. (1996) Indus Valley Civilization. UNESCO. Retrieved from: https://en.unesco.org/silkroad/sites/silkroad/files/knowledge-bank-article/vol_Isilkroad_theinduscivilizationBIS.pdf

Kramer, S. N. (1963) The Sumerians: their history, culture and character. The University of Chicago Press, Chicago & London. Retrieved from: https://oi.uchicago.edu/sites/oi.uchicago.edu/files/uploads/shared/docs/sumerians.pdf

Van der Crabben, J. (2011) Agriculture in the fertile crescent. Ancient History Encyclopedia, Article, 23 February 2011. Retrieved from: https://www.ancient.eu/article/9/agriculture-in-the-fertile-crescent/

Allen, M. (2014) Ten ways the bible was influenced by other religions. Religion, Article, June 20, 2014. Retrieved from: https://listverse.com/2013/06/30/ten-influences-on-the-bible/

Mark, J.J. (2011) Akkad, Definition. Ancient History Encyclopedia, Article 28 April 2011. Retrieved from: https://www.ancient.eu/akkad/

Whitehead, F. and Yuter, S. (Dr) () The Collapse of the Ancient Akkadian Empire and Climate Change.North Carolina State University Retrieved from: www.environmentanalytics.com/pdfsposter/071111whiteheadposter_final.pdf

Gibbons, A. (1993) How the Akkadian Empire was hung out to dry. Science, volume 261, 20 August 1993, pg 985. Retrieved from: https://science.sciencemag.org/content/261/5124/985/tab-pdf

Mark, J. J. (2018) Hammurabi, Definition. Ancient History Encyclopedia, Article 16 April 2018. Retrieved from: https://www.ancient.eu/hammurabi/

Sasson, J. M. (1995) King Hammurabi of Babylon. Retrieved from: https://ir.vanderbilt.edu/bitstream/handle/1803/3863/King_Hammurabi.pdf

Lewis, M. and Feldman, M. (2015) The Ancient City of Babylon.

Mark, J. J. (2018) Nebuchadnezzar II, Definition. Ancient History Encyclopedia, 07 November 2018. Retrieved from: https://www.ancient.eu/Nebuchadnezzar_II/

Belibtreu, E. (1991) Grisly Assyrian record of death and torture. Biblical Archaeological Society. Retrieved from: www. faculty.uml.edu/ethan_spanier/Teaching/documents/CP6.0AssyrianTorture.pdf

Smit, J. L. (2019) Ancient civilizations timelines: 16 oldest known cultures around the world. History Cooperative. Retrieved from: https://historycooperative.org/ancient-civilizations/

Snape, S. (2019) Estimating population in ancient Egypt. Brewminate. Retrieved from: https://brewminate.com/estimating-population-in-ancient-egypt/

Mark, J. J. (2017) Ancient Egyptian Agriculture. Ancient History Encyclopedia. Retrieved from: https://www.ancient.eu/article/997/ancient-egyptian-agriculture/

El-Behary, H. (2017) Sudan claims that their pyramids are 2000 years older than Egypt's. Egypt Independent. Retrieved from: https://www.egyptindependent.com/sudan-claims-their-pyramids-are-2000-years-older-egypt-s/

Omer, I. (2008) Daily life: agriculture ad diet. Ancient Sudan-Kush. Retrieved from: http://www.ancientsudan.org/dailylife_01_diet.htm

Lekson, S.H. (2016) Chaco Canyon. Colorado Encyclopedia. Retrieved from: https://coloradoencyclopedia.org/article/chaco-canyon#Roads-and-Waterworks

Guiterman, C. H., Swetman, T. W. and Dean, J.S. (2015) Eleventh century shift in timber procurement areas for the great houses of Chaco Canyon. Retrieved from: https://www.pnas.org/content/113/5/1186

University of Cincinnati (2018) Ancestral people of Chaco Canyon likely grew their own food. ScienceDaily. Retrieved from: https://www.sciencedaily.com/releases/2018/07/180703154919.htm

Eaton, R. (1985) Chaco Canyon. Retrieved from: http://www.robert-eaton.com/wp-content/uploads/2013/05/Chaco-Canyon.pdf

Clark, L. (2000) Pioneers of Eater Island. Retrieved from: https://www.pbs.org/wgbh/nova/article/pioneers-of-easter-island/

Than, K. (2006) View of Easter Island disaster all wrong, researchers say. LiveScience Retrieved from: https://www.livescience.com/616-view-easter-island-disaster-wrong-researchers.html

Mark, J. J. (2011) Sumer. Ancient History Encyclopedia. Retrieved from: https://www.ancient.eu/sumer/

Chapter 11

Dale, A. (2015) Production and consumption of wood pellets in the European Union. Ekman and CO AB, WPAC Conference November 2015, Wood Pellet Association of Canada. Retrieved from: https://www.pellet.org/images/2015/ArnoldDaleEkman.pdf

Mlay, G., Turuka, F., Kowero, G. and Kachule, R. (2002) Agricultural Policies and forestry development in Malawi, Mozambique, Tanzania and Zimbabwe-Complimentary and conflicts. Retrieved from: www.tanzaniagateway.org/docs/Agricultural_policies_and_forestry_devel_malawi_moz_tz_zim.pdf

Baumhardt, R. L. (2003) Dust Bowl Era. Marcel Drexel, Inc., New York, USDA. https://www.researchgate.net/publication/43255753_Dust_Bowl_Era

Assuncao, J., Lipscomb, M., Mobarak, A.M. and Szerma, D. (2016) Agricultural productivity and deforestation in Brazil. INPUT, Climate Policy Initiative. Retrieved from: https://climatepolicyintiative.org/wp-content/uploads/2017/06/Agricultural-Productivity-and-Deforestation-in-Brazil-CPI.pdf

Albert, E. and Xu, B. (2016) China's environmental crisis. Council on Foreign Relations Retrieved from: https://www.cfr.org/backgrounder/chinas-environmental-crisis

Elassar, A. (2019) Amazon deforestation rates hit highest levels in over a decade. CNN. Retrieved from: https://www.edition.cnn.com/2019/11/19/americas/brazil-deforestation-amazon-2019-trnd/index.html

Conrad, J.M. and Kobildjanova, K. (2011) The economics of an environmental disaster: The Aral Sea. Cornell University. Retrieved from: www.cs.cornell.edu/courses/cs6702/2011sp/readings/AralSea2011.pdf

Metternicht, G. (2017) Global land outlook: land use planning. United Nation Convention to Combat Desertification (UNCCD). Retrieved from: https://knowledge.unccd.int/sites/default/files/2018-06/6.+land+use+planning +g_metternicht.pdf

US EPA () Land use. US EPA. Retrieved from: https://www.epa.gov/report-environment/land-use

UNESCO () Water and our health. Drops of Water 3. UNESCO, Venice Office. Retrieved from: https://www.unesco.org/new/fileadmin/MULTIMEDIA/field/venice/pdf/special_events/bozza_sheda_DOW03_1.0.pdf

FAO. The role of wood energy in Asia. Retrieved from: www. fao. org/3/w7519e/w7519e08.htm

THE ROLE OF WOOD ENERGY IN ASIA (fao.org)
USEIA (2014) Increase in wood as main source of household heating is most notable in the Northeast. Retrieved from: https://www.eia.gov/todayinenergy/detail.php?id=15431

Ong, S., Campbell, C., Denholm, P., Margolis, R. and Heath, G. (2013) Land use requirements for solar power plants in the United States. National Renewable Energy laboratory NREL Retrieved from: https://www.nrel.gov/docs/fy13osti/56290.pdf

Denholm, P., Hand, M., Jackson, M. and Ong, S. (2009) Land-Use requirements of modern wind power plants in the United States. National Renewable Energy Laboratories (NREL). Retrieved from: Https://www.nrel.gov/docs/fy09osti/45834.pdf

National Wind Coordinating Collaborative (2010) Wind turbine interactions with birds, bats and their habitats Retrieved from: https://www1.eere.energy.gov/wind/pdfs/birds_and_bats_fact_sheet.pdf, _ Wind Turbine Interactions with Birds, Bats, and their Habitats: A Summary of Research Results and Priority Questions (energy.gov)

Derwent, R. G (2018) Hydrogen for heating: atmospheric impacts- a literature review. BEIS Research Paper Number 2018: no 21. Department of Business, Energy and Industrial Strategy, England. Retrieved from: Hydrogen atmospheric impact report.pdf (publishing.service.gov.uk)

Balakrishnan, A., Jamis, A., Reyes, W., Strutner, M., Sinha, P. andGeyer, R. (2019) Environmental impacts of utility-scale battery storage in California. Bren School of Environmental Science & Management, University of California, Santa Barbara. Retrieved from: https://www.firstsolar.com/-/media/First-Solar/Sustainability-Documents/Enivironmental-Impacts-of-Utility-Scale-Battery-Storage-in-California.ashx

Chapter 12

Hickey, D. (2016) Ireland has great woodland but the lowest forest cover of all European countries. Irish Examiner, March 28 2016. Retrieved from: https://www.irishexaminer.com/lifestyle/outdoors/donal-hickey/ireland-has-great-woodland-but-has-the-lowest-forest-cover-of-all-european-countries-389700.html

Forest Research (UK) Woodland Statistics. Retrieved from: https://www.forestresearch.gov.uk/tools-and-resources/statistics/statistics-by-topic/woodland-statistics/

Forest Cover Current Affairs (2020) FSI: 21.4 percent of forest cover prone to forest fire. The Ministry of the Environment, Forestry and Climate Change, India. Retrieved from: https://currentaffairs.gktoday.in/tags/forest-cover

CIFOR (2008) Measuring and Monitoring Forest Degradation for REDD. Info Brief, No 16, November 2008 Retrieved from: https://redd.unfccc.int/uploads/2_134_redd_20090209_cifor_measuring_and_monitoring_forest_degradation.pdf

IPCC () Good Practice Guidance for LULUCF. Retrieved from: https://www.ipcc-nggip.iges.or.jp/public/gpglulucf/gpglulucf_files/Chp4/Chp4_25_to_4210.pdf

Thrall, P.H., Bever, James D. and Burdon, J.J. (2010) Evolutionary change in agriculture: the past present and future. Evolutionary Applications. Retrieved from: https://www.ncbi.nlm.nih.gov/pmc/articles/PMC3352499/

Dudley, N., Jeanrenaud, J-P. and Sullivan, F. (1995) The timber trade and global forest loss. WWF. Retrieved from: www.equilibriumresearch.com/upload/document/thetimbertradeandgl484.pdf

Czartoryski, A. (2011) Amazing hunter-gather societies still in existence today. Retrieved from. https://www.academia.edu/31129371/Amazing_Hunter-Gatherer_Societies_Still_In_Existence

Hardin, G. (1968) Tragedy of the commons. Science AAAS. Retrieved from: https://pages.mtu.edu/~asmayer/rural_sustain/governance/Hardin%201968.pdf

Characteristics of Sustainable Forest Management. Retrieved from: https://www.fs.fed.us/nrs/pubs/gtr/gtr_nrs90/gtr-nrs-90-chapter-3.pdf

Xin, L., (CHINA) (2019) National Report of the People Republic of China on Progress towards the Implementation of United Nations Strategic Plans for Forests (UNSPF) 2017-2030, the United Nations Forest Instrument (UNFI) and Voluntary National Contributions(VNC). Retrieved from: https://www.un.org/esa/forests/wp-content/uploads/2019/12/China.pdf

Mann, M. E. () Little Ice Age. University of Virginia, Charlottesville, Virginia. Retrieved from: http://www.meteo.psu.edu/holocene/public_html/shared/articles/littleiceage.pdf

Howard, J. L. and Liang, S. (2018) United States Forest Product, Annual Market Review and Prospects 2015 -2019. Retrieved from: http://www.unece.org/fileadmin/DAM/timber/country-info/statements/usa2018.pdf

Berg, P. and Lingquist, O. (2019) Pulp, paper and packaging in the next decade: transformational change. McKinsey & Company. Retrieved from: https://www.mckinsey.com/~/media/McKinsey/Industries/PaperandForestProducts/OurInsights/Pulp-paper-and-packaging-in-the-next-decade-Transformational-change-2019-vF.ashx

The history of gold. National Mining Association. Retrieved from: http://nma.org/pdf/gold/gold_history.pdf

Hur, J. (2020) The history of gold. BeBusinessed.Com. Retrieved from: https://bebusinessed.com/history/the-history-of-gold/

Gauger, A., Rabatel-Fernel, M. P., Kulbicki, L., Short, D. and Higgins, P. (2013) The ecocide project. Human Rights Consortium, School of Advanced Study, University of London. Retrieved from: https://sas-space.sas.ac.uk/4830/1/Ecocide_research_report_19_July_13.pdf

Hunt, T. L. and Lipo, C.P. (2009) Revisiting Rapa Nui (Easter Island) "ecocide". Pacific Science October 2009. Retrieved from: https://scholarspace.manoa.hawaii.edu/bitstream/10125/22778/1/vol63n4-601-616.pdf

Norrington, B. (2018) The rats of Rapa Nui. University of California, Santa Barbara. Retrieved from: https://geog.ucsb.edu/the-rats-of-rapa-nui/

Harris, N., Goldman, E.D., Weise, M. and Barrett, A. (2018) When a tree falls, is it deforestation? World Resources Institute. Retrieved from: https://www.wri.org/blog/2018/09/when-tree-falls-it-deforestation

Wallheimer, B. (2019) Invasive pest kill so many trees each year, it equal to 5 million car emissions. Perdue University, Agriculture News. Retrieved from: https://www.purdue.edu/newsroom/releases/2019/Q3/invasive-pests-kill-so-many-trees-each-year,-its-equal-to-5-million-car-emissions.html

Sabu-Jaddi: The site revealing the Sahara's verdant past. BBC, Travel, Sudan, Climate Change. Retrieved from: http://www.bbc.com/travel/story/20200607-sabu-jaddi-the-site-revealing-the-saharas-verdant-past

D'Atanasio, E., Trombetta, B., Bonito, M., Finocchio, A., Di Vito, G., Seghizzi, M., Romano, R., Russo, G., Paganotti, G. M., Watson, E., Coppa, A., Ananoustou, P., Dougoujon, J-M., Moral, P., Sellitto, D., Novelletto, A. & Cruciani, F. (2018) The peopling of the last Green Sahara revealed by high-coverage resequencing of trans-Sahara patrilineages. BMC, Genome Biology. Retrieved from: https://genomebiology.biomedcentral.com/articles/10.1186/s13059-018-1393-5

Mann, B. (2017) Climate change could green the Sahara and unleash monster hurricanes on the US. NCPR. Retrieved from: https://www.northcountrypublicradio.org/news/story/34232/20170704/climate-change-could-green-the-sahara-and-unleash-monster-hurricanes-

Boissoneault, L. (2017) What really turned the Sahara Desert from a Green Oasis into a wasteland? Smithsonian Magazine. Retrieved from: https://www.smithsonianmag.com/science-nature/what-really-turned-sahara-desert-green-oasis-wasteland-180962668/

Chapter 13

Strongman, J. (2002) Sustainable mining development: from concept to action: a presentation made in mining and the community, Madang Papua, New Guinea, September 2002. Retrieved from: https://www.ombudsman.gov.ph/UNDP4/wp-content/uploads/2013/PrimerPolicy-Brief-on -sustainable-mining.pdf

Printed in the United States
by Baker & Taylor Publisher Services